Advanced Praise

"Simply the BEST, most comprehensive, no nonsense, step-by-step guide to Indie film producing ever!"
—Michel Shane, Executive Producer, *Catch Me if You Can*, *I Robot*

"Finally, a how to film book that combines personal experience with brilliant advice and enlightening behind-the-scene stories. An excellent read!"
—Chris Wyatt, Producer, *Napoleon Dynamite*

"I've always loved Suzanne Lyons' gift for communication and explanation, and now she's applied that to her vast experience as a producer of low budget movies. She takes you through the process in a step-by-step, practical, direct, and honest way that only Suzanne can do. You're not just going to love this book, it's going to be your production bible!"
—Mark Rosman, Director, *A Cinderella Story*, *The Perfect Man*

"All you need to know about putting together an indie film, and more! One of the best and most comprehensive books I've read about this business, as good as a graduate degree! When anyone ever asks you "What does a Producer DO?" just give them this book, since they do EVERYTHING in it, and deserve more credit and respect for it all, too!"
—Sara Risher, former Chairman of Production for New Line Cinema

"Finally! A book about what I know and love – producing films – that smartly maps exactly what to do and how to do it – to prep, populate, finance, produce and get your film out into the world. Unlike most filmmaking books, Suzanne doesn't waste time on theory or useless generic forms. Just clear, sensible, powerful, actionable information so you get real world results. Suzanne's is the only book you need to confidently turn your film into a reality and make your dreams come true. No wonder she gets so many films produced!"
—Gary Goldman, Producer, *Pretty Woman*

"Suzanne knows the secrets to putting the business back in show business, but keeping it human, approachable and fun at the same time. An inspiring book - makes you believe you can do it!"

—Pen Densham, Producer, *Robin Hood:*
Prince of Thieves, Backdraft, Moll Flanders, Phantom

"A great 'how to' on low budget film producing. This book explains how you can be creative and business smart at the same time. Fulfilling your vision and making your investors happy. Now that's a winning combination."

—Ram Bergman, Producer, *Brick*

"Concise, simple, step-by-step plans and models for the indie producer. This is what most film schools never teach you – the business behind the making of a film. Suzanne takes the mystery out of the financing process. A must read for all aspiring and working producers."

—Anne Marie Gillen (CEO, Gillen Group LLC,
Producer: *Under Suspicion, Into Temptation, Fried Green Tomatoes*)

"If you're even thinking about making a movie... Read this book... Now! I've worked with Suzanne for years and she knows her stuff more than most people in this town!"

—Stacey Parks, www.FilmSpecific.com

"At each important step in the journey of getting a film produced we are reminded the importance each individual brings the project through the development of the script to a film that its audience will see. Ms Lyons reminds us to make the process a fun experience while not sugar coating the demanding job of a producer. Her enthusiasm for both the art and the business of film is highly evident in these chapters."

—Phyllis Laing, President, Buffalo Gal Pictures

"This is an invaluable book for indie filmmakers. Buy it now! You'll save a hundred times its cost in production and post-production."

—Kate Robbins, Former Co-founder of Snowfall Films, Director,
Candy Stripers

"Education is a force to enrich our humanity, being so, I highly recommend *Indie Film Producing*, a complete and comprehensive guide to film student, filmmaker and educator. Suzanne Lyons, a person of wisdom and goodness, with years of practice and experience presents filmmaking's most profound facets in clear and simple terms. I gained insight while reading *Indie Film Producing,* which I highly recommend."

—Nicolas Nelle, Chairman, African Film Commission

"If there was an Academy Award for film books on producing your movie... This one's a winner!"

—Jim Orr, Award Winning Cinematographer

"A film school in a book. I wish I had such a book when I was starting out. Suzanne Lyons covers everything a filmmaker needs to know about developing, producing, and marketing a feature film in a succinct nuts and bolts approach."

—Terence M. O'Keefe, Writer, Producer, Director Vanguard Productions

"Susanne Lyons' book *Indie Film Producing: The Craft of Low Budget Filmmaking* is an essential guide for all new producers about to begin their journey into the world of independent feature filmmaking. Suzanne conveys laser focused insights and invaluable practical advice with infectious enthusiasm."

—Alan M. Shafer, Careyes Pictures, LLC

"Suzanne's been there and done it. Now with *Indie Film Producing: The Craft of Low Budget Filmmaking*, you can, too! A page-turner for all Indie Producers!"

—Rob Buckham, Owner, ChinaFilm Productions

"Suzanne illuminates every important aspect of film producing—from script option to deliverables—in the most engaging and thorough manner. And, her enthusiasm is catching. It's like reading tales from a producer's diary with the true expertise to back it up. For everyone considering producing their own movie, from low budget and even beyond, *Indie Film Producing* is a MUST READ!"

—Alison Lea Bingeman, Screenwriter, Indie feature, *HURT*

"Suzanne Lyons brings us the lessons from the trenches from her own experience and those of other filmmakers. She shows how producing is not all swimming with sharks but everyday practical work with countless details to attend to. And she reminds us of the importance of the human side of producing that requires creative thinking, deliberation and consideration of the creative work of others."

—Alyn Warren, Associate Professor,
Digital Cinema MFA program director, National University

Indie Film Producing
The Craft of Low Budget Filmmaking

Suzanne Lyons

Focal Press
Taylor & Francis Group

NEW YORK AND LONDON

First published 2012
by Focal Press
70 Blanchard Road, Suite 402, Burlington, MA 01803

Simultaneously published in the UK
by Focal Press
2 Park Square, Milton Park, Abingdon, Oxon OX14 4RN

Focal Press is an imprint of the Taylor & Francis Group, an informa business

Library of Congress Cataloging-in-Publication Data
Application submitted

ISBN-13: 978-0-240-81763-7 (pbk)

Contents

Chapter 7 Soft Prep   76

Chapter 8 The Casting Process   84

PLEASE NOTE: I am not an attorney. The deal memos and information in this book should not be construed as legal advice. Please use your own council for anything contractual and anything pertaining to an LLC.

Acknowledgments

If I were to thank all the people I want to, this section would be longer than the book itself. So I will try to keep it as brief as possible. A big giant thank you to Kate Robbins, my brilliant and talented film partner for over ten years. Kate's input, suggestions, and advice during my writing process was invaluable, and her partnership over the years has been a gift.

A sincere thank you to Michele Cronin at Focal Press for believing in me and my book. Michele's professional guidance and never-ending encouragement saw me through the entire process.

I am extremely appreciative to my generous colleagues who gave their time to be interviewed for the book: Ellen Pittleman, Becky Smith, Jim Pasternak, Richard Marshall, Jerome Courshon, JC Calciano, Stacey Parks, Marc Rosenbush, Alethea Root, and Justin Trefgarne. Their stories and experiences are far more than informative – they're brilliant and inspiring!

Thank you to Mike Tarzian for the much-needed help defining the important differences between the responsibilities of the producer and the line producer. I want to thank Laura Brennan and Heather Hale for their input and guidance on the glossary. And attorney Rick Rosenthal for defining legal terms related to the business plan package. Eve Honthaner deserves a big thank you for introducing me to Focal Press and for letting me use part of her amazing Filmmaker's Website Resource Guide. And I'd like to thank Amy Campione for her help with the Resource Guide's updates.

I really want to thank the hundreds of people who participated in my Indie Film Producing workshops. Their commitment to this industry was contagious and their excitement and passion to produce films inspired me to write this book. Also, I think my film investors and all my talented cast and skilled and knowledgeable crew deserve a standing ovation and my heartfelt thank you.

I have had incredible mentors over the years, and I want to specifically thank Michel Shane, Ram Bergman, and Pen Densham for contributing their brilliant knowledge of this industry and for their guidance and encouragement. My coaches deserve a special thank you as well. Like my mentors, I have been blessed with the best. I truly appreciate Heidi Wall (my partner for ten years in the Flash Forward Institute) and Geanne Frank, who pushed me lovingly beyond what I thought possible. And thank you to a couple of my early coaches, Pontish Yeramyan and Judy Billman. Long before I moved to Hollywood, they saw me as far bigger and greater than I ever saw myself. I chose their picture of me. All my coaches had the patience of a saint and the wisdom of a master.

A gigantic debt of gratitude goes out to my parents; although both deceased, they are with me every day. I thank them for giving me life, love, and guidance and for setting the brilliant example of living life with dignity and grace. Thank you to Dad for his calm and stable presence and to Mom for her contagious passion and unquenchable thirst for knowledge. And thank you to my five sisters and two brothers for their encouragement and for their patience in allowing me to disappear for weeks at a time as I wrote this book.

Finally, a humongous thank you to my adorable husband. He is the love of my life, my best friend, my genius collaborator, and the funniest man I know. He takes unconditional love to a whole new level, and without his undying support, this book could not have come to fruition. Life with my husband is a magical ride . . . a continual exploration of possibility and expansion.

About 13 years ago, I worked on a film executive produced by Heidi Wall, cofounder of Flash Forward Institute, a series of programs dedicated to fostering successful careers in the entertainment industry. I had never heard of Flash Forward until I met Heidi, but once the film was over, she invited me to one of their seminars. The audience was packed that evening, and Heidi's business partner, Suzanne Lyons, started the event by addressing the audience. I was immediately captivated – not just with what she had to say but with her passion, sense of humor, and personality. All I kept thinking about was how much I wanted to meet and get to know this woman. I wanted some of whatever it was she had. So the very next day, I asked Heidi if she'd introduce me to Suzanne. She did, and we arranged to meet for breakfast and have been friends ever since. Even after all this time, I am continuously awed by her accomplishments and have achieved more in my own career in part because of the confidence and motivation she inspires in me.

Suzanne is a force of nature. Her joy at being in this industry is infectious, and her positive energy is magnetic. She's not only a skilled producer but also a fabulous teacher/coach/mentor/role model who has devoted years to inspiring and helping tens of thousands succeed in our very competitive and challenging business. She's incredibly generous about sharing her wealth of knowledge with others, and this new book is no exception.

Throughout my career, I've often come across people who decide to make low-budget movies without doing their homework. They jump directly into the deep end before even knowing if they can navigate the waters. They may survive the journey and complete their films, but the experience is often a bumpy one. And it's not uncommon for them to squander valuable time and money along the way. If producing is what you want to do, understand what you're walking into, exactly what to expect, and what's expected of you *before* you start. And know that you don't *have to* do it the hard way. This book will propel you over that learning curve and take the mystery out of the entire process – one step at a time.

Indie Film Producing is the equivalent of an entire course in one book, and it's presented in an easy-to-understand, conversational tone. As you read it, you'll feel as if a friend is explaining what you need to know (my friend, actually, who – lucky for us – injects her passion and infectious personality into her writing). And you'll be a better producer because of it. Not only that, but you'll impress the hell out of all those you're working with.

Enjoy the book, savor the exciting experience of producing your own film, and – as Suzanne would tell you – don't forget to have fun along the way!

Eve Honthaner

Production Management Professional

Author: *The Complete Film Production Handbook* (4th Edition) and *Hollywood Drive*

Instructor: USC School of Cinematic Arts Summer Program

Founder: Film Industry Network (FIN) 2000–2008

Chapter 1

Getting Ready to Produce

It was the fall of 2004, and I was riding high. I had produced three award-winning films with another one in postproduction. I was on my way to the Osaka Film Festival, where my first film was being honored and I was the star attraction! My film partner, Kate Robbins, and I had three more films lined up, packaged, financed, and ready to shoot in Australia, when bang – the bottom fell out. The UK laws governing film production changed, Australia followed suit, and all three of my projects collapsed. Overnight, all that work was lost. We needed to stop and reassess.

THE TIME WAS RIGHT

As it turned out, the timing couldn't have been more perfect. The same month that the UK changes were happening, the US federal government announced Section 181. Section 181 allowed investors in the United States the opportunity to invest in films and enjoy an incredible tax deduction. The Directors Guild of America (DGA) had lobbied for years to get Section 181 passed with the intention to help prevent "runaway" production. At the same time, the Screen Actors Guild (SAG) was doing its part by offering more reasonable rates to support low-budget indie filmmaking in the United States. We were based in Los Angeles and really wanted to stay home and produce our films. Section 181 gave us that opportunity. So we immediately called our business coach and sat down with her to map out the next phase of our filmmaking adventure.

After speaking with a number of sales agents about what genres were hot, marketable, in demand, yet doable at the SAG ultra-low-budget level, we decided to focus on horror. It was a genre that was selling well at that time and also one that didn't require a big A-list actor. So we opened up a genre division – WindChill Films, Inc. – and started on our first horror film. We produced three and executive-produced one, all within two years, from 2005 to 2007.

THE LANDSCAPE IS CHANGING

Something I'd like to point out here is the dramatic shift that has occurred since I produced these films. I know it's only been a few years, but a lot has happened in that short time. One of the most important changes has been – you guessed it – the social media explosion! The landscape of indie film producing has been altered so much recently by this change that I feel it's important to address. Not too many years ago, we relied on sales agents, producer's reps, and distributors to both sell and market our films. The producer's job for a over a century was to develop the screenplay, raise the funding, cast the movie, produce it, deliver it to the sales agent, and for the most part, move on to the next project. In fact, in my earlier films, the sales agent even made the decisions as to which film festivals my films would be submitted. Today, as film producers, we are taking full advantage of the access the Internet has made possible, and in many cases we are self-marketing and self-distributing.

Because this is an area that is fairly new and certainly new for me, I will include stories, advice, and suggestions from producers who are currently using and exploring these exciting new avenues.

A STEP-BY-STEP APPROACH

In this book, I will take you through the overall timeline for our horror/ thriller, *Séance*. It is my intent to give a very specific overall timeline for making a film. I will break it down into clear chronological segments so you can be guided through it a step at a time. I will refer to *Candy Stripers* and *Portal* from time to time as well. All three of these films were produced in the United States. This book will focus on US laws, specifically those of the State of California. So, although I invite you to map everything you need from this book onto your own production, please keep in mind that you will want to research the laws and requirements applicable to your own area.

I actually think it is easy to produce a low-budget film. I look at filmmaking in a step-by-step, A-to-Z fashion. Don't get ahead of yourself. Really start with A, the first step. I think what stops people is when they look at the whole thing at once. It can look so daunting and overwhelming.

No matter how honorable our intentions are and how passionate and excited we may be about producing our film, we're human. When we hit roadblocks or when things look overwhelming, we all too often get stopped. Breaking it down into steps and stages will make it not only doable, but enjoyable. And isn't that why we're in the entertainment business? We want to provide "entertainment" to people! So shouldn't we be having a blast while we're doing it?

With so many amazing tax incentives around the world and with the remarkable digital cameras and technology we have at our fingertips, there is no reason why we cannot produce our films, see our visions realized, and make our dreams come true. Whether you are an actor, writer, director, director of photography, or editor, anyone who wants to produce a film can now do so – and with the firsthand knowledge you will be getting in this book, you have no reason not to.

WEARING TWO HATS: BUSINESS AND CREATIVE

I know that you are creative. That is fantastic. In fact, it's what drew you to this industry. That is what has you so excited about wanting to produce your film. However, what I so often notice is the unbelievable number of mistakes and problems faced by producers who think that being creative is enough. I am here to tell you that it's not. We have to wear two hats. One is creative and the other one is business! We have to wear the business hat and we have to wear it *all the time*.

I have friends who have produced films that will never see the light of day because they were so busy being creative they forgot to get the paperwork done on the chain of title, others who did not get proper clearance done on their script, and others who did not get signed actors' contracts. *This is a business!* Remember, it is called "show business," not just "show." There is a great quote by English economist Josiah Charles Stamp that is brilliant and should be kept in mind during your entire production: "It is easy to dodge our responsibilities, but we cannot dodge the consequences of dodging our responsibilities."

My friend John called recently from the Cannes film market, all excited that a sales agent was interested in picking up his film. As the sales agent was going over some of the delivery items with him, John realized that he had never had the option for the screenplay signed. When he called the writer to complete the process (something that should have been done before ever moving forward with producing the film), the writer told him that she'd had a falling out with the director. She told John that she refused to sign the agreement, leaving him with no chain of title and therefore no right to sell and distribute the film. It was over just like that! A year and a half of John's life had gone into making that film, and it would never be released. Neither he nor his investors would recoup their investment. If you are going to read the rest of this book and go out and make your film, you must be prepared to wear both your creative and business hats.

THE BUSINESS OF FILM PRODUCING

The reason I am writing this book is that I learned so much of this stuff the hard way. I don't want you or anyone to make the mistakes I have made. This book will save you thousands and most likely tens of thousands of dollars. My intention is that the information in this book will educate you about the business aspects of filmmaking; with this education, not only will you avoid my mistakes, but you will also have fun during the entire process of producing your film with no unforeseen surprises along the way.

I remember when my filmmaking partner Kate Robbins and I were finishing up shooting our first horror film, *Candy Stripers*, and we had made a point to get the still photos from the film off to a number of sales agents along with some great articles that had been written about us on various horror film websites. We received an encouraging response from sales agents and actually had a few of them wanting to sell our film. We got the delivery list from one of them and it was seven single-spaced pages! It was like reading another language. I had no idea what any of it meant. Sales agents and distributors need things like a dialog spotting list, a script clearance report, a pan-and-scan version, an HDD5, and a clone of an HDD5. I thought clones were something that happened to sheep in Scotland.

There were endless lists of these things, including E&O (errors and omission) insurance, and they were all essential if we were to do a domestic sale. I didn't even know what E&O insurance was. I knew that we had had our film production insured and that was all I knew. As it turned out, E&O insurance was an extra $5,000! As I started adding up all these delivery items, it was heading into the $15,000 to $20,000 range – and we had not raised that extra $20,000. This was a hard and expensive lesson to learn. It was then that I knew I would teach a class in low-budget filmmaking and write this book. I had done four films before moving into the low-budget world. I had produced three and helped raise the money as an executive producer on another. They were all budgeted in the millions of dollars, so when Kate and I decided to do these smaller $200,000 budget films, I thought, "This will be a joke! This will be so easy I can do them with my eyes closed." My arrogance cost nearly $20,000. On the larger-budget films, there is a lot of money set aside for postproduction and delivery and there is always a postproduction supervisor to handle it. When you're doing an ultra-low-budget project, you don't necessarily have that luxury: you, as the producer, may have to wear that hat as well.

So now that you're wearing your business hat, let's do what business owners do: commit to a specific goal with a deadline attached. Or, as I would say if I were teaching my workshop, "It's time to put your butt on the line." Take a look at Figure 1.1. I think you'll get the picture.

FIGURE 1.1

There is something very powerful about setting goals. It makes what you are taking about real! You are giving your word. This is happening!

Exercise: Project Goal

What's the game?

A **goal** is a clearly worded, single, focused statement that has you commit to a specific, measureable result by a specific date.

PROJECT GOAL

By _____ I will _____

_____

_____

_____

_____

FIGURE 1.2

Chapter 2

Timeline for *Séance*

Before starting a film (or any project), I do a timeline. I buy a big piece of paper or poster board and break down the entire project into a reasonable, doable timeline. Even if I don't know exactly when I'll be starting principal photography, I make up a date to force myself to put this step on paper. Even if it is just the highlights to get me focused, I find it helpful in many ways. It gives me something tangible that I can actually see before my eyes. It takes the project out of the world of hopes and dreams and makes it real. It makes it look very doable. In our heads, the process can feel daunting, but on paper, broken down over a period of time, it is surprising how easy it begins to appear. Most important, it forces me to become accountable and totally responsible for my project. This part sounds scary, but it's actually a good thing because it has you "put your butt on the line," and the more real it becomes for you, the more real it will seem to everyone around you.

I truly think that this step is part of why Kate and I were able to raise the funds and produce these films so effortlessly. We were so clear that it was going to happen that everyone around us got the same message. It was real! We weren't kidding. We weren't hoping or wishing or dreaming. We were making a movie and we had a timeline to prove it.

I am going to give you a detailed timeline to help you with this exercise (not that yours should be this detailed at first). The following timeline is a look back at our SAG ultra-low-budget film, *Séance*. I found that when I was teaching the "Indie Film Producing" workshop, people were really having a hard time with this exercise. I typed up this timeline for *Séance* to give people a little upfront information so they could get an overall look at the specific aspects of making a film and breaking it down into chronological segments and steps.

Don't worry if you don't understand all the terms and language used in this chapter. It is just a brief overview of the timeline. I will go into detailed explanations of each section in the following chapters.

TIMELINE FOR THE FILM, *SÉANCE*

September/October 2005: Optioned Screenplay

a. Optioned and developed screenplay. (Note: Séance had already been registered with the copyright office long before we did the option. If the script that you are optioning has not been send to the copyright office, please do this first.)

b. Did a table read so that the writer/director and I could hear the script out loud and make any necessary changes at this early stage. We had some actor friends do the read for us as a favor (also smart of them, as it's a great chance to meet the director). Given that we were going to be doing this project as a $200,000 SAG ultra low budget, we were really listening for places in the script to cut without affecting the integrity of the story. If you can have your line producer there for the table read to give feedback, that would be excellent.

c. Got the budget done. I know it seems early, but I wanted to be sure that the script could really be done for the $200,000 budget we were aiming for. This preliminary budget and shooting schedule might cost between $750 and $1,500 to do, but Kate and I felt that it was an investment. We reimbursed ourselves for the cost when we started preproduction on the film. I just want to point out here that in regarding to spending money, there are four places that you will need to spend money up front:

  1. Budget/schedule (I have paid anywhere from $750 to $1,500).
  2. Opening your Limited Liability Company (in California it's $70 to open your LLC).
  3. Script clearance report (the prices vary, but it's approximately $1,500).
  4. Legal advice (this will vary depending on what you need at this early stage).

> **Note**
>
>
> Producing this film today, I would add an additional expense: social media. This could include a number of items, such as a website, one-sheet poster, trailer, and the like. I recently did this for a current project, *Omarr the Camel*, and that cost came to $1,000. So this cost is something to keep in mind today; even if you are going the traditional route of sales agents and distributors, you will still need to do a certain amount of self-marketing. In addition, having an online presence today also helps attract investors at this early stage in the process.

November/December 2005: Business Plan and PPM

a. Did the business plan. As you will see from my chapter describing our business plan, we kept it quite brief. It may only take a few weeks, but because there is a certain amount of research involved, allow yourself the time.

b. Did the private placement memorandum (PPM), the operating agreement, and the subscription agreement. We read a number of PPMs and operating agreements that we borrowed from other producers. We pulled out the best from all of them, typed up our own versions, and then had our attorney look them over.

> **Note**
>
>
> As I mentioned earlier, if I were producing *Séance* in today's market, I would begin a serious, well-planned social media campaign using every possible online networking platform to help launch the brand that is my movie. I would make a concerted effort to begin the process of building a dedicated fan base. Jon Reiss stresses the importance of "creating a dynamic website" ("My Adventure in Theatrical Self-Distribution," *Filmmaker Magazine*, Fall, 2008). He urges us to do this long before we produce our movie. He cautions that "old-style film websites are out and blogging and a constant flow of information are in. Blogging and tagging is what the little bots out in cyberspace will recognize and bring you up in the rankings. A great website also helps you cultivate your niche audience."
>
> I interviewed JC Calciano for my chapter on alternative forms of distribution, but one of the items he suggests is worth mentioning here as well. "What I do," JC says, "is start with grassroots and free marketing like Facebook and Twitter. The Internet is the best value for an indie film producer looking to build an audience

for cheap. So I concentrate my efforts there. One thing I've done which has been extremely successful for me is to create a webisode. I figured I'd make something simple and sexy that would draw my target audience weekly. I started the webisode a year before my first movie and I've build a fan base on the Internet to market my movies through my webisode. Each of my webisodes average between 20,000 to 50,000 views a day!" Okay, so JC started a year before his film, and if you're reading this book, chances are you want to start getting ready to producing now, but I think what JC is saying is brilliant advice. So why not start something now – something that is different and unique and will grab an audience and expand your fan base long before your film comes out?

January 2006: Opened an LLC

a. *Opened an LLC.* There were three steps involved. The first was going online to the California secretary of state's site and doing a name search, which was free. Our first choice, "Séance, LLC," was available. The second step was to download the application to apply for our Séance, LLC, filing number. I mailed it off, and less than two weeks later it was back with an assigned number and a red stamp. Now it was time to get our federal Employer Identification Number (EIN), which was free. That took a few minutes online filling out a one-page application; an hour later, I got the EIN number. You need both numbers to open your bank account. I will explain this in more detail in Chapter 5.

b. Completed packages. It was time to type up some professional-looking labels with Séance, LLC, written on them to stick on the front of the professional-looking folders that we had put together with the business plan, PPM, operating agreement, and subscription agreement. We did not include a one-sheet poster of the film in the package. However, for *Candy Stripers*, we did create a poster, which was very visual and gave a great depiction of the film at one glance. So it was worth the additional cost ($40) in that case.

c. Created a detailed timeline. The timeline took us from early January through to the American Film Market in November; we included in the timeline how many units (shares) we needed to sell given our start date for principal photography: May 21, 2006.

d. Created a list of possible finders and investors we were going to be calling and a list of people to whom we wanted to mail our business plan/LLC packages.

January/February/March: Funding the Film

a. Began the calls and mail-outs.

b. Scheduled and prepared for a sales presentation. In the case of *Séance*, we actually didn't need to do a sales presentation because we had over 50 percent of the investors from *Candy Stripers* come back on board, and our writer/director took on selling units as well, so there was not as much work involved as there was with our first low-budget film. With *Candy Stripers*, we scheduled and held two sales presentations. A total of 110 packages went out to potential investors on *Candy Stripers*, and only 35 went out on *Séance*. Raising the money for *Candy Stripers* took five months; for *Séance*, it took less than one month. So please keep that in mind when you are doing your timeline. You will probably need several months (or more) to reach your goal the first time you raise money.

c. Script clearance. This is the time to get your script off to a script clearance company. The script clearance paperwork will be needed for delivery when the time comes, so the sooner the better. This step may cost as much as $1,500, but it is required. We reimbursed ourselves for the cost out of our delivery costs budget when we started production.

March: Finalized Details

a. Met with our line producer and director to do additional work on the budget and schedule. We also discussed location ideas and some of the keys (department heads) that we all wanted on board and scheduled an early April table read with as many keys as possible. Because we were going to be a SAG signatory production, our line producer sent in the SAG signatory paperwork. Getting

---

Note

We are just about to enter the soft prep stage; in today's market, I would be getting my fans (from Facebook, Twitter, YouTube, and so on) involved. I would be doing fun YouTube videos sharing about the fact that we are going into soft prep and what that entails. I would really be taking advantage of every social networking avenue at this point. We're about to get in to the really fun stuff – what a great opportunity to get fans on board! In fact, I would continue this intense social networking throughout the entire filmmaking process.

your number can take a couple of weeks, so it's important to do the paperwork early.

b. Met with the director regarding his storyboard for the film.

April: Soft Prep – Four Weeks

a. The beginning of soft prep: four weeks.
b. Did a table read of the screenplay (again with actor friends) for the line producer, writer/director, director of photography (DP), visual effects supervisor, and 1st assistant director (AD). Anyone else you may have on board should be there as well. There is no money being spent at this time, and you may lose some keys to other projects, as they are not locked in financially, but it is still extremely valuable to have an early table read. The feedback is invaluable.
c. Posted *Séance* production start date in the Industry trade publications (*Hollywood Reporter* and *Variety*, for example).
d. Started pinning down locations and getting that paperwork ready to sign.

April: Casting

a. Began the casting process.
b. Received our SAG signatory number from SAG.
c. Started my weekly email to the investors to keep them posted. This email continued throughout principal, postproduction, and delivery.
d. Contacted the Humane Society to inform them that we would be using an animal in our film.
e. Week of April 3: Typed up and sent in the Character Breakdowns to Breakdown Services.
f. Week of April 10: Breakdown services headshots started to come in by email, so I forwarded them on to the director. He forwarded his choices back to me for each role and I started booking auditions for a week out. In other words, on Monday I booked the following Monday, and on Tuesday I booked the following Tuesday, and so on.
g. Week of April 17: Casting was done with the director, a reader, Kate, and myself. Chapter 8 will explain clearly how I organized every detail.
h. Week of April 24: April 24 and the morning of April 25 were actors' call-back days and the afternoon of the 25th was for "chemistry call-backs." These are necessary to see what the chemistry is like between the actors. For example, you will need them for

boyfriend/girlfriend, college roommates, sisters, and so on. I used Wednesday through Friday (April 26–April 28) to get the deal memos off to the agents/managers or to the actors themselves who were not SAG. Because *Séance* was SAG ultra low budget, we were able to use a certain percentage of non-SAG actors.

May 1: Preproduction Begins – Three Weeks

a. Now I officially started spending money. Our line producer, Mike Tarzian, moved into my office with his production coordinator and an assistant. It is the beginning of official preproduction. At this budget level and with a 14-day shoot, three weeks of preproduction is what works – and with a good deal of work accomplished in soft prep, it works perfectly.

b. Mike began confirming and hiring the rest of the keys.

c. Mike and I signed off on the location deals we began in soft prep.

d. Booked our parrot and did the paperwork with the bird's owner.

e. Mike and the 1st AD scheduled a table read meeting for all the keys for the week before principal photography.

f. I set up a table read for the actors, director, and head of wardrobe.

g. Talked to our editor about any suggestions/requests he might have to ensure we got everything he needed.

h. Met with Chris Robbins, our stills and "Making Of" photographer, to discuss what was needed and prepared the schedule for his days on the set.

i. I also finished up some last-minute cast deal memos, met with my director about his storyboard, worked with the director and 1st AD on any changes to the schedule, worked closely with Mike as he confirmed his keys and finalized with him any permits needed for our locations, and went over the budget again with Mike to make sure we were ready to roll.

j. Kept the actor's agents/managers updated with revised schedules.

k. Emailed our investors the film shooting schedule with suggestions as to which days they could come to visit the set.

May 21: Principal Photography – Two Weeks

a. Was on set constantly to ensure that everything was running smoothly.

b. Kate and I prepared for postproduction by interviewing and hiring our composer, color correction specialist, and sound designer.

c. We sent press releases and still shots to horror/thriller websites and magazines and started looking into possible film festivals.
d. We also started planning for the wrap party.
e. Talked further to possible sales agents/distributors.
f. Sent daily still photos off to our investors and was available to meet the those investors who came to the set.

Note

Making *Séance* today, I would absolutely get my actors supporting my online social media campaign. I would request that they each use their own fan base to help get the word out as well.

June 5–September 29: Postproduction

a. During the week of June 5, Mike moved back into my office and tied up all the loose ends, paid bills, did the SAG delivery book, and created wrap books for the director, DP, and producers.
b. June 5–June 9: editor's assembly.
c. June 11–June 23: director's cut.
d. We scheduled our audience testing.
e. July 5: audience testing.
f. July 10–14: final pickup shots and director's and producer's final edit.
g. July 15: lock picture.
h. July 17–September 29: it was in the hands of the composer, color correction, and sound designer. The director and I did spotting with each of them during that time.
i. I used the DVD with temp music to send off to interested sales agents and to film festivals with a note to both that the final version was forthcoming.
j. We were preparing our front and end roll credits and hired our "Making Of" photographer to design a great opening and closing sequence for the titles. We made sure our ten-second WindChill Films company logo was ready. We hired Power Design, who had created our Snowfall Films logo a few years earlier, and they were fast, brilliant, and professional. WindChill was going to be the overall brand name, so we wanted the best possible logo.

k. We started to assemble some delivery items, as we were very close to the American Film Market (AFM) start date.

l. We signed a deal with a sales agent. Sent them a DigiBeta to send off to the film market.

Note

Today, self-distribution is an alternative option that film producers are taking full advantage of. I address this topic in greater detail in Chapter 13.

October: Prepared for Market

a. Our sales agent scheduled a screening during AFM and prepared the posters, one-sheets, and trailer.

November 1–8: Attended the American Film Market

a. Went to our AFM screening and were available if our sales agent needs us or anything else from us.

November 9–December 15: Delivery

a. Kate and I really got to work on the entire seven-page, single-spaced list of delivery items we received from our sales agent. We made an extra copy of everything for ourselves and because we sold *Séance* to a domestic distributor during the AFM, we researched E&O insurance companies as well during this time period.

Exercise

Now that you have a sense of the timeline for *Séance*, get some poster board and do a brief timeline for your film. Obviously, you don't have to be as detailed as we were here, but it is really important to get something on paper now!

Chapter 3

The Script: Option and Development

TIME TO DO THE PAPERWORK

Let's get a few things straight right away. You may be thinking, "I don't really need to read this part because I am optioning my friend's script." Or you are saying, "It's my sister's script, for heaven's sake; I'm not going to ask her to sign an option, she's family." I don't care whose script it is – you have to do the paperwork. It's a business, right? *Do the paperwork.* Also, people can get really weird about their baby, "the screenplay." I made that mistake early on with a very close friend of mine. She was the nicest, sweetest woman – very trustworthy. The minute we started to get solid interest in the script from some of the big production companies, the writer wanted the moon – extremely unreasonable and unrealistic. We had to walk away from the project and attempt to scrape the egg off our faces. If we had signed an option agreement with her and made certain that everything was clear on paper first, none of that would have happened.

As I mentioned in my introduction, my friend John called me from the Cannes Film Market and said that a distributor was interested in the selling and distribution of his film. He was overjoyed until he called the writer and she told him that because she and the director had had a falling out "there wasn't a chance in hell she was going to sign the option." When I asked him why he hadn't had her sign the option agreement at the beginning, he said that the writer was his friend, and why do the paperwork if it's your friend? As bad as I felt for him, the fact is that he had failed to address the business part of the business and get everything signed off on before moving ahead.

RESEARCH AND READ OPTION AGREEMENTS

When it comes to option agreements, please do your research and read a few of them to get educated as to what is required. There are many templates out there in books and online. I know that when you are doing a low-budget film, you will not have money to pay for an attorney to create the option, deal memo, contracts, and other items that you will need for your film. However, what I do is research the ones that are already out there and get copies of other producers' option agreements and deal memos and then take the best of all of them. Then I create my own versions and give them to an attorney to make sure they cover everything that needs to be covered. Better to pay for that one or two hours of the attorney's time than to hire him or her to do an entire deal memo.

On my bigger films, I always have attorney fees in the budget, but at the SAG ultra-low level it just isn't possible to pay for an attorney to create your option agreement and all necessary deal memos from scratch. This was a perfect alternative, and I was able to get a lot more educated on deal memos and contracts along the way, which I feel as a producer is of critical importance. Even if you have a great attorney, *please* read every deal memo that you will be signing off on. Ultimately, it is your responsibility.

WHAT'S NEEDED IN AN OPTION/PURCHASE AGREEMENT

My option/purchase agreement covers all the necessary legal points. Most are self-explanatory, but I will explain briefly those areas that might be confusing, and I've provided an example of an actual option/purchase agreement later in this section. But first, here's what it must cover:

1. Underlying rights option/purchase agreement.
2. Exercising the option. Here is the wording from the option agreement on *Portal*: "Producer may exercise the Option at any time on or before the expiration of the Option Period by delivering written notice to Writer of Producer's intention to purchase the Property and payment of $1,000.00, which shall be deducted from the total compensation." As you can see, we were able to exercise the option with a portion of the purchase price. However, there are other times when Kate and I exercise the option with the full purchase price. If you are dealing with a guild writer, you need to exercise with the full purchase price. "Exercising the option" simply means that the rights for the project transfer directly to you the producer.
3. Total compensation.
4. Writers' additional services.

5. Credit
6. Sequels and remakes
7. Representations and warranties. This section explains that the writer is the sole and exclusive author of the property and that the writer owns the sole and exclusive rights, title and interest in and to the property, free and clear of any right, claim, lien, title, or interest of any third party.
8. No obligation to use services and proceeds. This part of the agreement explains how the producer is not obligated to use all or any portion of the screenplay or the results and proceeds of writer's services.
9. Assignment. This section gives the producer the unrestricted right to assign, license, delegate, or otherwise transfer and convey this agreement to any firm, corporation, partnership, or entity for the express purpose of further developing and/or producing the picture.
10. Ownership of rights and services. This section is quite a long paragraph but is very important because it greatly protects the producer. Briefly, it states that the writer agrees that in the event the producer properly exercises the option, the producer shall automatically become the sole and exclusive worldwide owner of all rights, titles, and interest in the work.
11. Joint and several obligations. This section explains that all benefits and obligations shall be the joint obligations of each of the producers and each of the writers.
12. Notices. This section simply states that all notices and payments pursuant to this agreement must be in writing and sent to the appropriate party at the address set forth below.
13. Claims/liability. This section is used in every agreement I have ever seen; it basically states that once the writer is paid the purchase price, the writer shall not in any way constitute or give rise to the writer having a lien or claim upon the picture.
14. Indemnification. This section is a crucial point because it states that the writer indemnifies the producer and the producer indemnifies the writer. They agree to hold each other harmless from and against any and all claims, liabilities, and causes of action arising out of a material breach.
15. Choice of law and jurisdiction.
16. No partnership or joint venture. This section points out that the agreement does not constitute either party the agent of the other, or create a partnership or joint venture between the parties.

17. Entire agreement. This section is already fairly clear. It states that this agreement contains the full and complete understanding between the parties with regard to the subject matter and cannot be modified or amended except by a written instrument signed by each party.

18. Capacity to contract. This section refers to the fact that both the writer and producer represent and warrant that they have full power and authority to enter into this agreement.

Do some research on option agreements and look at a few of them before choosing a template that works for you. Then, *please*, once you have put yours together, have an entertainment attorney read it over. Figure 3.1 shows the agreement that we used on *Portal*.

March 14, 2006

Maurice Kelly
Kelly Blumetti Entertainment Group
Address

George Blumetti
Kelly Blumetti Entertainment Group
Address

RE: Portal (Screenplay)

Dear Maurice and George,

*This letter will confirm the understanding between Maurice Kelly and George Blumetti ("Writer") and Portal Film ("Producer") with respect to the development and production of the screenplay entitled **Portal** ("Screenplay") and the motion picture based hereon ("Property").*

DEAL POINTS

1.   UNDERLYING RIGHTS OPTION/PURCHASE AGREEMENT. Writer shall be paid a $ 10.00 initial option fee for a 12 month option period ("Option").

2.   EXERCISING THE OPTION. Producer may exercise the Option at any time on or before the expiration of the Option Period by delivering written notice to Writer of Producer's intention to purchase the Property and payment of $1,000.00 which shall be deducted from the total compensation.

3.   TOTAL COMPENSATION. If Producer elects to exercise the Option, Writer shall be paid the balance of the compensation as follows:

a.   Writer shall receive the balance of the total cash price, $ 4,000.00 on or before the date of commencement of principal photography.

b.   Writer shall receive a backend participation of 5% of Producers Net Profit.

FIGURE 3.1

4.   *WRITERS ADDITIONAL SERVICES. It is expressly agreed by the parties that the Cash Purchase Price includes full and complete compensation for the Writer's continued services as follows: Writer shall provide one rewrite and polish of the Screenplay. Such services shall be provided if and when requested by Producer.*

5.   *CREDIT. Writer shall receive on-screen credit, on a single card, in the main titles of the Picture, if there are main titles, and in all paid advertising in which the Producer or director receives credit and such credit shall be accorded in a size of type no less than that accorded the Producer of the Picture. Said credit shall be substantially in the following form:*

"Screenplay by Maurice Kelly and George Blumetti"

Notwithstanding the immediately preceding two sentences, Writer's credits in paid advertising shall be subject to the usual industry exclusions, which include but are not limited to, exclusions for nomination, congratulatory or award advertising.

No casual or inadvertent failure by Producer to comply with the provisions hereof, nor failure of any other person or entity to comply with its agreements with Producer relating to the aforesaid credits shall constitute a breach by Producer of its obligations hereunder. Producer shall use reasonable efforts to prospectively cure any credit error under this paragraph upon written notification that such credit error has occurred, and Producer shall use its best efforts to obtain a binding obligation from third parties involved in exploitation of the Picture to observe the credit obligations hereunder.

6.   *SEQUELS AND REMAKES. If Producer desires to develop any theatrical remake or theatrical sequel, television pilot/series, television mini-series or television motion picture (collectively, "Future Project"), then subject to Writer's availability as and when requested by Producer, upon reasonable prior notice, then Producer shall contact Writer and both Producer and Writer agree to negotiate in good faith with regard to Writer's writing services in connection with each such Future Project; provided further, however, that the financial terms hereunder with respect to the Picture shall serve as a minimum "floor" in connection with each such Future Project. Writer shall have first right of refusal. It is expressly agreed by the parties that nothing in this Paragraph 6 or elsewhere in this Agreement obligates Producer to produce a Future Project.*

7.   *REPRESENTATIONS AND WARRANTIES. As a material inducement to Producer to enter into this Agreement, Writer represents and warrants to Producer as follows:*

(a) Prior to the date hereof, Writer did not, and during the Option Period and any extensions thereof, and at any time after the Option Period if the Option is exercised, Writer shall not, exercise, authorize others to exercise, or permit the exercise by others of, any of the rights granted to Producer hereunder in the Property;

FIGURE 3.1   (*Continued*)

(b) Writer is the sole and exclusive author of the Property and Writer owns the sole and exclusive rights, title and interests in and to the Property, free and clear of any right, claim, lien, title or interest of any third party;

(c) To the best of Writer's knowledge neither the Property nor Producer's exercise of any rights granted to Producer hereunder will infringe upon or violate any right or interest of any nature whatsoever of any third party; and

(d) Writer is unaware and has no knowledge of any person(s) and/or entity(ies) that claim they have any lien, interest, right and/or title in and to the Property.

8.   *NO OBLIGATION TO USE SERVICES AND PROCEEDS. Producer is not obligated to use all or any portion of the Screenplay or the results and proceeds of Writer's services hereunder, and upon exercise of option Producer has the right to add to, subtract from, use, not use, or otherwise alter the whole or any part of the Screenplay and Writer's services and creations hereunder, free and clear of any "moral rights" of authors. Producer and/or its affiliates have no obligation to make, produce, release, distribute, advertise and/or exploit the Picture, and Writer hereby releases Producer and/or its affiliates from liability for any loss or damage they may suffer by reason of Producer's failure to do so, provided always that nothing herein shall relieve Producer of any payment obligation Producer may have hereunder.*

9.   *ASSIGNMENT. Writer hereby agrees that Producer shall have the unrestricted right to assign, license, delegate or otherwise transfer and convey this Agreement or any or all of Producer's rights, obligations, options or privileges hereunder, in whole or in part, to any person, firm, corporation, partnership or entity for the express purpose of further developing and/or producing the Picture. Any such reassignment of this Agreement to any third party shall include an assumption of all terms and conditions herein, and provided such condition is met, Producer shall no longer be primarily or secondarily liable under this Agreement after the date of such assignment.*

10.   *OWNERSHIP OF RIGHTS AND SERVICES. Writer agrees that in the event Producer properly exercises the Option, Producer shall automatically become the sole and exclusive worldwide owner of all right, title and interest in the Work and the Picture and all rights of every nature therein and thereto, whether now known or hereafter devised, including but not limited to: all copyrights therein throughout the world; the sole, exclusive, and worldwide owner of all motion picture, television (whether filmed, taped, or otherwise recorded and including series rights), theatrical, and incidental rights in the Work and all screenplays and any other adaptations thereof whether heretofore or hereafter written by Writer or any other person; all sequel, prequel and remake rights; all advertising rights (including publication rights); all rights to exploit, distribute and exhibit any motion picture or other production based upon the Work in all media now known or hereafter devised; all rights to make any and all changes to and*

FIGURE 3.1   *(Continued)*

adaptations of the Work, and Writer waives any rights of "droit moral;" all rights of every nature in and to the characters, story lines, and plots contained in the Work and the Picture; all merchandising, sound track, music publishing and other allied and ancillary exploitation rights; the right to use Writer's name in connection with the exploitation of the rights granted hereunder; and all other rights customarily obtained in connection with formal literary purchase agreements. Writer shall take all steps necessary to document the assignment and registration of such rights to Producer. Should Producer exercise the Option, then for purposes of United States copyright laws, Producer shall be the sole author of the Work and the Picture.

11.   *JOINT AND SEVERAL OBLIGATIONS. If there is more than one Producer or Writer hereunder, all benefits and obligations hereunder shall be the joint and several benefits and obligations of each of the Producers and each of the Writers, as the case may be. Moreover, all representations and warranties made hereunder shall be deemed as being made jointly and severally by each of the Producers and each of the Writers, as the case may be.*

12.   *NOTICES. All notices and payments to either party pursuant to this Agreement must be in writing and sent to the appropriate party at the address or fax number set forth below. Notices and payments sent by mail shall be deemed received three days after deposited with the U.S. postal service (ten days if deposited with the postal service of a foreign country) postage prepaid and properly addressed. Notices sent by telefax shall be deemed received on the date sent. Written notice may not be sent via computer generated electronic mail. Changes in either party's address for notice/payment must be communicated to the other party in writing.*

        To Writer: *George Blumetti and Maurice Kelly*
                              Kelly Blumetti Entertainment Group
                              Address

        To Producer: *Portal Film, LLC.*
                              2321 W. Olive Avenue, Suite A
                              Burbank, CA 91506

13.   *CLAIMS/LIABILITY. Writer acknowledges and agrees that Producer is under no obligation to make and/or distribute the Picture. It is expressly agreed that the compensation payable to Writer pursuant to the terms of this Agreement, shall not in any way constitute or give rise to Writer having a lien or claim upon the Picture, upon any rights therein and/or upon any proceeds received from the commercial exploitation of the Picture. Writer shall not have the right to seek equitable relief hereunder, including without limitation, the right to enjoin or restrain the development, pre-production, production, distribution or exploitation of the Work or Picture, or any rights therein.*

14.   *INDEMNIFICATION. Writer hereby indemnifies and agrees to hold Producer harmless from and against any and all claims, liabilities and causes of action (including costs and outside attorney's fees in connection*

FIGURE 3.1   *(Continued)*

therewith) arising out of a material breach of any of Writer's representations, warranties and obligations contained in this Agreement. Producer hereby indemnifies and agrees to hold Writer harmless from and against any and all claims, liabilities and causes of action (including costs and attorney's fees in connection therewith) arising out of (a) Producer's breach of this Agreement and/or (b) Producer incorporating into the Property or Screenplay any third party's ideas, material, or property.

15.   *CHOICE OF LAW AND JURISDICTION. This Agreement shall be governed by the laws of the State of California applicable to contracts entered into and to be wholly performed entirely within California. The parties hereby submit and consent to the jurisdiction of the courts located in Los Angeles, California, and stipulate that such courts are convenient to the resolution of any disputes relating to this Agreement or the formation, interpretation or breach hereof, subject, however, to any arbitration requirements contained elsewhere herein.*

16.   *NO PARTNERSHIP OR JOINT VENTURE. The Agreement does not constitute either party the agent of the other, or create a partnership or joint venture between the parties, and neither party shall have the power to obligate or bind the other in any manner whatsoever. Neither of the parties hereto shall hold itself out contrary to the provisions of this paragraph by advertising or otherwise. This Agreement shall not be construed to be for the benefit of any third party.*

17.   *ENTIRE AGREEMENT. This Agreement contains the full and complete understanding between the parties with regard to the subject matter hereof and cannot be modified or amended except by a written instrument signed by each party. This Agreement supersedes all prior agreements and understandings between the parties with regard to the subject matter hereof, whether such agreements and understandings were written or oral. Writer acknowledges that no representation or promise not expressly contained in this Agreement has been made by Producer or any of its agents, employees or representatives.*

18.   *CAPACITY TO CONTRACT. Writer and Producer hereby represent and warrant that they have full power and authority to enter into this Agreement, and neither is under any obligation, restriction or disability, created by law or otherwise, which would in any manner or to any extent prevent or restrict Writer and/or Producer from entering into this Agreement and fully performing hereunder. The assent of each party to this Agreement shall be indicated by the signature of its duly authorized agent below.*

Any controversy or claim arising out of or relating to this agreement or any breach thereof shall be settled by arbitration in accordance with the rules of the American Arbitration Association, and judgment upon the award rendered by the arbitrators may be entered in any court having jurisdiction thereof. The prevailing party shall be entitled to reimbursement for costs and reasonable attorney's fees. The determination of the arbitrator in such proceedings shall be final and binding.

FIGURE 3.1   (*Continued*)

If this concurs with your understanding of our relationship on the Picture, please sign below.

AGREED TO AND UNDERSTOOD

_____   _____

George Blumetti, Writer   *Date*

_____   _____

Maurice Kelly, Writer   *Date*

_____   _____

Suzanne Lyons for Portal Film, LLC   *Date*

FIGURE 3.1   (*Continued*)

OPTION PERIOD

In the three ultra-low-budget films (each costing around $200,000) we produced and the one we executive-produced, Kate and I knew we were going to be shooting within six to eight months of the initial option agreement date, so our options were for a twelve-month period. But in cases where we were optioning a project to pitch to the studios or to put together as a Canadian/UK coproduction, those options were eighteen months. In most cases, our option agreements were twelve months with an automatic six-month extension if we had certain elements attached. Because Kate and I offer only $10 for the option, we really tried to keep our agreement within the eighteen-month period and to work as quickly and effectively as possible, creating urgency with each phone call we made.

PAYMENT AND BACK END

At the SAG ultra-low-budget level, we offered the writer $10 for the option and $5,000 for the price of the screenplay. We paid $1,000 the first day of preproduction so that we could start the paperwork on the copyright transfer, and then we paid the final $4,000 on the first day of principal photography. We offered a percentage of the producer's net profits, but at this budget it's not necessary. Many times, at this budget level, it is a first-time writer and a first-time director who are getting the chance to see their dream of having their film produced. Your writer and director are getting a DVD. It's really like giving them a check for $200,000! It's their show-piece. And if it is a success, it is the writer and the director who will get the recognition. The agents and studios will be knocking on their doors.

You, as the producer, will be spending nearly two years (and beyond!) producing the film and your salary in the budget will no doubt be much less than $5,000. After having gone through the last few years producing these films, I believe that as much of the back end as possible (if there is any at all) should go to the producer. If there is any money coming in, this may be the only way you recoup your costs. If you think you want to share part of the producer's net profit, then offer a small percentage to the writer and director. However, if their name is helping you sell the units for your film or will help in the selling of your film to distributors, like your lead actor's name would, then that is different. That is worth some points on the back end.

DEFERMENTS

I try to avoid deferments at this budget level. It would be a pain to say to the investors when the first check comes in from a territory sale, "Oh, sorry, but I have deferments to the writer, director, and cast to make first." Kate and I had to do it only once on our low-budget films. I hear producers touting it all the time and I really don't get it. People talk about deferments as if they are not an issue, but they are. Personally, I don't think it's fair to the investors. When the money starts to come in, you want it to go the investors. You don't want a long list of cast and crew who are still owed money that you deferred. Keep it clean and simple. You know your budget, raise the money, and pay people during production. Everyone got paid on our films and everyone was happy.

CERTIFICATE OF AUTHORSHIP AND SHORT-FORM ASSIGNMENT

I always make a point of attaching two additional pieces to the option agreement, the certificate of authorship and the short-form assignment. The certificate of authorship states that the writer is the sole writer of the screenplay and that the writer has to sign his or her name to that effect. Figure 3.2 shows a sample copy that I use in my workshop.

CERTIFICATE OF AUTHORSHIP

I, _____ *(writer's name), hereby certify that all rewrites and other literary material of whatever kind or nature to be written by me, if any (all such literary material being referred to herein as the "Material"), for Snowfall Films ("Producer") pursuant to the terms of that certain Option and Purchase Agreement between me and Producer dated as of ----------------- (date) (as may be amended from time to time) (the "Option Agreement") in connection with the proposed motion picture presently entitled "project name" (the "Picture"), has been or will be solely created by me as a "work made for hire," specially ordered or commissioned by Producer for use as part of the Picture with Producer being deemed the sole author of the Material for copyright purposes and the owner of all rights of every kind or nature, whether now known or hereafter devised (including, but not limited to, all copyrights and all extensions and renewals of copyrights) in and to the Material, with the right to make all uses of the material in perpetuity throughout the universe and to make all changes in the Material as Producer deems necessary or desirable. To the extent that Producer is not otherwise vested with all the foregoing rights as the author-at-law, I hereby assign and transfer to Producer, subject to the terms of the Option Agreement, any and all rights of every kind, whether in writing or not in writing, in connection with the Material, throughout the universe, in perpetuity, including the copyright thereof and all extensions and renewals of such copyright, and the right to exploit any and all such rights in any and all media, whether now known or hereafter known or devised.*

To the extent permitted by applicable law, I hereby waive the "moral rights of authors," as said term is commonly understood.

I warrant and represent that I am free to execute this Certificate of Authorship; that I have made no agreements, grants, assignment, or commitments which will conflict with or impair the complete enjoyment of the rights and privileges granted to Producer hereunder; that the Material is wholly original with me, is not in the public domain, and does not and shall not infringe upon or violate any copyright, right of privacy or publicity, or any other right, of any person, and does not and shall not defame, libel, or slander any person; that no motion picture, television, radio, dramatic, or other version of the Material has heretofore been made, produced, or performed; that there is no claim or action pending, outstanding or threatened which might in any way prejudice the rights granted or to be granted hereunder.

I shall defend, indemnify, and hold harmless Producer and any corporations comprising Producer, its and their employees, partners, officers, directors, agents, assignees, licensees and attorneys from and against any and all liability, claims, costs, damages and expenses (including attorneys' fees and court costs whether or not in connection with litigation) arising out of or in connection with my breach of any of the covenants, warranties or representations made by me herein.

I agree to execute any documents consistent herewith and do any other acts as may be reasonably required by Producer or its assignees or licensees to further evidence or effectuate Producer's rights as set forth in this Certificate of Authorship. Upon my failure promptly to do so after reasonable notice, I hereby appoint Producer as my attorney-in-fact for such purposes (it being acknowledged that such appointment is irrevocable and coupled with an interest) with full power of substitution and delegation.

FIGURE 3.2

I further acknowledge that (i) in the event of any breach of the Option Agreement by Producer, I will be limited to my remedy at law for damages, if any, and will not have the right to terminate or rescind this Certificate of Authorship or seek to enjoin the Picture or any other work based on the Material, (ii) nothing herein or in the Option Agreement shall obligate Producer to use my services or the results or proceeds thereof in the Picture or to produce, advertise or distribute the Picture, and (iii) this Certificate of Authorship shall be governed by the law of the United States and the State of California applicable to agreements executed and to be performed entirely therein.

This Certificate of Authorship is subject to the terms and conditions of the Option Agreement, and in the event of any conflict between the provisions of this Certificate of Authorship and the Option Agreement, the provisions of the Option Agreement shall control.

I have executed this document as of _____ (date).

_____
Writer's name

FIGURE 3.2   (*Continued*)

The short-form assignment states that the writer gives you, the producer, the right to transfer the copyright when you have paid the full purchase price for the screenplay. It literally transfers the rights of the author and grants those rights to the assignee as if they were the author in perpetuity. I have looked at many templates for option agreements, and seldom do I see this short form agreement attached to it. I had a friend tell me about one of his early films on which he didn't know about the short-form agreement and thought the option agreement was sufficient. When it came time to transfer the rights and fill out the copyright paperwork, he needed the short-form assignment signed by the writer to allow him the right to do the transfer, and the writer refused to sign it unless he was paid an additional $10,000! No chain of title, no movie! It's that simple.

Figure 3.3 shows a copy of the short-form assignment for *Candy Stripers*.

SHORT FORM ASSIGNMENT

*For good and valuable consideration, receipt of which is hereby acknowledged, the undersigned, Jill Garson and Kate Robbins ("Writers"), hereby sells, grants, conveys, transfers and assigns to Candy Stripers, LLC ("Producer") and its successors, licensees and assigns, exclusively and forever, all right, title and interest in and to that certain screenplay owned and written by Writers presently entitled **Candy Stripers** (the "Property"), including, but not limited to, all motion picture, television, non-theatrical, home video, interactive, radio, dramatic, publication and allied rights thereto, including the worldwide copyright in the Property and all renewals and extensions of such copyright. The rights granted to Producer hereunder include, but are not limited to, the right to do any acts or things necessary to protect the rights granted hereunder, including the copyright, and to institute any actions for such purpose in the name(s) of Producer, Writers or any of them.*

This Short Form Assignment is expressly made subject to all of the terms, conditions and provisions contained in the certain Option and Purchase Agreement between Writer and Producer dated as of September 14, 2004 (as may be amended from time to time).

IN WITNESS WHEREOF, the undersigned has executed this instrument as of _____, 2004.

FIGURE 3.3

SCRIPT DEVELOPMENT

Once you have the option/purchase agreement, it's time to move to the next step: script development. It's common practice that option agreements state that the writer will provide a rewrite and polish. Note that I am not talking about Writer's Guild agreements. Guild agreements are different; at this budget level, for the most part, you are not dealing with Guild writers. However, if you are, please speak with the Guild in your country about rewrites and polishes. Whether you are going to the studio to pitch it as a bigger budget film or planning to go the low-budget indie route and raise the funds to shoot it yourself, you want the best possible script.

TABLE READ

I strongly suggest that you do a table read. It's free, and you can always have one of your actor friends manage it for you. Have the writer present and the director (if you have a director at this point). There is nothing like hearing the script read aloud to really give you and the writer a clear sense of the story, what can be changed to make it better and what can be cut to make it shorter and more budget-friendly. At the $200,000 budget, 90 to 95 pages is a great length.

Candy Stripers started at 115 pages with more than 60 speaking roles. During the table read, we could see where it could be cut to fit our budget without compromising the integrity of the story.

DIRECTOR'S NOTES

If you have your director on board at this point, he or she will have brilliant suggestions as well. However, many times, at this low budget level, you will have a first-time director, so you – as the producer, knowing your budget level – will have to oversee the rewrite and script changes to ensure that it can be done for the budget you have in mind. On the bigger-budget projects, it is customary for the director to have a much bigger say with regard to the rewrite and direction that the screenplay will take. Film is a director's medium, and it will be his or her vision on the screen. However, at the SAG ultra-low budget level, you – the producer – must work closely with the director and writer. At this budget level, you will have to monitor the changes to ensure they fit the budget. Your director is going to want things that at this budget, you cannot provide. Everyone – the writer, the director, the DP, and the keys – all must be flexible and reasonable, perhaps even willing to push their creative boundaries. Maybe you can't afford that crane for the day, so what are some alternative ways to shoot that scene that will be even more interesting, unique, and artistic?

Get the screenplay as perfect as you possibly can during the development stage. Of course, there will be changes as you move along, but really work to get it where you want it so that you can be confident that your line producer can sign off on the budget you are committed to having.

Chapter 4

Creating Your Business Plan

Great – so you have your option agreement and you've set up your time-line. You've done some development on the script, and you've even done a table read to give you a great sense of what you need to change and what needs to be cut. I know what you're thinking – let's open up the LLC and the bank account. You want to get started raising the money. Hold on. Before you even think about opening up an LLC or a bank account, you have to focus first on your business plan.

K.I.S.S.

Don't worry: setting up a business plan isn't the long, arduous, boring process that you think it is. Writing commercials and promotions in television for years taught me one very important thing: keep it short and simple. Also, I approach everything I do by putting myself in the other person's shoes, in this case, the potential investor. If I'm a busy person, do I want to read a 40- or 50-page business plan? Absolutely not!

TABLE OF CONTENTS

Let's start with the first page, the table of contents. If I were the investor, what would I want to know about the film project, the people involved, the marketplace, and of course, what's in it for me? How can I get involved and how can I possibly benefit from this investment? With these issues in mind, I decided that the following items should be in the business plan:

Quotation
Investor proposal

Project objective
The marketplace
Film comparisons
Company summary
The team
Synopsis
Revenue scenario
Los Angeles Times article
Section 181 (information)
Company mission statement

Note

This business plan was the one used inside the full packet that also held the PPM (private placement memorandum), the operating agreement, and the subscription agreement. If I were sending it out by itself, then I would not be including the investor proposal, revenue scenario, or Section 181 information. I'll explain more about this topic later.

These items literally gave all the information necessary to have the potential investor decide whether or not they were interested. If they were interested, the next order of business was for them to read the full packet, which included the PPM, the operating agreement, and the subscription agreement.

QUOTATION

The quote was easy to find. I just went online and looked up information on projects in the same genre and in the low-budget arena. I had tons to pick from. When I was putting together our first low-budget film, *Candy Stripers*, I decided to pick a quote based on the great success of *Cabin Fever*, which had come out a couple of years earlier. Everyone had heard of that film, and what was so great about this particular quote was that it included the success of the genre: "The audiences keep accepting these films. There doesn't seem to be a saturation point." The quote came from a credible producer and was featured in a respected paper, *Crain's New York Business*.

INVESTOR PROPOSAL

The next page, the investor proposal, was very clear and simple. Once again, I put myself in the investor's shoes. What would get me excited?

What would make me want to participate? Also, any time Kate and I took on any endeavor, we always made a point to stand in abundance, generosity, and graciousness. In the entertainment industry, there seems to be a pervasive feeling of scarcity. There is not enough – roles, jobs, shows, films, money. I have always refused to buy into that story and really work at coming from a place of, a mind set of abundance in everything I do.

So, with that in mind, with *Séance*, I started with three very short paragraphs. Please keep in mind that we were selling units in *Séance* in 2006 and the thriller/horror genre was thriving at that time.

Investor Proposal

 Séance, LLC, is offering a unique opportunity to investors. With the incomparable success of the horror genre in recent years, investors can become involved in a project that has the potential to make a profit, but to do so in a shorter period of time than the more expensive films.

Investors can purchase one or more interest (units) for $7,500.00 (seven thousand five hundred dollars). Commencing from the date of film delivery, investors will benefit by receiving 100% of all profits until they have recouped 110% of their original capital contribution. Thereafter, investors will receive 50% of the profits derived from exploitation of the film in the first five years after delivery.

Investors will be invited* to attend the Wrap Party as well as the Producer's Private Screening of the film (if there is a private screening). Also, Investors are welcome to visit the set to observe the filming of the movie.

Before I get into why the units were $7,500, I will address the other issues in this first part of the proposal. Kate and I had decided to go the traditional route of using a sales agent to sell domestic and foreign territories for us when the film was complete, and we were well aware that most of the sales would be done in the first two years (mostly the first year). There are three major markets worldwide: AFM, Berlin, and Cannes, where most of the sales are done. A lot has changed in the last few years, and there are now numerous ways to self-distribute; I will address this issue in chapter 13. I did not want to keep the LLC open indefinitely, paying taxes and paying an accountant every March to do all the K1s. I knew that would be money coming out of my personal pocket, so the decision was made to keep the LLC open for five years, and to make it very fair, we make it five years from delivery, knowing that it would take nearly a year just to complete the film.

Also, because Kate and I were planning to do a full slate of these films, we wanted to make our investors very, very happy, so before we would get a cent, we offered our investors all the profits until they reached 110 percent. Then and only then would we begin the 50/50 split. You don't have to do it that way at all. You could do what is called a "corridor": a 90/10 split or an 80/20 split from the beginning. As checks begin to come in (and after the sales agent has taken their expenses and commission), your investors would get 90 percent and you (as the producer and manger of the LLC) would get 10 percent, for example. If you do decide to use the corridor, then I would increase the amount the investors receive before you move to the 50/50 split. It could be worded like this:

Commencing from the date of film delivery investors will benefit by receiving 90 percent (with 10 percent going to the producer/manager) of all profits until they have recouped 120 percent of their original capital contribution.

In the third paragraph in the investor proposal, I invited the investors to the wrap party and the screening (if there is a screening), but please note that I put an asterisk (*) on invite. *This is a low-budget film*, so you don't want to make a promise to your investors that you can't keep. And if you just say they are invited to these events, they will assume that you will be paying for their plane ticket and hotel. The sentence at the bottom of the page that followed the asterisk said "All invitations mentioned above are at investors' own expense." *Please* be conscious when you are drawing up your proposal, PPM, and so on: wording is everything. The same holds true when you are speaking about your film project. Don't be misleading in any way. It could cost you dearly. It all goes back to what I talked about in Chapter 1: it's a business!

WHY $7,500? HERE ARE FOUR GOOD REASONS

We mention the price of $7,500 per unit (interest or share). Where did that number come from? The whole idea was to use the SAG ultra-low-budget agreement, which is $200,000. However, where so many producers make their first mistake is right here – and it's an expensive, painful mistake. There is much more to making the movie than the budget of actually producing the movie. A line producer tells a producer that he or she can shoot this movie for $150,000 and then the producer goes off and raises that exact amount. Bad move.

There are other costs that you have to take into account, and these need to be added to your final number before you can open your LLC and start raising funds. There are operating costs that you will incur and for which you will need to be reimbursed when the time comes; there may be fees to be paid to your executive producers (finders), who will be helping to bring financing to your project; and the part that nearly everyone forgets is delivery. There will be expensive delivery costs.

The film's budget is only one part. As you can now see, there are four distinct parts. So keep that in mind and do the math before you complete your business plan package. In fact, if you are anticipating self-distributing your film, you may want to have a separate category for that. There will be additional, perhaps substantial costs associated with this category, including creating a film website, planning a festival circuit, carrying out extensive social media campaigns, and doing a possible four-walling of your film.

1) Let's Start with Delivery

Delivery is not even mentioned in a budget. The words that describe the items needed for delivery don't exist anywhere except on the delivery list – which producers often don't see until the film is long finished. Yet that list can cost anywhere from $15,000 to $30,000. With *Candy Stripers*, *Séance*, and *Portal* and when Kate and I were consulting on *Desert of Blood*, we decided to allow $20,000 for delivery costs. I describe some of the delivery items in Chapter 12.

2) Operating Costs

We knew we wanted around $15,000 for operating costs. We would be spending money on an attorney, budget/schedule, tons of photocopies as we put the LLC/business plan packets together, a possible one-sheet poster, mailing costs, table reads, and sales presentation hotel costs. Also, I don't believe in putting the wrap party in the film budget, so that is a cost you may have to incur. In addition, I know how important it is to be able to have treats for your cast and crew, but in a low-budget film, there's no room for that in your budget, yet it is something you want to have available funds for. Now, of course, none of the money needed for expenses before preproduction came from the investors. It was all our own money, but we kept our receipts and reimbursed ourselves the first day of preproduction from the operating costs budget.

3) Executive Producer Fee

Once again standing in abundance, we decided on an executive producer's fee of 10 percent for those who worked with us to help raise the financing. In some states, you are able to use the term "finder" for those who come on board to help with funding, but because it varies from country to country and in the United States from state to state, ask your attorney about the best and most appropriate term to use.

I know 10 percent sounds ridiculously high – the norm in the industry is 2½ to 5 percent –but our units were going to be so small that it would hardly be worth the effort for someone to make a phone call for $200 or $300. And I knew I needed help. I didn't want to spend a year raising the money for the first project, *Candy Stripers*, so why not be generous and have some of our colleagues work with us and therefore move the project forward with velocity? That way it's a win/win for everyone and your executive producers get to come and be on the set of the film, act in the film, write a song for the film or do any number of the fun jobs that are available.

4) Budget

Your line producer will do your budget. That's not your job. Knowing how to read a budget and a schedule is your job, but you don't have to create the actual budget or schedule. It is one of those areas that stop producers from moving forward. They think they have to do everything, which is just not the case. Line producers are specialists when it comes to budgets, so take advantage of that knowledge. Also, this is one of the places that I do spend money early in the process: hiring someone to do the budget before we even try to start raising funds. As I've mentioned before, make sure to keep track of any out-of-pocket money so that you can be reimbursed during preproduction. When we were doing the SAG ultra-low-budget projects, it was important to keep the budget at $200,000. So, to be safe, we asked our line producer to bring it in at closer to $190,000, allowing us some breathing room during the production of the film.

EXTRA BONUS

On the investor proposal page, there is also an extra bonus that helped us raise the money so quickly that it was amazing. And it's just one more instance of putting yourself in the other person's shoes. Looking at it from their perspective, here is what I came up with:

Should an individual buy and/or sell three to five units, that individual will receive an Executive Producer credit on a shared card in the main titles of the picture.

Should an individual buy and/or sell six or more units, that individual will receive an Executive Producer credit on a single card in the main titles. And in addition, their credit will appear on the movie poster and DVD box.

On the film *Portal*, we sold two sets of six units immediately to two individuals who wanted the credit of executive producer because they were in the process of starting up their own production company. It was an important business move for them to have their company credit in the main title of our film. It was that kind of unconventional – and generous – thinking that had the units sell more quickly. It doesn't take much, just thinking as if you were the investor. What would get *you* excited, make *you* happy, have *you* want to play? Keep that in mind when you are writing up your own investor proposal. In the low-budget world, when the units are this small, it's not as much about making a big profit as it is about playing in the entertainment industry and having fun.

RISK

Please note that on the investor proposal page, I allowed one-third of the page to talk about the risk involved. The risk references are all in capital letters. It begins with this sentence: *ONLY PERSONS WHO CAN AFFORD TO LOSE THEIR ENTIRE INVESTMENT SHOULD PURCHASE THE INTERESTS.*

Then it goes on to tell them to read the OPERATING AGREEMENT and the CONFIDENTIAL PRIVATE PLACEMENT MEMORANDUM. Any time you are mentioning investing in your film, whether on paper or verbally, you have to mention the risk factor.

Once again, the page I have just talked about – the investor proposal – is only part of the business plan that was actually included in my full PPM packet. If I were sending out just the business plan to pique people's interest, separate from the full packet, I would not be permitted to include this page. When you are requesting funds, explaining the process by which people can invest and the benefits they may receive by investing, you are dealing with items that fall under government regulations. Therefore, it's important that these types of proposals be included only when your PPM is attached.

PROJECT OBJECTIVE

The project objective page is fun to write. Mine is only one-third of a page – and it's double-spaced – but it explains the objective very clearly. At the time we were putting together the business plans for these genre films, the game plan was to do a full slate of ten films. No one could foresee what was to take place: the glut of horror films, the worldwide pirating, and the economy breakdown that affected territory sales around the world. Okay, so maybe my timing was a little off! Here is the project objective that we used on *Candy Stripers*:

Our objective is to produce Candy Stripers as a successful feature film that will be one of many "horror" movies that are part of our genre division here at WindChill Films. WindChill Films will be a major contributor of horror films committed to producing a minimum of two projects per year. Our films will be extremely well written with exceptional plots . . . edgy, unique, scary stories that will leave our audiences trembling in their seats and wanting more. In addition to creating quality projects, we are one hundred percent committed to having each and every film generate a healthy profit for our investors.

As you can see, it is something that only you can write. You should never hire someone to write this for you. The project objective makes you think about why you are doing this film or this slate of films. It benefits you as much as the investors, and it forces you to get very clear about what you are trying to accomplish.

THE MARKETPLACE

The marketplace page is fun to work on and very easy to do. I just went on the Internet and found articles on horror films and how great they were doing (at that time) internationally. My page started like this:

The "horror" and "thriller" genres have always done extremely well in the marketplace. Year after year, these films outperform all other genres except action and animation. And action and animation require huge budgets, and therefore a huge risk. Projects like Séance can be produced for a low budget, thus allowing for higher profits.

Then I included a number of quotes that backed up that statement. For example, "It's alive! Horror flicks help restore pulse at box office" and "Massacre appeal: no matter how you slice it, horror movies are making a real killing at the box office." Both these quotes were from reputable sources, in this case, the *Los Angeles Times* and *Entertainment Weekly*, respectively. Once again, there is no guarantee that your film will perform the way the other films performed, but it does give some real credibility as to why you chose your particular film and genre. Others have done it before you and proved to be successful and profitable.

FILM COMPARISONS

I personally think the film comparison page is useless, but everyone seemed to love it. It speaks for itself: it is a list of films in the same genre and budget size as your film, along with the budget amount and how much the film has grossed worldwide. Once again, with the Internet and access to sites like IMDb, it is easy to get both the domestic and worldwide numbers.

The problem that I ran into was finding current films that were done at the budgets we were planning to do – budgets ranging from $200,000 to $600,000 (SAG ultra and SAG modified). There are many cases in which these films have done extremely well and were exceptionally profitable, but because they are often straight to DVD or VOD (video on demand), there are no box office numbers. And because the sales agents who are selling these films often do full buy-outs on each territory sale (which seldom has any back end associated with the deal), there is no way to track the profits.

For example, we sold *Candy Stripers* to Screen Gems as a full buy-out for a specific amount of money, yet Screen Gems went on to make a huge profit. Or so we were told. But we have no way of getting that exact information, and it's not listed online like the numbers are for the box office. That is why it is so important that when you do territory sales, you get a back-end participation so that the distributor will be required to give you quarterly records. That way you will have the numbers you need to help you put your package together for your next project.

COMPANY SUMMARY AND TEAM

Because our company had already completed four films, had won awards, and had been featured at a number of high-profile festivals, we had a great company bio. We also included bios for the writer, director, DP, and line producer. In addition, we added the bios of other keys who had impressive backgrounds. Our composer, for example, had been honored at Sundance and had worked on a number of award-winning films. It is very important to make a note at the bottom of their bios that says "subject to availability." In fact, on *Candy Stripers*, our line producer and our special effects producer had to be replaced a couple of months before production because they got bigger jobs. I love disclaimers and I love being completely honest with people. You are dealing with other people's money, and it is extremely important that they are aware of all of this information.

SYNOPSIS

This one is obvious: you always add the synopsis to your business plan. People have asked me if they should include the entire script or offer the script to investors with the business plan. The answer is "no!" Of the 54 investors who bought a total of 82 units in *Candy Stripers*, *Séance*, and *Portal*, only one investor requested the script, which I of course gave to him. But you don't have to offer it to them. For the most part, investors are not in the entertainment industry, and they wouldn't know how to read a script. It's not easy for people outside the industry. It doesn't read like anything they would have seen before and it will only bring up a ton of questions, comments, and suggestions from someone who doesn't know the world of filmmaking.

REVENUE SCENARIO

As I mentioned earlier, when we were planning to produce *Candy Stripers*, the Internet was not as advanced as it is now in terms of allowing for easier, more efficient ways to self-distribute. So we planned to go the traditional route of having a sales agent sell domestic and foreign territories for us when the film was complete.

We made a point of getting to know sales agents, and we spoke with them about the project very early on. I highly recommend that you do the same. Even if you are planning to go the self-distribution route, I would still get to know sales agents and distributors because you never know what direction your film might take when the time comes. Be open and be educated on all fronts. We asked one of the companies that we had created a great relationship with for sales estimates on our film – and we got them.

In the case of *Candy Stripers*, we were not going to have any major stars, but we were going to have great aliens, and it was going to be a fun, campy horror film being done for the ultra-low budget. So with that information, we got the estimates back. From there, we just did the math: based on the high end sales agent's expenses and commission at that time, we figured out the possible percentage the investors could make, should the sales agent fulfill their estimated sales. Of course, as always, please put a disclaimer at the bottom of the page, because you never really know exactly what the final number will be. They could be much higher or lower, depending on so many variables: the economy, pirating, a glut of films in your genre, the success of your stars, and so on. We wrote in bold block letters: "THESE SCENARIOS ARE FOR ILLUSTRATION PURPOSES ONLY AND SHOULD NOT BE CONSTRUED AS A PROMISE OR AN EXPECTATION OF FUTURE REVENUE."

The revenue scenario also mentions "high-risk investment"; it is important to mention this on any and every page where you are talking about sales estimates, possible profits, and anything that has to do with money. Figure 4.1 shows a sample revenue scenario.

CANDY STRIPERS, LLC

The chart below illustrates how revenues would be distributed in three different earning scenarios. These scenarios are for illustration purposes only -- to show how revenues flow -- and should NOT be construed as a promise or an expectation of future revenue.

Having said that, these ranges are realistic targets for movies like **Candy Stripers**, and the Managers will be working hard to create a product and negotiate a distribution deal that will return as much profit as possible to the Investors. Independent film is a high-risk investment. There is NO GUARANTEE that the Managers will secure a profitable distribution deal or that the film will generate any revenue to the Investors or Managers

Revenue Distribution: Three Scenarios

Total worldwide sales	$600,000	$900,000	$1,200,000
EXPENSES			
Distributor's commissions (25% of sales) *	$150,000	$225,000	$300,000
Distributor's billable expenses ($50,000 cap)	$50,000	$50,000	$50,000
Revenue after expenses:	$400,000	$625,000	$850,000
RETURN ON INVESTMENT			
Return of Investors original capital	$245,000	$245,000	$245,000
Return to Investors of 10% premium	$24,500	$24,500	$24,500
50% of remaining profit to Investors	$65,250	$177,750	$290,250
Total return to Investors:	$334,750	$447,250	$559,750
Total dollars returned per unit:	$9,564	$12,779	$15,993
Profit ir: dollars per unit:	$2,564	$5,779	$8,993
Projected return on investment:	37%	83%	128%

* Fees and expenses charged by the distribution company are negotiable and the Managers will endeavor to execute the best possible deal. Figures shown above are reasonable estimates and could be higher or lower.

THESE SCENARIOS ARE FOR ILLUSTRATION PURPOSES ONLY AND SHOULD NOT BE CONSTRUED AS A PROMISE OR AN EXPECTATION OF FUTURE REVENUE.

FIGURE 4.1

NEWSPAPER ARTICLES

In 2005, there were tons of articles on the amazing success of horror films. We picked one from the *Los Angeles Times* Calendar section that was called "Horror Returns to Make a Killing." How great was that? It was a two-page article with a photo from *The Grudge* on the first page, and the caption under the picture gave the budget of the film at $10 million, stating that it had already made $110 million domestically. The article was written at the same time that we were sending out our PPM/business plan packages. I highly recommend that when you are putting your business plan together, you find a fantastic article that really helps back up what you have been saying in your proposal and gives it additional credibility.

SECTION 181

Our timing was perfect with the film projects we were planning to shoot here in the United States. Section 181, part of the American Job Creation Act, had just been passed, which allowed investors to get an incredible tax write-off if they invested in films that were shooting on American soil. So find out if there are incentives like that in your country and also include any possible local incentives that may benefit investors in any way. In many cases, provincial and state incentives are something you might want to explain in your business plan if your plan is to give them back to the investor. If you are shooting in an area that offers a 25 or 35 percent labor/tax incentive (based on the local spend ... what % of the budget was spent in that state or province), then you might want to do a conservative estimate of what that amount would be and find out approximately when you will see the return from that incentive. That could be a substantial check that could go directly to your investors the minute it arrives, and it's safe, guaranteed money.

MISSION STATEMENT

It is important to write a mission statement for your company. In fact, you should already have one. If you don't, stop reading and go work on your mission statement. Now! I had an investor call to tell me that it was solely because of our company mission statement that he made the decision to buy a unit in one of our films. Plus, it gives more credibility to your company and to you. It makes it all more real. People are not just investing in your film; they are investing in you and your company. Figure 4.2 shows our mission statement.

MISSION STATEMENT
Snowfall Films and WindChill Films

WHO WE ARE:

*Snowfall Films and WindChill Films produce feature films and
television for audiences worldwide.*

We are committed to:

Being on the cutting edge of entertainment.

Creating projects that make an emotional, psychological, or social impact.

Generating vast revenues.

Having fun!

*Snowfall and WindChill provide the opportunity for people to excel, expand, risk,
laugh,
be nurtured, and have creative breakthroughs.*

*People around us prosper financially and personally and experience a new level of
enjoyment and fulfillment in their work.*

*We can be counted on to bring our voice, our passion, and our vision to the screen
in ways that delight, inspire, inform and entertain.*

*We operate with integrity, creativity, and an undauntable stand for quality and fun
in every aspect of our work.*

FIGURE 4.2

YOUR ONE-SHEET POSTER

Ordinarily, in the low-budget world I hate to spend money before preproduction because anything before preproduction will be out of my own
pocket. Yes, I will get reimbursed, but it is still money that is at risk at
this stage. However, if a small, 8½ × 11 good-quality color poster of
your film is so compelling and so visually stunning that it will entice the
investor, then do it – spend the money and make the poster. Call in some
favors if you need to. Our poster cost us $40, and that was for buying the
candy striper outfit for the photo. Everything else was a gift from friends.
Of course, today, with social media playing a major factor in building your
fan base well in advance, having a poster on your website or YouTube
channel is essential.

I didn't do a poster for the business plan for *Séance* or *Portal*, but by that time, I already had 50 percent of the investors from *Candy Stripers* coming back on board. But for the first one in this slate of new genre films that we had decided to do, it was important to take advantage of every marketing tool available, and because the poster so clearly depicted the film, it really was a smart decision. I had investors write a check based on the poster alone.

Figure 4.3 is the final poster with the billing block included. The one we used in our business plan package for *Candy Stripers* was identical,

FIGURE 4.3

but in the billing block section we had just our names, the writers' names, and the line producer's name. It is a pretty fantastic poster, if I do say so myself, and you can see why some of the investors wrote their check based on this amazing one-sheet!

PPM/OPERATING AGREEMENT/SUBSCRIPTION AGREEMENT

This is the part that can be expensive – anywhere from $15,000 to $25,000. So what I did was borrowed four business plans/LLC packages from other successful producers. I really don't believe in reinventing the wheel, especially if it will save me money. A PPM is easily 25 pages, and so is an operating agreement – so I had a lot of reading to do. I wanted to know exactly what was in these intense documents, so reading them was well worth the time. I took what I thought was the best from each one and literally created my own, typing it up one word at a time. Then once I read it over a few times and Kate read it over, I handed it off to our attorney and was charged by the hour (in some cases, an attorney will sign on for 5 percent of producer's net profit in exchange for this type of work), which was a whole lot better than the $15,000 we'd been quoted to have an attorney create the PPM and operating agreement from scratch.

Because this is an extremely important topic and because I am not qualified to describe to you what is involved in a PPM, operating agreement, or subscription agreement, I have asked attorney Rick Rosenthal to go into more detail. Here is Rick's explanation:

The Private Placement Memorandum ("PPM") is a document that describes the interests that are being sold as an investment in order to comply with various state and federal securities laws which require that an investor be given a comprehensive description of the investment. The purpose of this document is to protect the producer from certain liabilities related to selling unregistered securities. A PPM should contain a complete description of the security (interest) being offered for sale, the terms of the sale, including any and all fees being paid to finders; and a detailed business plan that includes the nature of the risk associated with the investment.

An operating agreement is an agreement among Limited Liability Company ("LLC") members governing the LLC's business and the member's financial and managerial rights and duties. Many states in the United States have specific requirements as to what terms and conditions need to be in the operating agreement at a minimum. It is similar to a partnership agreement when there are more than one member, with each member protected from personal liability in most cases (except for such things as fraud, for example). It will provide for the governance of the LLC and who the managers are that are authorized to act on its behalf. It will also address the ownership and the voting rights of each member by allocating shares or percentages of membership interest. The operating agreement does not need to be filed with the state, but without it the LLC may not be considered a complete legal entity. Operating agreements can be amended at any time by the company members or managers.

The subscription agreement is in the form of an application to purchase LLC membership interests. The subscription agreement requires the applicant to disclose financial information relevant to his or her suitability to participate in the LLC. It is in the form of a questionnaire that asks the applicant specific questions about the nature of the investment, his or her finances, and an understanding of the risk involved. It also contains a signed pledge by the investor to invest a certain amount of money on or before a certain date. The subscription agreement is often made a part of the PPM.

Please familiarize yourself with the Security and Exchange Commission in your area for information regarding filing. Because our budget was under $1 million, we were able to use what's called Rule 504 under the Regulation D Offering. In the United States, for information about the SEC's registration requirements and common exemptions, go to www.sec.gov.

It is important that you follow government rulings at all times. Because phone calls to their office (and their attorneys) are free, why not call and get educated on the proper procedures? For example, one of the things I found out when I called was that in the State of California, under our LLC, we were able to go to only 35 nonaccredited investors. You can go to as many accredited investors as you want, but you are restricted to 35 nonaccredited. That is important information to be aware of. An accredited investor is someone who has at least $1 million net worth that's liquid (does not include a house or alternatively) and someone who's made $200,000 in income in two of the last three years. A married couple must have made $300,000 in two of the past three years. The bottom line here is to get educated. One of my students refused to listen to me regarding this issue, and I got a call from him a couple of years ago telling me that he was fined $25,000 for not following government rulings. Wouldn't it be a whole lot more fun to make a movie with that $25,000?

Chapter 5

Setting Up Your LLC and Opening Your Bank Account

An LLC (limited liability company) is separate from your corporation. A corporation is more like your umbrella company that depicts your brand. You don't raise funds under your corporation. I have a company called Snowfall Film, Inc., under which I produce my art house and family films. When Kate and I decided in the fall of 2004 to produce some horror films, we wanted to keep them separate from Snowfall Films and to instead create a company with its own brand, so we launched WindChill Films, Inc.

Every film you produce that you are raising money for will be a separate entity. If anything goes wrong and there is a lawsuit filed against your film, it will not affect your corporation. Also, for tax purposes, each film is kept separate, which will make your life much easier at tax time.

So let's open your LLC.

OPENING YOUR LLC: YOU CAN DO IT!

Do you have to use an attorney to open your LLC? Well, I thought we did, at first. I hate to spend money before preproduction, but when Kate and I were beginning to work on *Candy Stripers*, the thought of opening an LLC by ourselves sounded scary and complicated. So we called an attorney and paid him a lot of money – money that should have gone toward production. I found out after the Candy Stripers' LLC was open just how ridiculously easy it is to open an LLC! It literally takes a few minutes and in the State of California it costs only $70. So there is no excuse to pay an attorney $2,000 or more to do it for you. In California, it's as easy as going to www.sos.ca.gov.

However, if you really don't want to open the LLC on your own, there are companies that will do it for you for a fraction of the price of an attorney. Just Google "opening an LLC" and you will get a number of companies that will help you do it for a small fee. There are companies and sites like legalzoom.com/llc, incfile.com, www.smallbiz.com, incorporate.com/llc, and many more. Also, in your state, province, and country, there are obviously different ways to open your LLC, so please go online and do your research or call your state/provincial government office for information. I take advantage of their staff and attorneys all the time. They are free, so why not call them and learn from them? Even if you are using an attorney of your own or having a company like Legal Zoom do the work for you, I still recommend doing your own research, just to educate yourself in this area. You are the producer, which is in fact the manager/president/CEO of your company. Take full responsibility for holding that position at all times.

WHERE DO I OPEN MY LLC?

When I was teaching the Low Budget Film workshop, that question came up in every single class. I know that in the United States the cost of having an LLC varies from state to state. People would ask if they should open their LLC in a state where LLC taxes were less expensive. My attitude is: don't mess with the government. Your film company is like any other company, so be professional about it. The law states that you should open your LLC in the state in which you will be doing business. So if California is where you will be "doing business," then open your LLC in California.

WAIT UNTIL YOU'RE READY

When we were preparing to open the LLC for *Candy Stripers*, we were so anxious to get started that we just went ahead and opened the LLC. We had finished development on the screenplay and were busy working on the business plan and private placement memorandum, so we thought, why not go ahead and do the LLC paperwork at the same time? It was November. We were finished putting the PPM packages together, which wouldn't go out to investors until January – but we still went ahead and opened the LLC in November. Crazy! We ended up having to pay taxes for the year we opened it even though we weren't ready to do anything with it at that time.

Also, in the State of California, there is not only a yearly $800 cost for the franchise taxes for an LLC but there is an $800 charge that has to be paid four months after you open your LLC. That charge is required as a payment for the following tax year. So there we were, barely ready to go out and raise the funds, and we were spending money out of our pockets. Be conscious of your timing.

STEP # 1: CLEAR THE NAME

Okay, let's open your LLC. The first thing that Kate and I did was list our first three choices for the name of our company. For example, Séance, LLC; Séance Films, LLC; and Séance Productions, LLC. Then we went online to www.sos.ca.gov and found the form for the name clearance. We entered our three choices in order of preference. It didn't cost anything at all, and in minutes we got notice that our first choice was available. You can also fill out a hard copy and mail it in. You will get your notice back within a week. Figure 5.1 shows what the form looked like.

Name Availability Inquiry Letter
(Corporation, Limited Liability Company and Limited Partnership Names)

To check on the availability of a corporation, limited liability company or limited partnership name in California, complete the form below, and submit the completed form by mail, along with a self-addressed envelope, to Secretary of State, Name Availability Unit, 1500 11th Street, 3rd Floor, Sacramento, CA 95814.

Note: Checking the availability of a corporation, limited liability company or limited partnership name does not reserve the name and has no binding effect on the Secretary of State, nor does it confer any rights to a name. Please refer to our Name Availability webpage at www.sos.ca.gov/business/be/name-availability.htm for information about reserving a name.

Email and/or online inquiries regarding name availability cannot be accepted at this time.

Requestor's Information

Your name: _____

Firm name, if any: _____

Address: _____

City / State / Zip: _____

Phone #: _____ FAX #: _____

Entity Type (Select the applicable entity type. **CHECK ONLY ONE BOX.**)

[ ] Corporation   [ ] Limited Liability Company   [ ] Limited Partnership

Name(s) To Be Checked (You may list up to three names to be checked.)

1st Choice: _____

( ) is available.   ( ) is not available. We have:

2nd Choice: _____

( ) is available.   ( ) is not available. We have:

3rd Choice: _____

( ) is available.   ( ) is not available. We have:

The space below is reserved for office use only.		
Date:	I #	By:

BE - NAAV INQ ORDER FORM (REV 08/2010)   Page 1 of 1

FIGURE 5.1

STEP # 2: ARTICLES OF ORGANIZATION

In the State of California, at the time we were opening *Candy Stripers*, *Séance*, and *Portal*, the form that we had to fill out was one page long and the cost was $70. Filling out the form takes a few minutes. Basically, the information you have to give is your name, address, phone number, and how many managers there are. That's about it!

Be careful with the number of managers. Even if you are going to have 25 or 30 investors, they are not managers. If you are the only person involved and it is your LLC and your film production company, then check "one manager." In the case of our films, there were both Kate and myself, so I checked off "more than one manager." That is all the information you need. Pretty simple and basic and certainly something you can do yourself. You can do this online or fill out a hard copy and mail it in to the Secretary of State's office.

To get the hard copy back with the red stamp and state number on it takes at least a few weeks. When you get that number, you can move on to the next step: the LLC form. The LLC form is shown in Figure 5.2.

FIGURE 5.2

STEP # 3: GETTING YOUR EIN NUMBER

Once we had our assigned state number, I went online and filled out the one-page form to get our federal EIN (Employer Identification Number). This was completely free and literally took only a few minutes to get back from the federal government. Go to www.ein.com. Figure 5.3 is the first page of the EIN online form.

IRS EIN ONLINE
Obtain Your EIN (Employer Identification Number) / TIN (Taxpayer Identification Number) Instantly Using Our Easy us
Online IRS Assistant.

ENTITY TYPE SELECTED [CLICK TO CHANGE ENTITY TYPE]

Limited Liability Company (LLC)

STEP TWO OF THREE: PLEASE ENTER YOUR LIMITED LIABILITY COMPANY INFORMATION
ENTER THE LIMITED LIABILITY COMPANIES OPERATING INFORMATION

NAME OF LLC:

DOING BUSINESS AS (Optional):

Where was the LLC organized?
⦿ USA   ◯ Foreign Country

STATE ORGANIZED IN:

NUMBER OF MEMBERS OF LLC: 1

FISCAL YEAR ENDS IN: December

☐ CLICK HERE IF THE LLC IS OWNED BY ANOTHER BUSINESS

MANAGING MEMBER / OWNER / COMPANY INFORMATION

FIRST NAME:

MIDDLE NAME (Optional):

LAST NAME:

TITLE: Owner/Individual

SOCIAL SECURITY NUMBER:

ENTER THE BUSINESS ADDRESS [NO P.O. BOXES]

ADDRESS:

CITY:

STATE:

ZIP:

COUNTY:

CONTINUE TO STEP THREE

EIN APPLICATION PRIVACY - SITE CREATED AND MAINTAINED FOR IRS EIN AND IRS TIN CREATION BY MATT BRANDENBURG

FIGURE 5.3

CERTIFICATES AND SEAL

The one disadvantage of doing it yourself is that you don't get investor certificates or the seal packet that gives your company the embossed seal. Don't worry; there are companies online where you can get those items (and more) if you want them. I never bothered ordering the certificate but I did order the seal and ended up using it only once on one film. The seal and certificates are not at all expensive. You can probably get 20 or 25 certificates for around $30 and the seal for about the same. Your investors may be impressed with having a certificate with their name on it stating that they invested in your film. It might be worth the cost to order them.

OPENING YOUR BANK ACCOUNT

You're thinking, come on, a section about opening a bank account, really? I know, it sounds like it would be commonsense and pretty easy. Well, it is easy, but even opening a bank account comes with a certain learning curve when it's for a business – specifically, a film. Plus, I have a few tips for you that I learned along the way that may save you some money.

WAIT UNTIL YOU'RE READY TO OPEN YOUR ACCOUNT

Don't open your bank account until you are absolutely ready and know you have investor's checks about to come in the door. Why pay the $10 or $12 dollars a month in banking fees for an account if you're not ready? I made that mistake and ended up having an account open for months and months before we received our first check. In addition, you will need both your assigned LLC Secretary of State number and your EIN number if you are opening an account in the United States. This process may differ depending on which country you are planning to open your business in. With each film, you need a different LLC, and the same goes for your bank account: you'll need a new one for each film.

OPEN TWO ACCOUNTS

Of course, you will need to open a business checking account, but there is another account you can open that will give you interest! I hate to pay for the wrap party out of the budget, and although I set aside money for the party as part of the operating expenses, I found an even better idea when I was opening the bank account for *Séance*. At Bank of America it's called a "maximizer account." It's a business savings account that allows you to earn interest on your money. On *Séance*, by the time we were ready to shoot and I needed to move the money into the checking account, we had earned $835 in interest, which more than paid for the wrap party. So check to see what your bank offers in regard to a business savings account. For the few minutes it takes to open the account, it's worth it.

If you want to go ahead and open your accounts before you have checks from investors – but you know it's close and you want to be ready – then you can usually open both accounts with as little as $100 in each. Kate and I have done that each time, and if you decide to this, just keep the deposit receipt so you can be sure to get reimbursed when you enter preproduction.

WHAT TYPE OF CHECKBOOK SHOULD YOU ORDER?

We looked at all the different types of checkbooks that Bank of America offered and decided on the one that offered three checks per page, each one numbered and each with a check stub attached. Figure 5.4 shows one of the checks.

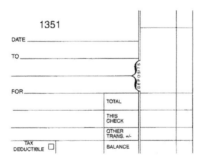

FIGURE 5.4

The checks were available in different colors, so with each film we chose a distinct color. There is no carbon paper to bother with and the checks and stubs are plenty big. I love using the check stubs, so let me tell you a bit about how to use them. I learned this one the hard way. I was doing the taxes for *Séance*. It was March and we had shot the film in May and June the year before. Trust me, remembering details from eight or nine months before is not something you want to do.

Because of the budget size on these films, I was the one who would be doing the detailed outline for the annual taxes. I always send everything off to an accountant, but only after I have done all the paperwork. It can be the difference between a bill for five hundred dollars and a bill for five thousand.

When I began the accounting on *Séance*, I had broken down my sheet into all the categories related to the film. Then I started going through the checkbook stubs and adding up all the items related to each category. I had been pretty good with details, even including which items were budgeted, operating expenses, and finder's fees. However, when it came to petty cash that was spent during preproduction and principal photography, I hadn't made a note of exactly what it was needed for. It totaled nearly $7,000. So I called Mike, and together we tried to recall what each of the petty cash checks had been used for. I remembered $1,000 going to craft services one day and Mike remember something else, and eventually, after an hour on the phone, we remembered each category that each check was allotted to. What a waste of time and energy!

If I had asked each time and written it on the check stub the moment I got the check request and wrote the check, I would not have had to go through that painful exercise. The moral of this story is to keep detailed (very detailed) records on your check stubs. That's what they are for, so use them – no matter how busy you are at that moment.

MAKING DEPOSITS: DETAILS

Speaking of details, here is another area where you want to be conscientious. You will get a good-sized book of deposit slips and a stamp with all the company checking account information on it. So when you flip the check over that you are going to deposit, you just have to stamp it. When you fill out the deposit slip, once again, put as much information on it as possible. Once I fill it out, I remove the carbon paper and on my copy I write even more information. I write the name of the person that check is from, for example, which has come in handy more than a few times. I've had calls around tax time from investors asking when they sent their check and when I cashed it. Instead of going through old bank statements, I can just glance at the deposit book and there is all the information. Any little time-saving device is valuable.

GET YOUR VISA OR MASTERCARD NOW

Here is a step that is very, very important, yet is also something that many producers forget to handle. On the day you are opening your account, fill out the paperwork for your film company's Visa or MasterCard. It will take a little time to come in, so don't leave it to the last minute. Also, you and your line producer will need the Visa/MasterCard the minute you begin preproduction. Your line producer will need to use it to make deposits to certain vendors. You won't necessarily be putting any money on the credit card itself, but it is often required to hold vendors.

THE CHECKS AND VISA ARE IN YOUR NAME ONLY!

You are the producer. You are the *only* one who gets to sign the checks and the credit card is in your name *only*. Please read that sentence again a couple of times. Of course Mike (our line producer) would get to use the credit card to hold vendors, but the cards themselves were in our names only. Kate had one and I had one – period. Also, regarding the checks, they are in your name and only you have the check-signing authority. Anything else is crazy. This is a business, and you are accountable to investors. You don't have the right to play this game any other way than as a business professional.

One of my students just didn't listen, and because he was the writer/ director in addition to producing the film, he felt overwhelmed and gave his line producer full check-writing privileges. He also gave his line producer a credit card in his own name. The line producer was a great guy and even came highly recommended, but toward the end of the shoot he fell off the wagon and took the credit card and ran up personal charges of over $25,000! My student was liable for this money. In the end, he needed to go out and raise additional money for post and delivery.

As much as Kate and I loved our line producer (he and his wife are personal friends of ours), there is still no way I would ever give him either the right to sign checks or a credit card in his name. It is not about me and my personal relationships or about how busy I might be. It is a business and I am responsible to the investors associated with that business.

CHECK REQUEST FORM

When your line producer needs money, he or she will bring you a check request form; this is when you look it over, approve it, write the check, sign it, and hand it back to him or her. Figure 5.5 shows the one that Mike used on our low-budget film projects.

CHECK REQUEST

SHOW SÉANCE	PROD # 002
COMPANY SÉANCE, LLC	
ADDRESS 2321 W. Olive Ave. Suite A	PHONE # 818-558-5005
Burbank, CA 91506	FAX # 818-842-4112
DATE	AMOUNT $

CHECK PAYEE

ADDRESS

PHONE #   FAX #

ATTN:

PAYEE SS # OR FED. I.D. #

DESCRIPTION	CODING	AMOUNT

TAX:

TOTAL: $

☐ PURCHASE
☐ RENTAL   CHECK NEEDED: ☐ IMMEDIATELY
☐ DEPOSIT   ☐ WITHIN NEXT DAY OR TWO
☐ ADVANCE   ☐ WITHIN NORMAL PROCESSING TIME
☐ 1099
☐ INVENTORY

WHEN READY: ☐ PLEASE MAIL CHECK
                   ☐ PLEASE GIVE CHECK TO

CHECK REQUESTED BY   DEPT.

APPROVED BY   DATE

(INVOICE SUBSTANTIATION MUST FOLLOW THIS REQUEST)

PAID BY CHECK #   DATE

© ELH Form #09

FIGURE 5.5

PAYROLL COMPANY OR NOT?

During your actual film production, if you are doing the film as a SAG sig-natory project, your line producer will need to hire a payroll company to pay the SAG actors. However, for all the rest of the cast (the ones who are non-SAG) and the crew, Mike drew up a list of everyone and how much their salary was each week. He would bring me the list on the day every-one was being paid. I would write out the checks and give them back to Mike for him to deliver to people on set before we left for the day.

Also, long after the film is completed and sold, you will have to con-tinue to use a payroll company to make your residual payments if your film is SAG signatory. It is not at all expensive and well worth it, as they are the experts in working with your sales company's report and figuring out the SAG residual payments for both your international and domestic sales.

Chapter 6

Sales Presentation and Finding Investors

The truth is that I had not planned to do a sales presentation. It came about by necessity, and I'm thrilled it happened that way. It actually helped create an urgency that was needed at that time. Prior to producing *Candy Stripers*, my whole focus was on international coproductions – and raising funds for coproductions was a whole different ball game. Much of it was done through government soft money, sale and leaseback deals, labor/tax credits, and territory presales. Even raising equity funds in other countries at that time was fairly effortless because of the tax benefits provided to the investors.

So here we were, raising funds for our first low-budget film in the United States, and we had a pretty arrogant attitude. We thought, "This will be easy – a piece of cake, right?" Wrong! What happened was that we froze! We did a great job of putting together all the paperwork and prided ourselves on our PPM, our operating agreement, our amazing business plan, and opening an LLC for the first time. But when it came to selling the units in the film, we seemed to go totally unconscious.

I remember looking at the calendar and realizing that it was March 1. Two months had drifted by and we had sold two units . . . and that was to each other! At that moment, Kate and I sat down, created a solid timeline, pushed our start date forward by two months, and made a decision to do a couple of things. First, we would start including what we were doing in *every single* conversation we had with people. Second, we would plan two sales presentations. There was something about planning for and scheduling a sale presentation that created a sense of urgency. We needed to move forward and we needed to do so with velocity. It turned out to be useful in more ways than one. Just the act of preparing for a presentation forced us to get very clear about our pitch and made it very real, completely altering how we spoke about the project. It was real. We were making a movie!

And it worked: within three weeks from our sales presentations, we went from 2 units sold to 22!

PREPARATION

Preparing for the sales presentation was great fun. As I mentioned earlier, what I always do when I am planning any event or workshop is put myself in the shoes of those in the audience, as if I were the one sitting out there listening. So with that in mind, I had to consider what my potential investors would want and need to hear. How much time would they be willing to sit in the room? I decided that 45 minutes was enough time to get through the presentation. Kate and I would be able to get through the essential materials in that time. In addition, I allowed 45 minutes for a question and answer session. So we estimated an hour and a half for the entire sales presentation.

OUTLINE

Next came the outline. As I had never done anything like this before, it took me a few days to create the outline for the event. I wrote and rewrote it quite a few times, and here is what I ended up with:

1. Welcome
2. Purpose of the evening
3. Outline of the evening (including room logistics)
4. Introductions: Producers, Suzanne, and Kate
5. Introduction to Snowfall Films
6. Launching WindChill Films, why this film and budget
7. Director's vision
8. Introduce team
9. Explain the LLC offering
10. Q&A session
11. Thank you for coming and good night
12. Sign out packets and answer private questions

With the outline complete, I proceeded to expand each area. Once I felt comfortable and confident that I had covered all the essential points, I went ahead and set the date.

BOOKING THE VENUE

I decided to hold two separate sales presentations in order to accommodate as many people as possible. I chose a Monday and a Wednesday evening a week apart. As I researched possible venues, I kept in mind that I wanted a fairly small room that would hold around 40 people. I really wanted the event to look like there was standing room only. In addition, I looked for added perks, like easy highway access and free parking. And because Kate and I were paying for this out of our own pockets (keeping all receipts for reimbursement later!), the cost of the room was also something I needed to consider. I found a great room at a hotel only a couple of blocks from my office.

GETTING THE WORD OUT

As you have probably realized by now, I like to keep things as simple and clear as possible. I wrote the invitation and emailed it to our entire database (people we knew personally). I sent the emails off in blind copies in groups of ten to avoid being categorized as spam. Kate and I also made the decision to go through our database, highlighting specific people to call personally to extend the invitation. Some of these people we knew were potential investors; others were friends and colleagues we wanted to come on board with us as possible executive producers. We requested that they bring potential investors to our event.

All these calls and emails provided a great reason to get back in touch with people and to let everyone know what we were planning. It also forced us to get crystal-clear about our pitch.

Here is a copy of the email that we sent out.

E-mail Invitation

 As you may know, Kate and I are in the process of selling units for our Candy Stripers, LLC, for our horror movie, *Candy Stripers*.

We will be holding a small presentation in the Studio Room at the Anabelle Hotel on West Olive Avenue in Burbank on Monday evening from 7:00 to 8:30 pm, April 4.

You are invited to attend and feel free to invite friends who may be interested in investing money in *Candy Stripers*.

Following the presentation, we will be available to answer questions and we will have PPM/LLC packages with us as well as one-sheets on the film. We will also have the trailers and one-sheets from our previous films to show you during the evening.

Our line producer will be there to discuss the budget and our director of photography and director will speak about the look and style of the film.

If you and your guests are interested in attending, please let us know as soon as possible. Or if you have any questions, please feel free to give us a call at 818-555-5555.

Warmest regards,
Suzanne Lyons
Kate Robbins

LOGISTICS

I've been leading seminars for 25 years and I believe I've mastered the art of logistics. Yes, I call it an art because it is something that you have to really work at perfecting. Nobody realizes how important logistics are. It is essential that you make a list of everything you will need for your sales presentation. Just think about it for a minute, and you can picture how critical it is. If people arrive at your event and need a pen to take notes and you've forgotten to bring them, it's a reflection on you. If you're flustered because you forgot the sign-in sheets, people will notice. It is all a reflection on you, and those potential investors are watching you closely. It's like when you're on a plane and notice that your seat is ripped. You can't help but wonder about the condition of the engine. If I'm an investor and you're flustered and disorganized and there are no pens, I'm already worried about my investment and the evening hasn't even started yet.

Everything about the presentation represents you and who you are. Are you coming across as professional and accountable? Are you someone I can trust with my money? I know it's just logistics, but as you can see, it's important. The investors may want to invest in your film because it sounds like good business, but they need to put their faith in you first. Your professional demeanor is critical. So please plan and type up your logistics list – every detail! That way, you will have everything you need at your event and you won't have to be at all concerned about logistics, leaving you free to focus on your presentation and on the people in the room.

Here is the logistics list from the *Candy Stripers* sales presentation:

Logistics List

Sign-in sheet (Name/Email/Phone #)
Pens/paper
Masking tape
Copies of bios (our bios and our team's bios)
Business cards
Copies of our company mission statement
One sample script
Our BAFTA Award
One-sheets of the *Candy Stripers* poster (with our contact info)
Copies of the synopsis (with our contact info)
Copies of the *Los Angeles Times* article on the success of genre films
Copies of the director's vision notes
Quotes on poster boards for the walls
Posters of our previous films
PPM/LLC numbered packets with sign-out sheets

Small TV and DVD player (to show trailers)
Cookies, fruit, and water for the refreshments table

SETTING UP THE ROOM

When Kate and I were preparing for the *Candy Stripers* presentation, we gave a lot of thought to how the room should look. We decided on a visual display that supported our presentation. We took a number of the quotes from the "marketplace" section of our business plan and had them blown up on colored posters and put them on the walls around the room.

We also took the *Los Angeles Times* article from our business plan and had it blown up and put on an easel in the front of the room. The title alone was impressive: "Horror Films Return to Make a Killing at the Box Office." Find quotes that give credibility to the type of film you are producing. There is a good chance you will already have them in the business plan, so just use them as a visual display. It will look great.

In addition, we brought movie posters of our previous films and put them on the wall in the front of the room. We took quotes and articles that had been written about us and our previous projects and displayed those on poster boards. For example, *Hollywood Reporter* and *Variety* had written rave reviews of our very first film, *Undertaking Betty*, so we took advantage of that and put it on display. If you have not yet produced a film and this is your first, you might want to display the posters of projects completed by your director, writer, or DP.

We had a side table set up with a variety of items that people were free to take: copies of the director's vision notes, the film synopsis, our company bio, and copies of the *Los Angeles Times* article. We also had 8{1/2} × 11 posters of our film with a brief synopsis and contact information on the back. I know that sounds expensive, but in the case of *Candy Stripers*, the posters were so stunning and said so much that I think it was worth the cost. We also brought our BAFTA award and put that on the table.

Arrive at your event early to allow a good amount of time for setup. Make sure that you have lots of help. When choosing your assistants – who will be at the sign-in table – make sure to also request that they help with setup and that they are completely accountable and prompt. You don't want to be putting posters on the wall or giving instructions to your assistants when your guests are arriving.

YOUR ASSISTANTS REPRESENT YOUR COMPANY

Make sure your assistants are prepared to welcome people as they arrive. I know you will be there welcoming people as they come in the door, but keep in mind that as you are chatting with one person, a few more are arriving and going directly to the sign-in table. Have at least two people at the sign-in table and prep them in advance to dress and look professional. They are there representing you, your project, and your company. You want to start on time, so you don't want long lines at the table. Have your assistants sign people in without any chatting. They should be focused on making sure that everyone is filling out the sign-in sheet clearly and correctly. This all sounds like common sense, but I have missed opportunities to follow up with people because I couldn't read the handwriting on the sign-in sheet. All these little details matter.

IT'S SHOWTIME: WELCOME EVERYONE

It's now 7:00, people are seated, and it's time to go to the front of the room and formally welcome everyone and thank them all for coming. Take the time to really thank them for coming:

Hello, I'm Suzanne Lyons and this is my film partner Kate Robbins. Before we begin, we want you to know that we appreciate your being here. I know there are a number of things you could be doing this evening, and the fact that you are here to find out about our film project and possibly participate as an investor is something that we truly appreciate.

PURPOSE OF THE EVENING

It is very important to explain the purpose of the evening. Don't just launch right into your presentation. In fact, this is a great practice to adopt for every call, meeting, and event. Be honest and direct and say why you have invited them here this evening:

The purpose of the evening is for you to hear about Candy Stripers, LLC, and to have any questions answered. We would love for you to invest in our film project and we look forward to doing this sales presentation for you this evening.

OUTLINE FOR THE EVENING

Tell the attendees what you are planning to cover and exactly how the evening will unfold. Go over the timeline, and if you are planning a break, now is the time to let people know that. People will have a hard time fully listening to you if they don't know the timeline and exactly how the evening is structured. In our case, it went like this:

Here is how tonight's presentation will go: Kate and I will talk for 45 minutes. We will introduce ourselves and our company and tell you about the film and the offering for the project. We will introduce our line producer and our director of photography and

Kate will discuss her vision as the director of the film. At the end of the 45 minutes, we'll open it up to a 45-minute Q&A, and at the end of that time we will complete the evening. However, Kate and I will stay here to be available for as long as you need us to answer any further questions and of course to sign out our LLC/PPM packages.

At this point, it's also important to go over the hotel logistics. For example,

The bathrooms are just outside the door to the right and the refreshments table is at the back of the room. Our two wonderful assistants, James and Ruby, whom you met on your way in, are seated at the back of the room and are available if you need something throughout the evening.

IT'S YOUR TIME TO SHINE: HAVE FUN!

Remember people are investing in you and putting their faith in you. *Please* keep that in mind during the entire evening. In fact, in the car on the way to your event or with your partner, remind yourself of why you chose this particular project, this career, this amazing life in the entertainment industry. You are going to get a chance to pitch yourself, your company, and your project, so it's important to get completely in touch with your passion, your joy, and your love of this industry. The truth is that it all comes down to enrollment. You will be enrolling people into playing with you. If you're not having fun, people won't want to play with you. It's not just about the money, and in many cases it's never about the money – it's about having fun. That's why we're here. That's why we all chose this career in this industry. We get to make movies. We get to bring joy and magic to people's lives. We get to provide an escape for people. We get to create memories for families. We impact, enhance, and make a difference in the lives of people on a global scale. You have a great sandbox in a magnificent playground, and you are providing an opportunity for people to come play with you . . . how cool is that? Remind yourself of that on the way to your sales presentation.

INTRODUCE YOURSELF

Be careful not to jump right into the conversation about your film or the details of the offering. Remember that they are investing in you, not just your film. This is the part of the evening when you get to speak about yourself and your background: possibly the most important part of the presentation. Really take time during your planning stage to outline what you are going to say. Make a point of speaking about the areas of your background that highlight your strengths, drawing from both your career and personal life. This stage will create credibility for you and a comfort level for your potential investors. Here is a form that I took from my Flash Forward (FFI) seminar and adapted to use in the Indie Film Producing workbook.

Career and Personal Highlights

What is your story?

Your STORY is the evidence, from your career and your life, that will establish your professional credibility and your personal connection to the project.

Whether you are pitching to potential investors over the phone or in a meeting, or pitching to a full room at your sales presentation, it is important to put together a pitch that will clearly show that you and your project are not only credible, but well worth investing in.

Complete the list below of at least **12 HIGHLIGHTS from your career and personal life**. Be vivid and specific!

The purpose of the **career highlights** is to give you maximum credibility. Include your major credits, accomplishments, and success stories – awards, problems you've solved, good reviews you've gotten. Make sure to drop NAMES and NUMBERS.

Personal highlights show you as an interesting, three-dimensional person with life experiences that are relevant to you producing your project. These should be the most dramatic, illuminating facts or accomplishments of your personal life.

Combine the career highlight with the personal highlights and create the perfect pitch that will wow your investors.

GOLDEN RULE: Do not mention or apologize for anything negative. Put their attention where you want it – on the GOOD STUFF ONLY!

Career Highlights:

_____
_____
_____
_____
_____
_____
_____

Personal Highlights:

_____
_____
_____
_____
_____
_____
_____

This exercise will help you choose the areas that will highlight your expertise in the areas that are important and relevant to your film project. I chose three specific areas. I mentioned my background as the head of marketing and promotions at a television network and affiliate in Nova Scotia. I talked about my job in sales for a film and TV distribution company in Philadelphia. And I highlighted the fact that I was cofounder of the successful entertainment industry company Flash Forward Institute, having led workshops for well over 15,000 participants and having guest-lectured at nearly 50 entertainment industry organizations, colleges, and guilds. I did some name-dropping here and noted that the participants in my workshops had gone on to great success.

Kate mentioned that she had studied acting at NYU and how that would enhance her talent as a director. She also shared about the number of prestigious awards she had won for her screenwriting, including the Spielberg Chesterfield Fellowship and the Diane Thomas award. Kate wrote *Candy Stripers*, so mentioning her awards as a screenwriter was invaluable.

It is important to get specific numbers whenever you can and include them in your talk. It is so much more powerful to the listener. For example, you have produced five short films, winning six festivals. Or, your script won best screenplay at La Femme Film Festival competing against more than 300 entries.

YOUR COMPANY INTRODUCTION

Once you have introduced yourself, tell them about your company. Kate and I started with our trailers. We had produced four movies at our Snowfall Films company, and the trailers were around a minute and a half each. It was worth the time because the trailers were impressive and the casts in our previous films were big names that everyone knew. It gave us immediate credibility and proved that we were able to take a film project through to completion. We were now doing a series of SAG ultra-low-budget films for $200,000, so the fact that we had already proven ourselves in the higher-budget world created a comfort level for our potential investors.

However, if you don't have a background in film and this is your first project, don't worry about it at all. When it comes time to introduce some key members of your team, like your director or DP, they can always share their industry background and show a couple of their trailers.

During this introduction, we shared about what Snowfall Films was planning for the long term. I know that if I were the one sitting in the room listening to the presentation, I would want to know that you and your company were planning to be around for years to come.

Another suggestion is to read your mission statement. We made a point of including copies of our mission statement on the information table and reading it aloud. I found out months later from one of the investors that he made his decision to invest solely on the strength of our mission statement. So if you don't have one, write one! The Snowfall Films/WindChill Films mission statement is available in Chapter 4.

LAUNCHING WINDCHILL FILMS: WHY THIS FILM? WHY THIS BUDGET?

It's important to share why you are producing your specific project and what made you decide on this particular budget. Because genre films were doing so well at the time of our *Candy Stripers* sales presentation, we talked about the fact that we had just launched WindChill Films, a new genre division of Snowfall Films. We were serious about producing *Candy Stripers* as our first project in a series of genre films for WindChill Films. We talked about how great those films were doing (at that time) worldwide and we shared our plan to shoot them at an ultra-low budget of $200,000. We explained how, with high-quality yet inexpensive digital cameras along with our huge number of contacts in the industry, we could keep our budget low without sacrificing quality.

We told them about the Screen Actors Guild offering a fantastic deal for those producers interested in staying within certain budget levels. When runaway production was hurting film production in the United States, the unions and guilds reformatted their policies to make allowances so that producers could shoot their indie films in the United States. The cost per day for SAG actors in the ultra-low-budget agreement was $100, so it made it very doable for our project. I believe it's important to explain to the investor why you decided on your budget and how you plan on staying within your budget. Of course, your line producer can expand on that conversation during his or her part of the presentation.

When we were writing our business plan, we researched film comparisons, so we read aloud numbers from some of the similar films, highlighting specific examples of other projects that had performed well. Of course, we clearly explained that there were no guarantees that *Candy Stripers* would have the success that these other films had. We chose this opportunity to read the quotes we had posted on the wall as well as sections from the *Los Angeles Times* article that talked about how extraordinarily well horror films were doing worldwide. Some of the quotes included the following:

"Horror titles continue to sell extremely well," said Martin Blythe, chief of publicity at Paramount Home Entertainment.

"They have a fiercely loyal fan base." Hollywood Reporter

"Horror film makers slash and earn: Low cost, high returns, wider audiences mean bloody good business." Pop Culture

"Massacre Appeal: No matter how you slice it, horror movies are making a real killing at the box office." Entertainment Weekly

The TV series *Project Greenlight* just happened to be about the making of a horror film that year, so we showed a clip from the pilot in which Matt Damon and Ben Affleck spoke about the success of genre films. The timing couldn't have been more perfect. If you can find anything like that to back up your claim for why your project is marketable and has profit potential, that would be a great addition to your presentation.

If you chose your project for a personal reason, share that. Is there something about the story that resonates deeply with you? Is it something you are truly passionate about? Is it based on events that affected you personally? This type of information is extremely important, so be sure to include it in your presentation.

THE DIRECTOR'S VISION

Introduce your director and let him or her have the floor to share his or her vision for the film. Make sure your director is well-prepared and has rehearsed with you exactly what he or she is going to say. It shouldn't be long and drawn out – and it shouldn't catch you by surprise. The idea is to give your audience a sense of how your film will look and to show them that it is well planned and well thought out.

In our case, Kate was to be the director on *Candy Stripers*, so she shared her vision in a crystal-clear, visually stunning way. As she spoke, you could clearly see the look and feel of the film she had in mind. She had typed up her speech in advance, so I had it copied and put on the information table for people to pick up at the end of the evening.

When I asked her to share some advice for this book about the director's vision, Kate said, "When communicating your director's vision, always include the color palette of the film as well as the angles of shots and the mood and emotions those angles will evoke over the visual progression of the story. Remember that the listeners are not likely to be media-savvy, so speak to them from the point of view and emotions of an audience member, and you'll be amazed by their enthusiasm."

Here is a copy of Kate's director's vision for *Candy Stripers*.

Director's Vision
Kate Robbins

We open wide onto a beautiful night sky. The moon reflects across the wide-open landscape. Farmers' fields are lit only by moonlight. Nothing bad could happen here.

An old Ford truck's headlights shine on the road ahead. Inside the cozy cab of the truck, the color is vivid – reminiscent of a 1950s movie. We feel like we're almost eavesdropping on the two midwestern teens concerned with the moment. But the two are about to be brought face to face with life and death as they come upon a mysterious crash on the road. Suddenly the night is not innocent; instead, it is cloaked in smoke, and through the wreckage the girls can see a young woman, soaked in blood, running from them in fear.

This opening scene is representative of the rest of the story. Shot wide at first and then closer and closer until, even outdoors, we're feeling claustrophobic and afraid as if the world were coming in at us, about to destroy us.

Visually, the hospital is a simple, happy place – reminiscent of the Midwest of the 1950s. There is a small-town, perky air about it. Things don't become frenzied until the dying girl is brought in (symbolizing the introduction of evil).

The early scenes with Matt, Crystal, Cherie, and others will be shot with bright happy colors that snap off of the screen – shots that catch the sky's vivid blue.

As the story progresses, the color palette will dim, making the hospital more and more eerie. As the Candy Stripers take control, the shots become more claustrophobic; even the long shots of the hallways seem oppressive and almost green-gray. Close-ups become more prevalent – we need to see their fear as one by one they die. In the final hospital hallway scenes, gray, black, and red will permeate the screen.

When Matt and Cherie are pulled from the wreckage, it is a rebirth into blinding white light. The world is bright again, packed with color. There is an openness about the shots; everything feels like there is space again.

Until they find the one surviving Candy Striper: then the world spirals in again, and at the end we fade to black as if being pulled into evil.

INTRODUCE YOUR TEAM

Who is on your production team? I would highly recommend getting a few key people on board before you have your sales presentation. In fact, by that time, you will have done your budget for the film, so have your line producer present. You should certainly have your director by this stage, and because the director usually brings on his or her favorite DP, you have a great start already. You are not paying anyone at this point, and there is always the chance that you may lose them to another project, but for now they are part of the team. Have their bios on the information table and of course in your business plan that is part of your PPM package; be sure to note on each bio "subject to availability."

In addition, if your writer has existing credits or has won awards, he or she would be a great addition to the evening. If there are any other major keys that might be especially important to the type of film you are producing, consider having them there as well, even if just for a quick introduction. For example, in the case of the horror genre, having your special effects artist there with his or her portfolio would be excellent.

I had invited our line producer and our DP. Our line producer spoke about how we could shoot our film for the budget we had planned, reinforcing what Kate and I had already discussed. He shared his relationship with professional, experienced keys, crew, and vendors and how with his years in the business, he could bring on board a professional team while still keeping costs at a minimum. Our DP, Geoff Schaff, had 25 years' experience; he shared his past successes and his vision for our project. They were both amazing in front of the room.

If you don't have any film credits or trailers of your own, now would be a perfect time to take advantage of your team and show a few of their film trailers.

YOUR OFFERING

Here is the part that your audience has been waiting for. And now that you have built sufficient relationship and given enough background, you can move comfortably and confidently into this section.

Let me just stop and explain what I mean by having "sufficient relationship" and why it is important to establish relationship before moving into action and making your request.

I worked with a management consulting firm for a time in Philadelphia that specialized in small business consulting. One of the most important things I learned there was to never jump directly into action. It's a guaranteed way to have your business fail. I took that to heart. First, create relationship, then possibility, then opportunity, and then take action. Notice what comes first is relationship! It is extremely important to create relationship before ever jumping into action. It is a business model that is used in companies worldwide; when you are standing in front of the room doing your sales presentation, you are the president and CEO of your company. So follow this model. It works.

So far in the presentation we have created relationship and we've provided the possibility of fun, participation, and involvement in the project. Now we're presenting the opportunity to potentially make a profit, and finally, we're taking action: requesting they consider investing in our film and signing out a PPM/LLC package upon competition of the evening.

WHAT'S IN IT FOR ME, THE INVESTOR?

I was clear about what exactly our offering provided (see Chapter 4 for details) and felt very comfortable speaking about it. I specifically made a point of telling them that it was a high-risk investment throughout this section of the evening.

Kate and I had a sales agent do estimates for us, and although these estimates were listed in the PPM packets, we also made a point of putting the information in a handout for everyone at the presentation. We called the handout a "revenue scenario"; it showed clearly what return on their investment they could receive if the estimates came in as planned. This handout was a huge success. It showed that we had done our homework and it looked great. Of course, even on the "Revenue Scenario," we noted at the bottom of the page that there was "no guarantee."

If you are not planning to go the traditional route with a sales agent and you are planning to self- distribute, then you may want to type up a handout explaining how you envision the revenue flow. Or, if you are planning to distribute to a specific niche market, then I would have the statistics available to back up your claim.

We also explained to our audience exactly what our "private placement offering" was going to be, clearly laying out the percentage we were offering, the time period the offering would be open, and the estimated time schedule for return on territory sales. We explained that we had the full PPM/operating agreement packages available to sign out if they were interested in investing in the project. However, we told them that if they were interested and had made a decision to invest, they still had to take the packet home with them and read it carefully before writing us a check and investing in the film. We also shared some of the perks here, a few of which included being on the set, perhaps being an extra, an invitation to the wrap party, getting a copy of the DVD, and getting a credit on the film – depending on the number of units they purchased.

Also, during this session, if you have any investors who have already invested or made a commitment to invest, have them in the room and call on them to share about why they decided to invest in your project. If they can't be there, have them put it in writing so you can read it to everyone in the room. One of our investors, a retired stockbroker, was in the room; he stood and said, "Thirty-eight years on Wall Street taught me to look for four things in investment opportunities: (1) a good product, (2) a market for that product, (3) good company management, (4) good profit potential. *Candy Stripers* contains all four things. I'm happy to be an investor."

At our second sales presentation, that investor couldn't be there, so he emailed us what he had said and I read it during the evening. In addition, a woman who had been at our first event and bought a unit came to our second presentation and shared why she had decided to invest. Endorsements like that are invaluable. Make a point of doing this when you plan your sales presentation.

QUESTION AND ANSWER SESSION

After we formally ended the first 45-minute session of the evening, we moved on to the scheduled 45-minute Q&A session. It's important to stay on schedule. At our sales presentation, the Q&A took the full 45 minutes. Plan for every possible question. Talk to people who have raised money for films, talk to your mentors, and ask people you know who have done sales presentations. What are some possible questions that potential investors may ask? Some of the questions that were brought up at our event included: How long before we could see our first check? Could you clarify exactly what happens when the film is done? Is it going to be in film festivals? Are you going to be having a premiere of the film? Is there any chance it will be at theaters?

When the questions are answered, remind people that you and your team are going to stay for as long as possible to answer any further questions one on one. And of course remind them that the PPM packages are available to be signed out for those who are interested in investing in the project.

WRAP-UP

Keep your wrap-up short and sweet:

Thank you so much for coming this evening. Feel free to come up and say hello. We truly appreciate you coming to our event to find out more about Candy Stripers, LLC. It was a pleasure meeting you. Thank you, good night, and drive carefully.

MOCK SALES PRESENTATION

One of the participants in the Low Budget Film Workshop had a great idea. She organized her entire sales presentation and invited the class to her house for a mock sales presentation. She treated it exactly like the real thing and got her feet wet doing the presentation with friends. She learned what her weak areas were, and the mock presentation gave her the confidence to book the date for the real thing.

A PROMISE IS NOT A CHECK

Just a quick word of caution here. There may be people who will tell you that they are going to be investing in your film and you might take them at their word. Don't do that. A promise is not a check. Until the money is in the bank, it isn't real.

ADDITIONAL PERKS

Don't forget that people are often attracted to this industry because of the cachet and because they want to play and have fun. It's not always about the money. In fact, because of the high risk, it's seldom about the money. So keep that in mind when you are creating your investor proposal, preparing your sales presentation, speaking with potential investors, and even while sharing about your project with friends and colleagues.

When an investor approached me after the sales presentation and asked if there were a possibility for his sons to write and sing a song for the end roll credits, I was more than thrilled to say yes – why not? Another investor asked if his wife could have her picture taken with the stars in the film. He ended up buying three units! As I mentioned in my chapter on business plans, I make sure to be generous to all at all times.

TIPS TO GETTING INVESTORS

In my workshops on indie film producing and at every speaking engagement I have ever done on this topic, the number-one question is, "How do I get investors to invest in my film project?" I got asked the question so often that I sat down and wrote a short booklet that focused solely on this question. I came up with 13 valuable tips. Here is a brief summary of the booklet:

1. **Mine your own network of people.** Call everyone you know and tell them exactly what you are doing – and make a request!
2. **Do more networking.** Go to events and get to know more people and tell them what you are up to (be clear, brief, and specific).
3. **Find other great people who can help you.** Have friends and colleagues introduce you to potential investors, get to know them and see if they are interested in reading your business plan package.
4. **Offer a bonus: an executive producer credit.** Offer this credit on a single card in the main titles and on the DVD cover and poster to people who buy and/or sell a larger number of units (i.e., our

number was six units). Many people who are looking to start their own film company really liked this opportunity.

5. **Credibility is key: partner up . . . way up.** If this is your first film or if you are moving into a bigger budget arena and have done only low-budget films, team up with a powerful partner. Having a partner who has more experience and more credibility will help give potential investors a better feeling of security.

6. **Hold a fantastic sales presentation.** Have some of your team/key attachments there if possible: for example, your director, line producer, DP, or anyone on your team with great credits.

7. **Talent means money.** If you can get talent on board early, that is great. But make sure the talent is worth something from a domestic and/or international sales point of view. *Always* check names that you are considering with a sales agent to get a sense of whether they are really going to help sell your film when the time comes.

8. **Buy a unit yourself.** It really means a lot to investors that you have invested in your own film. (Buying just one unit is fine.)

9. **Get educated on state and provincial incentives. And think globally.** It's important to know all of the state and provincial incentives. It can save you a lot of money and it's great information to include in your business plan. And remember that there is a lot of money out there in the world. My first few films ($5 to $10 million) were coproductions with different countries. It may mean teaming up with a producing partner in another country but this is well worth it if it means getting your movie made.

10. **Talk to sales agents.** Ask if they know anyone who might be interested in investing in films or if they themselves are interested in buying units. One of our sales agents was interested in purchasing two units on one of our films.

11. **Ask your state/provincial film commissioner** (if you are shooting in your own state or province). Ask if they would be willing to get investors together for you to do a sales presentation. This tactic has proven to be very, very successful for some of my students in my Low Budget Film class. One of the participants raised her entire budget of $650,000 during the two meetings set up by the film commissioner in her state.

12. **Look for common ground.** If you have a project that has a niche market, then use that to your advantage when looking for funding. For example, a faith-based project would have an excellent appeal

to potential investors who are committed to seeing more of those types of films produced.

13. **Give investors a chance to play.** Offer the possibility to investors to really have some fun with you by offering a number of things – having a line in the film, being an extra, just being on the set (make sure you have headsets and chairs for them), getting pictures taken with the stars, inviting them to the wrap party (at their own expense, of course), and perhaps even doing the song for your end roll credits. It's all about having *fun*! If you are not having fun with all of this, they won't have fun, and they will go play somewhere else. Of course, it is a business and you are a professional, but they are not just investing in your film, they are investing in *you*. And of course offer them a really great deal. Be generous when you write up your business plan.

BE PREPARED

I am giving this tip its own heading because it's something that I'm just now learning about and I think that it deserves special attention. I had the pleasure of meeting Justin Trefgarne at a Women In Film and Television event in Toronto, and he shared something that I think is invaluable when it comes to finding the money. His motto: "Be prepared." It was that type of thinking that got him the entire budget amount he needed for his science fiction film. Here is Justin's story:

When pitching my futuristic thriller, Junk, the same question was asked again and again: "What's it going to look like?" As a first-time director, I had only my passion and my shorts to convince people, so when we received some funding from a regional agency to develop story and script, the idea came to me: why not use the money to make a trailer? When I think of the kinds of films that reach out and grab my attention, I so often think of the first teaser trailer as the thing that hooked me. At the time we were thinking about this, the first teaser for Inception had just been released. I thought it was amazing – the impact that 30 seconds of film had on me was enormous.

The fact was that I knew exactly how I wanted my film to look and feel. I sat down and wrote the teaser script in about an hour – all I had to do was imagine that we'd made the film and that I was some marketing person charged with the challenge of selling the film. The film deals in distorted reality, so I decided to pose a series of questions culminating in the shot I had wanted from the start: the protagonist aiming a handgun at himself. So I designed the big moment of the film around this final enigmatic shot of the protagonist gazing out across the radically altered cityscape.

Cut to three months later. I was now looking for a producer and an investor. The work I had done on this film had pushed me into a new orbit. I needed to find someone who had as much passion about producing and funding this film as I had about directing it. I was so proud of the trailer that I decided to put it on my iPhone, mainly as a tool to cheer me up. As it turned out, it did a whole lot more than cheer me up. It became my self-marketing gold mine!

I was at my brother's 40th birthday party, of all things, when I bumped into a guy I'd met a few times before. When he asked me what I was up to, I decided to be open, and showed him the trailer on my phone. He watched it and said, very succinctly, "How can I get involved in that?" It just so happened that he and his brother had just sold their company – for millions and millions of dollars! So we chatted some more and then again he said, very seriously this time, "I mean it. I want to produce a film. I want to produce that film."

Could I have just made one of the most important connections of my life? The answer is yes, and I know that I would not be where I am today, with my first feature film in postproduction, had I not had the foresight to shoot the trailer. When my producer/financier saw it, he saw it. Whatever I had to say afterward, he had already looked through a window into the world I was creating, and those images were indelibly etched on his mind.

BE INNOVATIVE

When I interviewed JC Calciano for chapter 13 on alternative distributive methods, I was super impressed with his entrepreneurial spirit and business savvy. He was not only thinking outside the box but was also planning for and thinking about his investors potential profits from the very beginning. Because the economy is unstable and investors are looking to invest in films that have an additional safety net, I asked JC what he did in his initial planning stages to give investors a comfort level and get them excited. He said,

My movie, eCupid, is a movie about an app that comes to life and helps this couple in jeopardy fall in love. So what I did is I went out and I actually designed an eCupid app that is part of the movie. So you can actually go to iTunes and download the eCupid app, and in the movie, Morgan Fairchild is the voice of the app. So Morgan Fairchild's voice talks to you, and in the integration of the game (or love tester), you can play with the game on the app or can go on "About the Movie" and it takes you to the website, Facebook, Twitter, screening times, and trailer. I've created this app that is not only a fun device but is also a tool that integrates the marketing and promotion of the film – all of these things talk to each other.

LET'S GET VISUAL

The Internet has changed just about every aspect of our lives, and the film industry is no exception. There are YouTube videos on everything, and people are starting to expect something visual. Recently, while selling units on my Christmas animated feature *Omarr the Camel*, potential investors wanted to see a trailer. The cost of an animated trailer would be around $75,000! Not going to happen. However, I knew that I had to get with the program, so I shot a four-minute video of me talking about the project, focusing on the overview and the synopsis. I added some colorful one-sheets, and it looked fantastic. It gave the information on how to contact me for further information. It went up on my film's website and on YouTube in late fall, and by Christmas I had over 16,000 hits, some of which generated calls from investors.

Also, companies like Kickstarter and IndieGoGo provide an incredible opportunity to raise money for your film. Usually, posting a trailer is required, and it is up to you to get the word out and drive people to your site. It doesn't conflict with the selling of your own units, as those online companies help you raise funds as *donations* toward your project. People will not be making an investment in your film. Instead, they will be pledging a certain amount of money. Producers use these online companies to raise development funds, finishing funds, and money for delivery and even for raising enough money to produce their film.

I spoke with *Part Time Fabulous* indie producer Jules Bruff and director Alethea Root. They made the decision to raise the finishing fund needed for their film using this method:

We choose IndieGoGo to host our campaign because unlike some other crowd funding websites, we would be able to keep all the money we raised, even if we missed our goal. Thankfully, we surpassed our goal! We believed in the film and so did everyone else. We sent out tweets, Facebook updates, and personal emails to everyone we knew. We were shameless in our quest, but we had no shame. I (Alethea) even got a person I met on an airplane to donate to Part Time Fabulous. Raising the funds this way also helped with the promotion of our film. Indiewire and Shinkrap ran articles about the film. We were thrilled. Our 30-day finishing funds campaign was successful. We had enough money to complete post, and we had a huge list of supporters of our film. So far, Part Time Fabulous has gone to two festivals – the Monaco Charity Film Festival and the Berkshire International Film Festival – and we have two wins! So our advice: just do it, and do it with a film you can stand behind, a film that you love, a film that makes you proud to ask for money.

Chapter 7

Soft Prep

WHAT IS SOFT PREP?

You may have heard the statement, "The lower the budget, the longer the prep." Well, is it absolutely true. However, when the budget is as low as a SAG ultra-low, like the projects I was producing, there is certainly no money at this stage. I don't want to start spending money and writing checks until the first day of preproduction. I promised my investors that I would not start soft prep until 80 percent of the funding was complete; in the case of the first one, *Candy Stripers*, I had promised the investors that I would not be moving forward on the film until 100 percent of the funding was complete. So the minute I knew we were in good shape percentage-wise, I started soft prep. To me, it means doing a ton of work and getting plenty of what would normally be considered preproduction done without spending money.

In the case of my low-budget films, Kate and I – together with our line producer – decided that our actual preproduction would be three weeks. Our shooting schedule was fourteen days. So Mike would be moving into my office exactly three weeks before we started shooting each film. However, there was no way I was going to wait until then to start the casting process or location scouting. I would not be able to sleep nights. My goal was to have the entire casting process over, complete with signed deal memos as well as the major locations penciled in. We wouldn't be able to write a check for the locations, but at least we could get the initial deals in place so that on the first day of preproduction, we could have them signed and locked in.

I thought that four weeks would be a good amount of time for what I was calling soft prep. I had a list of things that needed to be done and

I used every minute during that four-week period. Here are five specific items that I feel need to happen during this time period and that can be accomplished with almost no money – all of which will save you a lot of stress during preproduction. Believe me, you will have enough to do during preproduction, so why not get some major items off your plate now? Here's an approximate time line:

Soft prep	Preproduction	Principal photography
4 weeks	3 weeks	2 weeks

1) GET SAG SIGNATORY NUMBER

In the case of *Candy Stripers*, with 33 speaking roles and a budget of $200,000, there was no way we were going to be SAG. However with *Séance* and *Portal*, we wanted to use SAG actors, so that meant getting a SAG signatory number for these films. It is one of those jobs that your line producer is responsible for; however, please check in to make sure the paperwork has been ordered and handled. Mike was so busy doing multiple jobs for us on *Séance* prior to soft prep that he had filled out the paperwork but had not had time to send it back to the SAG office. So here we were four weeks from preproduction and a week away from starting the actual casting process and we didn't have a SAG number. I had Mike send it to the SAG office immediately and I called them and asked if we could get our number as soon as possible because we really wanted to get our character breakdown into Breakdown Services so that we could begin scheduling auditions. They were very accommodating and got us our signatory number within a couple of days.

It is important that you have your number assigned to you by the beginning of soft prep, four weeks before preproduction, so that you'll be ready to begin casting well in advance of preproduction. Also, it is always wise to learn about the guilds and unions you will be using on your film. So call them to see if they are offering any seminars on their policies. I know that SAG has a seminar with a question and answer session at least one evening a month. At the very least, go online and do some research on their rules and regulations. Or feel free to call and speak to someone at the Guild office.

Even working under the low budget that I am discussing here, I wanted to know as much as possible about SAG. That was the only guild we would be using, so why not spend time learning about their policies?

If you are using other guilds or unions, I recommend that you do the same for each.

Please note that the SAG signatory is only for each individual film that you produce. Do not use your umbrella company if you have one. For example, Snowfall Films, Inc., and WindChill Films, Inc., are not signatory companies. Each time I prepare for a new film and I want that film to have SAG actors, I will have that project, which is an LLC (like Séance, LLC), be the signatory company.

2) TABLE READ

We'd already had a table read during script development. That table read was for a couple of reasons: to tighten the script so that we could keep the budget where we wanted it and to catch any areas that needed to be enhanced in any way.

This second table read served a different purpose. At this one, we would of course be looking for any additional ways to enhance the script, but the main reason for scheduling the read was for the heads of department who were now on board to get a chance to hear the script out loud and for us to sit and discuss the project in detail following the read.

I was not going to be paying anyone at this point, but believe me, anyone on board will want to be there. We invited our director, writer, line producer, DP, stunt coordinator, special effects artist, and 1st AD. I could have held the meeting in my office, but in the interest of having an uninterrupted read, I booked a hotel for three hours for the read and discussion. We paid for it personally, and as always, kept the receipt. It was only $100 for a small room, so it was well worth it, and when we started preproduction, we reimbursed ourselves as part of our operating costs and not out of the film budget.

Don't even think about getting and scheduling the actors yourself. Remember, you are the president and manager of this company, so you have to learn to delegate. It is essential. There are tons of actors out there who would love to take on this job for free. They will get to meet the producers and director. An actor friend of ours offered to schedule the actors for the table read. In the case of *Portal*, I told her that there were sixteen speaking roles, so booking seven or eight actors would be fine. I emailed her the script, gave her the location and the time they needed to show up, and I left the rest up to her. She ended up doing such a great job that the director asked her if she would be interested in being a reader during casting. Of course she said yes, and then she ended up getting a major role in the film!

A table read at this stage is invaluable. We were seven weeks away from principal photography and four weeks away from preproduction. This gave us some time to take a serious (really serious) look at the script and have a realistic discussion with the heads of some of the major departments. What was working and what wasn't? During the discussion following the read, we looked at what could be done, what couldn't, and where we might have to cut back or make some changes. Better now than during principal photography.

Mike had done an excellent job of creating the initial budget and schedule, but now we had the special effects expert sitting with us. We had the stunt coordinator and the director all talking about what we could make happen. At this budget level, some things seemed crazy and impossible, so it gave us a chance to brainstorm together and get really, really creative. Instead of saying "That's impossible at this budget," we thought up ways to make those scenes happen. Of course, your director has been working on his or her storyboards to date and perhaps the director has even had the opportunity to work with the DP and first AD, but there is nothing like having them all together in one room where you have just heard the script read aloud. It's kind of like when the rubber hits the road: you have to get real about what can be done at this budget, but you also get the opportunity to create. It's one of the best parts of the entire process of filmmaking.

Something else that came out of this table read was a surprise to me. I think in the first read, we were all so focused on where we needed to cut and trim that we never really concentrated on the emotional impact of certain scenes. At the end of this read, we invited the actors to stay for a few minutes and give us their take on the script. Was there anything they noticed that we should be aware of? We were so close to the script at this point that it was great to have a fresh perspective. During the *Candy Stripers* table read, the actors brought up the fact that our male lead, Brian, had no real emotional reaction to his girlfriend's transformation into an alien. Even though he had to act quickly and kill her in order to survive, the actors at the table read thought that there should be a moment where he gets to express his sadness and therefore give the scene that emotional punch for the audience. It was a great point; the writers and director totally agreed and made immediate changes to the script.

If you have a script supervisor on board at this point, please invite him or her to attend this table read. I wish we had done that on *Candy Stripers*. We had a ton of "hallway" shots, but there was no description differentiating one hallway from another, which posed a real problem for the script supervisor during our shoot. Hearing the script out loud at this early table read might very well have caught and solved that problem.

3) LOCATION SCOUTING

Although we were not spending money to lock in our locations until pre-production, but – like with casting – I would have had a nervous break-down if we didn't at least have our locations penciled in well in advance. Figure 7.1 shows a deal memo that we did with the motel we used during the entire filming of *Portal*.

PORTAL
LOCATION AGREEMENT

Agreement entered into this: by and between:

PORTAL, LLC ("Production Company")
La Crescenta Motel ("Grantor").

PORTAL LOCATION AGREEMENT - September 24th, 2006

1. IDENTITY OF FILMING LOCATION: Grantor hereby agrees to permit Production Company to use the property located at La Crescenta, CA ("Property") in connection with the motion picture currently entitled, PORTAL ("Picture") for rehearsing, photographing, filming and recording scenes and sounds for the Picture. Production Company and its licensees, sponsors, assigns and successors may exhibit, advertise and promote the Picture or any portion thereof, whether or not such uses contain audio and/or visual reproductions of the Property and whether or not the Property is identified, in any and all media which currently exist or which may exist in the future in all countries of the world and in perpetuity.

2. RIGHT OF ACCESS: Production Company shall have the right to bring personnel and equipment (including props and temporary sets) onto the Property and to remove same after completion of its use of the Property hereunder. Production Company shall have the right but not the obligation to photograph, film and use in the Picture the actual name, if any, connected with the Property or to use any other name for the Property. If Production Company depicts the interior(s) of any structures located on the Property, Grantor agrees that Production Company shall not be required to depict such interior(s) in any particular manner in the Picture.

3. TIME OF ACCESS: The permission granted hereunder shall be for the period commencing on or about: October 14th, 2006 and lasting until October 30th, 2006. The period may be extended by Production Company if there are changes in the production schedule or delays due to weather conditions. The within permission shall also apply to future retakes and/or added scenes.

4. PAYMENT: For each day the Production Company uses the location, it shall pay Grantor the sum of _____ for exclusive access to all the rooms on the upper tier of the motel for filming and 2 rooms on the lower tier for makeup and wardrobe, along with use of the office for 1-2 days to film in.   We will utilize the carport on the upper tier to build a dinning room set and if possible we would like to use the 2 car garage for our "basement" set), plus a $500 cleaning fee.

FIGURE 7.1

5. ALTERATIONS TO LOCATION: Production Company agrees that (with Grantor's permission) if it becomes necessary to change, alter or rearrange any equipment on the Property belonging to Grantor, Production Company shall return and restore said equipment to its original place and condition, or repair it, if necessary. Production Company agrees to indemnify and hold harmless Grantor from and against any and all liabilities, damages and claims of third parties arising from Production Company's use hereunder of the Property (unless such liabilities, damages or claims arise from breach of Grantor's warranty as set forth in the immediately following sentence) (and from any physical damage to the Property proximately caused by Production Company, or any of its representatives, employees, or agents). Grantor warrants that it has the right and authority to enter this Agreement and to grant the rights granted by it herein. Grantor agrees to indemnify and hold harmless Production Company from and against any and all claims relating to breach of its aforesaid warranty.

6. NO KICKBACKS FOR USE: Grantor affirms that neither it nor anyone acting for it gave or agreed to give anything of value to any member of the production staff, anyone associated with the Picture, or any representative of Production Company, or any television station or network for mentioning or displaying the name of Grantor as a shooting location on the Property, except the use of the Property, which was furnished for use solely on or in connection with the Picture.

7. BILLING CREDIT: Grantor acknowledges that any identification of the Property which Production Company may furnish shall be at Production Company's sole discretion and in no event shall said identification be beyond that which is reasonably related to the content of the Picture.

8. RELEASE: Grantor releases and discharges Production Company, its employees, agents, licensees, successors and assigns from any and all claims, demands or causes of actions that Grantor may now have for libel, defamation, invasion of privacy or right of publicity, infringement of copyright or violation of any other right arising out of or relating to any utilization of the rights granted herein.
The undersigned represents that he/she is empowered to execute this Agreement for Grantor.

IN WITNESS WHEREOF, the parties have hereunto set their names and signatures:
PRODUCTION COMPANY:

_____

GRANTOR:

_____

PRODUCTION COMPANY REP:
Michael Tarzian, Line Producer

FIGURE 7.1   *(Continued)*

On one of the projects, we paid for a location scout, but as it turned out, we got most of the locations by just putting the word out about what we needed. And our line producer was instrumental in securing some great locations as well. If you can put $1000 or $2000 in the budget for a location scout, go ahead, but if there is a way you, your director, and your line producer can pull it off, all the better.

You will be amazed at how helpful people will be if you start spreading the word as to exactly what you need. Even I forget to do this at first, so make a note of it. In fact, during soft prep I was mentoring a lovely young woman as part of the Los Angeles Women in Film mentor program. At the end of every one of our meetings, she would thank me for being her mentor and then she would ask if I needed anything. I always said no. I know, that was stupid. We were having such problems finding tunnels for the chase scenes in *Séance*. Everything we found was too small or too expensive. On her last mentor meeting with me, just around the end of soft prep, she asked me again if I needed anything. I was so concerned about our location problem that I started telling her about it and she started to laugh. When I asked what was so funny, she said, "Oh, by the way, I am the locations manager for the back lot of Universal Studios." I couldn't believe it. I had known her for months, and we were so focused on her future career in the mentoring program that I never even asked what her current job was! Anyway, we got a great deal, as you can imagine. Watch *Séance* and you will see a fantastic chase scene, as our killer ghost played by Adrian Paul chases our two female leads through the basement hallways at Universal Studios.

Any time you can save money, go for it! It also happened that our line producer was excellent at doing the negotiating and the paperwork involved in securing locations as well as city permits. Don't try to get around or avoid permits when they are required. It is a business like any other, so we don't have the right to cut corners when it comes to legal commitments.

4) LIST YOUR FILM IN THE TRADES

Another item to handle in soft prep is listing your film in the trades. This task is so much fun, and it's easy to do. Call your local industry trade magazines and get the information necessary to post your film. I think this is important for a couple of reasons. It is fun to see your film listed in the trades as being in preproduction, and it is also important, as you are about to start casting, that agents and managers see that your film is real. In addition, sales agents and studios will start tracking you. It puts you on their radar. It's also a great idea to scan a copy of the listing once it's been posted in the trades and email it to your investors.

5) INFORM YOUR INVESTORS

It was at this point, the first week of soft prep, that I started weekly emails to our investors. We were about to start the casting process, which was exciting. We were looking for locations and the film was getting listed in the trades – all great fun stuff to share with investors. As I really wanted to keep my investors informed and involved, I ended each week with a detailed email. I also informed them that the schedule would be available in a month and reminded them that they were welcome to come out to the set. I would be making recommendations for what days would be the most fun as we got closer to locking down the schedule. I continued this weekly email until well into postproduction. Without your investors, you don't have a movie. I know you are busy during soft prep, preproduction, principal photography, postproduction, and delivery, but don't forget to make a point of keeping your investors updated and informed.

Chapter 8

The Casting Process

PART 1: PREPARATION

I created a pretty brilliant schedule for the casting process and broke it down into four weeks that consisted of four categories that took place during the four weeks prior to preproduction. Our preproduction schedule was three weeks long, and there was going to be enough to do during that time. So I made a point of scheduling a full month, four weeks prior to preproduction, to handle the following:

1. **Week 7** we did our preparation, which consisted of planning the schedule with the director and line producer and getting the character breakdowns to Breakdown Services.
2. **Week 6** we did the scheduling for the auditions.
3. **Week 5** we did the auditions.
4. **Week 4** we did the callbacks and actors' deal memos.

Let's take it a step at a time, and you will see that once it's broken down into each section, it is actually a lot of fun.

Casting Director – Or Not

In an ideal world, you would have a casting director, but at this budget level, you may not be able to afford one. However, there is still a chance to get some help if you're smart about it. There are a lot of assistant casting directors who would love the chance to have a "casting director" credit and who will do it for a great price. In the low-budget world, you have to tell people what you have in the budget for them – not the other way around. If what you have is $500 or $1,000, then that's it. No negotiating. Perhaps you can compromise and have an assistant casting director help you call the agents to set up the auditions for that amount, and then you take it from there.

For the casting of *Candy Stripers*, we had help from a friend who was a former casting director. However, I strongly suggest that at this budget, you try taking on the job yourself. For *Séance* and *Portal*, I managed the entire casting process. And I did it for a couple of reasons.

My previous films had far bigger budgets, and we were dealing with the major agents from agencies like ICM (International Creative Management), CAA (Creative Artists Agency), and the William Morris Endeavor agency. That was a great experience, but at these SAG ultra-low and SAG modified budgets, I knew I would be dealing with a whole different group of agents and managers. Also, because Kate and I were planning a series of this type of films, I wanted to personally get to know the agents and managers involved. And because with *Séance* we had a first-time director, I wanted to make sure that I was very much involved in the casting process so that I would be there for him the entire time. At this budget level, it is all extremely easy, and I am going to take you through the entire process so that if you decide you want to take it on, you can do so with ease.

Guild Actors – Or Not

As I mentioned earlier, with *Candy Stripers* there were 33 speaking roles – and a 150 extras – so there was no way that we could work with SAG actors. The good news is that in the United States, the Screen Actors Guild has a group of actors that are "financial core," which allows you to access SAG actors without having to be signatory. So check in with your country's guilds and see what alternatives they provide. In fact, even when we did go signatory on *Séance* and *Portal*, because we were in the ultra-low-budget category, we were able to have quite a large percentage of non-SAG actors.

There are certainly benefits both ways. With SAG actors, you may not have to audition as many actors because you are dealing with actors who already have proven experience. During the *Candy Stripers* auditions, we saw more than 500 actors! During the *Séance* and *Portal* auditions, we saw around 250 for each film – half as many.

On the other hand, with *Candy Stripers*, we didn't have to be concerned with the scheduling and cost involved in overtime, or with the additional cost for the actors' table read prior to principal photography, or with the cost of ADR (additional dialog recording) during postproduction. In addition, there is the cost of the payroll company for your SAG actors' checks during production and the ongoing cost of the payroll company, as well as the percentages due as a result of the SAG residuals that are required with each territory sale. So don't just jump right into becoming signatory. Give it some serious thought before making your decision.

Guild Deposit

Something to keep in mind here is that there is a SAG deposit to be made prior to production. It is not a lot, but it is money that you will eventually need for postproduction and delivery, so just be aware that this check will need to be written and will not be returned until two or three months after you've finished shooting and delivered your SAG delivery book containing the cast deal memos and schedules. It will be your job to remind SAG (or whatever your actors' guild happens to be) periodically once your delivery book has been submitted to send you your money back.

Breakdown Services

If you make the decision to go with your local actor's guild then there is a good chance that you will need to go through an authorized company to post your character breakdowns. We used a company called Breakdown Services, an online communication service that publishes detailed casting information that is used by agents and managers. Figure 8.1 shows the information page we received at the time.

Click Here: To post a theatrical or commercial principal breakdown on Breakdown Express and/or Actors Access

Click Here: To post a background breakdown for Extras on Extras Access

Breakdown Services, Ltd. is the communications network and casting system that provides the most comprehensive and professional means to reach talent agents as well as actors when casting a project. In 1971 Breakdown Services started by delivering casting information to talent agents overnight via messenger. Today's Breakdown Service delivers casting information instantly via the Internet.

Breakdown Services has offices in **Los Angeles**, **New York** and **Vancouver** and maintains affiliate relationships with sister companies in **Toronto**, **London** and **Sydney**. With clients in most regions of the USA and Provinces of Canada our reach extends throughout North America.

Phone Numbers for Breakdown Services' offices are:

Los Angeles 310.276.9166

New York 212.869.2003

Vancouver 604.943.7100

Breakdowns are complete synopses of the characters contained within scripts. Our staff writers read scripts provided by casting directors and create approximately 30 television and feature film Breakdowns every day. Breakdowns approved for release are sent out REALTIME through our website at www.breakdownexpress.com. Talent Representatives are able to instantly view the Breakdowns and submit their clients' pictures, resume and videos via our website to casting directors.

Breakdowns that are released to talent representatives include episodics, pilots, feature films, movies for television, commercials, print projects, theater, student films, industrials, reality tv, and many other types of projects that require acting talent.

Breakdown Express is how your talent via the Internet and how casting views submissions of pictures, resumes, and videos. The site is organized to allow casting directors to review submissions and create audition schedules that notify talent representatives instantly.

Actors Access is how you can release your projects directly to actors. Actors view projects via Actors Access. It is entirely up to the casting director whether a Breakdown is released to actors or just to talent representatives. Submissions for both talent representatives and actors are viewed by the casting director on Breakdown Express. Actors Access is also an important tool for actors since they can upload new pictures, update their resume and add new skills and attributes to their profile, all online.

Extras Access is our new resource, now serving the Background/Extras community providing a fully integrated nation-wide online submission system between casting and Background actors through Breakdown Express. Extras casting can now post their Background Breakdown and Background actors can submit/respond to casting instantly online via Extras Access.

OUR ADDITIONAL DISTRIBUTION RESOURCES

Sides: Showfax provides actors with Sides. Since 1993, our Showfax division has been the number one resource online for distributing sides to actors. Don't forget to post your sides on Showfax when you need sides distribution. Fast, easy, efficient, Showfax will see to it that talent and representation receive your sides as well as any updated or revised sides. Sides distribution has never been easier or more convenient. Contact Showfax during office hours Mon-Fri 9 a.m. to 10 p.m. Pacific time at (310) 385-6936 or by email 24/7 to info@showfax.com

Scripts: Screenplay Online is our digital delivery service for distributing full scripts to representation as well as talent. Whether across town or across the world, Screenplay Online makes it possible to get your scripts delivered almost instantly. Contact Screenplay Online at Showfax during office hours Mon-Fri 9 a.m. to 10 p.m. Pacific time at (310) 385-6920 or by email 24/7 to scripts@gobetween.com

FIGURE 8.1

Remember that you don't have to submit every single character. In the case of *Séance*, we had only eight main characters, and they were all very distinct, so we did send in a character breakdown for each one. The character breakdown for the little girl is not listed on this page. Figure 8.2 shows what that looked like.

Seance

Film & TV / SAG /

Project created on 4/13/2006

Project Name: Seance	**Casting Dates:** April 20 - May 3, 2006
Project Type: Film & TV	**Audition Location:** WindChill Films/Snowfall Films
Category: Feature Film	Office
Union Status: SAG	2321 W. Olive Avenue, Suite A
Contract Status: SAG Ultra Low	Burbank CA 91506
Submissions Due By: 4/21/2006	**Callback Dates:** Start: 4/26/2006 End: 5/5/2006
Rate: Scale SAG Ultra Low	**Callback Location:** WindChill Films/Snowfall Films Office
Production Company: WindChill Films	2321 W. Olive Avenue, Suite A Burbank CA 91506
	Shoot/Performance Dates: May 22 - June 9, 2006
	Shoot/Performance Location: Los Angeles
	Mail Submissions To: WindChill Films 2321 W. Olive Avenue, Suite A Burbank CA 91506

Roles

LAUREN / Lead / Female / Caucasian / 19-22
Southern small town pretty. Survivor of a brutal childhood with the psychological scars to prove it. Now a student at NYU.
Wardrobe: Student

GRANT / Lead / Male / Caucasian / 19-21
Good looking in spite of being an introverted, reclusive computer geek.
Wardrobe: Student

DIEGO / Co-Star / Male / All Ethnicities / 19-21
American of minority descent. Diego is charming, sexy.
Wardrobe: Student

MELINA / Co-Star / Female / All Ethnicities / 19-21
A sophisticated, beautiful young Manhattanite student.
Wardrobe: Student.

ALISON / Co-Star / Female / Caucasian / 18-20
Student. Although she's a university student, she still sleeps with her stuffed turtle. Diego's girlfriend.
Wardrobe: Student.

SYD / Co-Star / Male / All Ethnicities / 40-55
Sloppy security guard.

SPENCE / Co-Star / Male / Asian, Caucasian, East Indian, Hispanic, Middle Eastern, Multi-Ethnic, Native American, Pacific Islander / 30-45
A ghost that has been summoned to the present. When he lived, Spence was a serial killer and an apartment building maintenance man who died in the electric chair for his crimes. He's back in his ghostly form intent upon killing again.

FIGURE 8.2

Portal had sixteen characters, so we wrote up a breakdown for eight of them, knowing that during the audition process we would be able to cast a number of the smaller roles based on the auditions we were holding for the main roles.

Because this stage occurs in the first week of soft prep, this would be the time to submit your film's character breakdown to your local breakdown service. You want to start scheduling actors at the beginning of week 6 (three weeks before preproduction), so get your paperwork in by Thursday or Friday of week 7 (four weeks before preproduction).

With *Candy Stripers*, we were not going to be SAG signatory, so we chose to post our character breakdowns on an online site called LA Casting because they did not require a signatory number. So depending on whether you choose to use the actors' guild in your territory, look into the various companies you can use to post your breakdowns.

Plan Casting Process With Your Director

Be in constant communication with your director. Review the storyboard with the director frequently and make sure that he or she is available for whatever casting process you have planned. With *Séance*, our director – Mark L. Smith – lived in North Carolina, so we decided that when I started getting the online head shots for the characters we submitted on *Séance*, I would send them to him directly.

Mark and I set up a daily schedule in which I would email him the head shots that had been submitted for each character and he would review them, sending them back to me and noting the actors he wanted to see by 4:00 p.m. each day. It worked perfectly. Also, because he was a first-time director, Kate and I made a point of going over the submitted head shots and picked out any actors that we thought might be worth auditing as well.

In some cases, if you have a casting director, you may choose to have him or her handle this initial stage and then you and your director can join the casting director during the callbacks. However, I wanted Mark, as a first-time director, to see the types of actors we were getting and to have the level of involvement that comes with seeing the audition process from the beginning. I also personally wanted to meet the agents or managers as well as the actors who would be coming into audition for us at this budget level so that I could also develop those relationships.

PART 2: SCHEDULING

Scheduling Auditions

With *Séance*, the director and I worked out a very clear schedule for work-ing together. I would send him the headshots that I received each morn-ing, and he would get his choices to me by 4:00 p.m. every day. I would then call the agents between 4:00 and 6:00 p.m. and book their clients to come in for an audition. To make it really easy, when I made the calls on Monday, I booked the following Monday. When I made my Tuesday calls, I booked the following Tuesday.

I also decided to try as much as possible to book the auditions in groups. Mark was a new director and I wanted him to see the contrast in the quality of the actors. So I booked back-to-back auditions for a number of actors who were coming for the lead role of Lauren. I did the same for the other roles as well. It really gave him a good sense of the talent and ability that the actors possessed.

Another little tip I figured out after a couple of days was to organize the actors' calls by the people who represented them. It took me quite a few calls to catch on that there had to be an easier way to do the scheduling. For exam-ple, I was making a call to book an actor for the role of Lauren, who was rep-resented by an agent at Bobby Ball's company, and then twenty minutes later I was booking an actor for the role of Grant who happened to have an agent at the same company. It was a waste of time and I was all about being extremely efficient with regard to the entire audition process. So, by day 2, when I got the list from Mark, I would check to see where each person was represented and then I would organize them into calls based on that information.

Mark, Kate, and I discussed at length our ideas for each character and what we felt they would or could look like. We focused on the headshots as our main source for finding our actors, and we decided not to review actors' reels or any other materials. However, when colleagues called with suggestions and referrals of talented actors, we made certain to fit them into our auditions. And of course Kate and I had a list of actors that we had gotten to know over the years and who we felt may fit some of the roles, so we booked them as well.

How to Schedule

Before I explain the process, I want to point out how important it is to put at least one name actor in your film. I know we are talking about really low budgets here, but regardless, you will still need to sell your film and name talent will help tremendously when that time comes. In fact, sales agents will tell you that a $100,000 film requires a marketable name to ensure sales. Also, with the digital camera allowing so many of us to produce our films, there is now a glut of films on the market. Add to that the downturn in the economy and the increase in film pirating around the world, and territory sales are far more difficult. So having at least one name actor gives you an edge.

With *Séance*, we wanted a name for our killer ghost, and we knew that we could shoot him out in five or six days, so we made a point of setting aside a certain amount of money for a marketable name that would help sales agents sell our film. We wanted Adrian Paul, and we went through the proper channels to get him attached. My husband had actually worked as a writer/producer on the *Highlander* TV series (the series in which Adrian was the lead). So an email was sent to Adrian in advance, telling him that Kate and I would be contacting his agent about the role in *Séance*, and when I called his agent, I made a point of mentioning that relationship. Even with that existing relationship, I still think it's important to go through the proper channels and handle the paperwork with the talent's agent/ manager/attorney.

With the rest of the roles, here's what I did: I called the actor's agent and basically said, "I would like to see your client, Tory White, for the role of Melina on our film *Séance*, next Monday morning at 10:00." Then I would give the agent the office address and the information on where to get the sides. Sides are something that you have prepared in advance of the auditions. They are scenes that you have pulled from the screenplay. When I was making the call, if I got an answering machine, I would leave the same message and add that if there were any problems to please let me know, but that I was going to assume everything was fine unless I heard otherwise.

Also, I had a special sheet made up for these calls. It looked like this:

Séance – Cold Read Schedule

DATE: _____

Character	Time	Actor's Name	Agent's Name	Agent or Actor's Phone #

So, if one of the actors that your director really wants to see doesn't show up for his or her scheduled time, you will have their agent's phone number right in front of you. If you don't have the agent's number on your sheet, it means you'll have to go look for it – and believe me, you don't what to be bothered with time-wasting problems like this during your auditions.

Once again, you don't have to do any of this. You can always have an assistant casting director on board to do this scheduling for you. It was only a couple of hours a day and, like I said, I wanted to know the process and to meet the agents and managers with whom I would be dealing on these low-budget films. Decide what matters most to you.

How Much Time to Allow for Auditions

During the auditions for *Candy Stripers*, we allowed three to five minutes because we knew we would be seeing more than 500 actors, the majority of whom were non-SAG, with a few who were SAG financial core. For the most part, it was extremely obvious within the first 30 seconds whether we wanted them to do a second read or wanted them to try different sides.

However, with *Séance* and *Portal*, the majority of actors we were seeing were SAG, and we knew that we might need time to have them do a couple of reads and perhaps a couple of scenes. Also, because we had a new director, I wanted to make sure that he had time to discuss an actor's possible callback with us after a great audition. So we allowed ten minutes. Fifty percent of the time, it only took a couple of minutes, but it was great to know we had the extra time if we needed it.

Book Your Readers

This step is easy. Most actors would kill for the chance to read opposite the actors during the auditions. They get to be with you for hours and get to meet and get to know the director and producers (and casting director, if you are using one). Plus, they get to hear the discussions that take place after the actors leave – invaluable! Once again, this is something you can delegate to an assistant, intern, or an actor friend.

Be sure that you have a number of them booked because it's a demanding job and you want to have quite a few on your team. Also, be sure they are people who can be counted on to be on time.

Choosing the Sides

What scenes should you choose for your auditions? I was lucky, in that Kate had studied acting and had been involved in theatre for years. She had a great idea: for each of the roles, we chose two very different types of

scenes from the script, making sure that one of the sides was a more difficult, emotionally challenging scene.

The scenes you choose – the sides – are something you send in to SAG
and to Breakdown Services (or whatever company you choose to use),
so the agents/managers and their actors can download them. Because the
agents and managers want to send their clients in to read for the lead roles,
we ended up with quite a few actors coming in to audition for a role that
they were really not right for at that time. So make sure you have a lot of
extra sides available because you will most likely be asking some actors if
they would be interested in reading for another role.

When actors agreed to read for another role, we gave them the new
sides, and they would go outside and take as much time as they needed to
get ready for that audition. We just continued auditions, and they would let
our outside assistant know when they were ready to come back in to audition for the other role.

In the case of *Portal*, we had only posted half of the roles on Breakdown
Services because we didn't want to be auditioning for all 16 roles, knowing that
we would find some excellent talent from the actors we were already seeing.

Also, keep in mind that some actors will forget to bring their sides with
them, so it is important to have extras available.

Typed Sign-In Sheets

Another thing to prepare for at this time is your sign-in sheets. I knew we
wanted to start at 10:00 a.m. and end at around 5:00 p.m. each day. Our
goal was to book around 45 actors a day. So I had sign-in sheets ready for
each day, and they were posted on the door. It was pretty simple, with just
three columns:

SIGN-IN SHEET

Name (please print)	Time Scheduled	Time Arrived

Okay, so the following week is fully booked, you've got your readers
scheduled, your audition schedule sheet completely filled out, and your
sign-in sheets ready. It's time to move on to part 3: auditions!

PART 3: AUDITIONS AND CALLBACKS

Auditions

I had booked auditions starting at 10:00 a.m., so I set up four chairs outside the office and posted the sign-in sheets on the door. My first reader
of the day showed up nice and early, and the director, Kate, and I – along

with one of our executive producers – had met even earlier to discuss the day and to be sure we were all on the same page with regard to what we were looking for with each role.

I had booked the actors ten minutes apart, and we knew that there would be some who would be early, some late, and some who would not show up at all. So be flexible. Also, because you will have some of your actors trying out for other roles, your timing will change slightly throughout the day.

One of the actors who came in for the lead role of Gibbs in *Portal* was Alex Martin – an amazing actor, but not how the director saw that role. However, he was absolutely perfect for the lead's sidekick, so we asked him if he would mind reading for that role. We gave him the sides for the role and he went outside and rehearsed, came back in, and did an incredible audition. We knew in a second that he had the part.

As I started to get to know the agents and managers and as they got to know a little more about what we were looking for, I began getting calls from them during auditions recommending certain actors who they thought would be important for us to see. Whenever possible, we made time to audition them.

When each actor arrived for their audition, he or she brought a couple of headshots, one of which I gave to the director so that he could make notes on the back. On *Portal*, our director, Geoff Schaff, had a ratings system. Each director has his or her own personal style that works for that director.

I kept a copy of each headshot as well, and as soon as we knew that a particular actor was coming in for a callback audition, I would set that headshot aside to call his or her agent a little later in the week to schedule the callback.

Lunch Break and Atmosphere

Don't worry about your lunch break. There will be enough flexibility with actors coming early and late, and no shows, that you will find ten minutes for lunch. The important thing is to not eat in front of actors during an audition. I know that seems like common sense, but I have heard horror stories from actors. They have told me that producers, directors, and even casting directors have had lunch during their auditions, have talked during entire auditions, and in some cases have been outright rude. If you want your production to run professionally, it starts by respecting the actors during the audition process.

When Kate and I would welcome each actor and thank them for coming in and then thank them again at the end of the audition, they would be shocked and tell us that this was unusual. They were sincerely moved by our politeness. I think politeness should be the norm, not an exception to the rule. It only takes a second and it really puts people at ease and means so much.

Scheduling Callbacks

Toward the end of the week, we got together and discussed callbacks. On each of the films, we ended up with around 40 callbacks. So on Thursday and Friday, I booked the following Monday. I really tried to fit them all in to the one day if the actors were available. And once again, I tried to book them in groups according to the role so that we could really see the differences in style and talent between the actors and therefore have a better chance of making an informed decision. If an actor was not available then I would book him or her for Tuesday morning, but I was really holding that time for the chemistry callbacks if they were needed.

We did not videotape the auditions. I know that some people do that and also videotape the callbacks as well. At this budget level, and in the interest of time, we never bothered to film the auditions. I truly don't think it's necessary. You can get such a great feel for the quality of talent and the genuine personality of the person during an audition and during their callback audition that I don't think you need to worry about filming them at this time. However, it is entirely up to you and your director. If your director feels comfortable having the auditions on tape, then in the interest of time, I suggest that you recommend limiting the filming to callbacks only.

Callbacks

Week four of soft prep means that just one week later my line producer, his production coordinator and his assistant will be moving into my office. So, my goal during this week is to finish up the entire casting process: callbacks and deal memos.

It's Monday, and I have booked more than 40 actors for callbacks. This is one of the best days in the process. You are going to be seeing all your favorite actors come in to audition. You will be pleasantly surprised to see how easy it is to distinguish which one is perfect for the role. This result always surprises me. However, keep track of your second- and third-favorite actors for each role, just in case your first choice is unavailable or – in the worst-case scenario – you need to recast.

Here is an example of one of these situations. On the first day of shooting *Candy Stripers*, I went into the office to pick up some papers before heading up to the hospital where we were shooting. Thank goodness I did. I checked the answering machine and there was a message from an agent who represented one of the main actors. It was 9:00 a.m. and he was to be on set at 1:00 p.m. She apologized and said that he was in Mexico because he had been offered a role at the last minute in a bigger film. Crazy! As the producer, I don't have the time to get upset, so I grabbed the headshots that

I had set aside for each of our second and third choices and called their agents. Within 15 minutes, I had one of them in a car on his way to the set. It was easy. But it could have been a real problem if we had not had the foresight to keep in mind a couple more actors for each important role.

There had been a red flag a few days before and I missed it. When I was double-checking the cast deal memos, I noticed that his was not in the file. I called his agent and she said not to worry, that he would bring it with him to the table read the next day (the table read was on Friday and we were shooting on Monday). He showed up the next day at the table read with no deal memo and said he had thought his agent was sending it in. I actually believed him and went ahead with the table read. He lied and his agent lied. It was that simple.

As we made our decisions, choosing our favorite actors, we had to keep in mind the importance of the chemistry that would be needed for some of the roles. Actors don't play in a void; they need to click with the other actors. So it was important to have our second and third choices in mind for that reason as well.

Chemistry Callbacks

If your film has roles that have best friends like we did in *Candy Stripers*, roommates like we did in *Séance*, and couples as we did in both those films and in *Portal*, then you will have to take into account the chemistry between the actors. I had scheduled Tuesday morning for our chemistry callbacks and I didn't realize how important they were until I saw it with my own eyes.

At the end of the callback day on *Candy Stripers*, we had picked our five actors and we were certain, 100 percent certain, that we had chosen the perfect five. However, because the roles were boyfriend/girlfriend, brother/sister, and best friends, we needed to see our first, second, and third choices on Tuesday morning to have them audition with each other.

I was absolutely amazed during the chemistry callbacks to discover, as they auditioned with each other, how certain actors that we thought were perfect for the role just didn't work as the lead's best friend or the female lead's brother, and so on. If I hadn't witnessed it myself, I don't know that I would be recommending it so strongly. We ended up with a completely different group; three of the five actors that were initially our first choice didn't end up getting the part.

Final Decisions

After all the callbacks were complete and the chemistry callbacks were over, we took a good part of Tuesday afternoon to just sit and talk about the lead actors we were going to hire as well as making our final decisions on all the supporting roles as well. In the case of the leads, the callbacks and chemistry callbacks had made our decisions effortless. However, with the supporting roles, especially in the case of the numerous supporting roles on *Portal*, we spread out the headshots of our choices on the floor; it was difficult, because in some cases our top two or three choices were equally excellent.

In some cases, we made choices based on the fact that one of us had a relationship with a particular actor and we knew that he or she would be great to have on set. Also, in some cases when actors were equally talented, we chose a percentage of non-SAG. At this budget level, we were permitted a percentage of non-SAG actors, and although we were paying them the same salary, we did not have to use a payroll company or worry about overtime restrictions or ongoing residuals.

As we made our decisions, one by one I pinned the actors' headshots on the door of the office with the role they would be playing attached to the bottom of each headshot. This whole process took a while, but it was one of the most important aspects of the film. What has a low-budget film stand out as bad – what screams "low budget" – is the quality of the acting. I see producers cutting corners here and rushing through this process thinking that it is just not important. I truly don't know why this happens. There are so many talented brilliant actors who are dying to do what they do best: act. You are offering an opportunity to actors here. You don't have to settle. Not ever. There is too much great talent out there for you not to take full advantage of that fact and have it be a win/win for both your film and for the actor. Taking your time here and really putting effort into the audition process will make all the difference in the quality of your film. Just watch *Séance*. We had to see a couple of hundred actors to choose our five college-age stars. Believe me, it was well worth the time.

PART 4: DEAL MEMOS

When you're dealing with contracts such as actor's deal memos, always have an attorney look them over. At this low budget level, I couldn't afford to have an attorney start from scratch, and I don't believe you need to. There are tons of books and online sources with great templates. In fact, I'm going to give you the one that was used on *Candy Stripers*, *Séance*, and *Portal* (see Figure 8.3). It's taken from one of my earlier, bigger budget films and was written originally by a fantastic entertainment attorney. You can use this one or even use parts of it, but as I have mentioned earlier, *please have an attorney look it over for you when you're done*. Of course, you want it as up to date as possible, and you should include any possible guild changes as well.

PORTAL FILM, LLC
2321 W. Olive Avenue, Suite A
Burbank, CA 91506
818-558-5917 (Fax) 818-842-4112

Date:

VIA FAX:

Name of Manager or Agent
Company Name of Manager or Agent

Re: MOTION PICTURE "NAME OF YOUR FILM" – NAME OF ACTOR

The present shall serve as an offer from YOUR COMPANY NAME, LLC ("Producer") to NAME OF ACTOR ("Artist") for the role of "NAME OF CHARACTER" in the motion picture "FILM NAME" subject to the following terms and conditions:

*1.   **TERM:** One (1) day for wardrobe fittings, plus four (4) non-consecutive days of principal photography acting services, plus one (1) day of post-production including ADR, looping and other customary post-production service activities if needed. Artist will be provided with a Day Out Of Days no later than one week prior to the start of Principal Photography.*

*2.   **GUARANTEED COMPENSATION:** $100.00 (One hundred dollars) per day for four days. This film is being produced under the SAG Ultra Low Budget Agreement. The Guaranteed Compensation shall be payable to Player when Player commences providing services, to be paid to Player weekly in arrears during the period of Principal Photography. Any additional days or pick up days will be at the rate of $100 per day.*

*3.   **BILLING:** On a separate card in the main titles (provided main titled credits are used and other cast member credits appear therein). Advertising Billing: Artist will be included in all paid advertising where the billing block appears.*

*4.   **GRANT OF RIGHTS:** Artist grants to Producer all rights, in perpetuity, resulting from the proceeds of Artist's services hereunder, necessary for the exploitation, production, distribution, merchandising and advertising of the Picture. Producer shall have the right to use a "double" for Artist in the case of hazardous stunts or similar type performances and to "dub" Artist's voice or performance at any time and for any reason upon meaningful consultation with Artist. Notwithstanding the preceding, Producer's right to "dub" Artist's voice in the English language shall be subject to Artist being offered the first opportunity to dub his voice in said language. Artist acknowledges that Producer shall be the sole and exclusive owner of all rights in and to the Picture, including, without limitation the copyright therein, and of all the results and proceeds of Artist's services hereunder and shall have the right to sue, exploit, advertise, exhibit and otherwise turn to account any or all of the foregoing in any manner and in any media, whether now known or hereafter devised, throughout the universe, in perpetuity, in all languages, as Producer in its sole discretion shall determine. Artist acknowledges that Artist has no right, title or interest in the Picture or any material on which it is based and Producer is the owner of the Picture and all such material. Any material written or contributed by Artist is intended by Artist to be*

FIGURE 8.3

a "work-made-for-hire" pursuant to Section 201 or Title 17 of the United States Code.
<u>*Rental and Lending Rights*</u>: *The Guaranteed Compensation payable to Artist pursuant to this Agreement shall be deemed to include fair remuneration and consideration for the "Rental and Lending Rights" (as such term is commonly and customarily defined and used pursuant to any European Economic Community ("EEC") directive, enabling or implementing legislation, laws or regulations engaged by any member nation of the EEC) licensed and granted to Producer. In connection with the foregoing, Artist irrevocably grants to Producer, throughout the universe, in perpetuity, the right to collect and retain for Producer's own account any amount payable to Artist in respect of Rental or Lending Rights and hereby irrevocably directs any collection society or other person or entity receiving such amounts to pay such amounts to Producer.*

5.   <u>**LOCATION**</u>: *Principal location of the Picture is Los Angeles, California.*

6.   <u>**START DATE:**</u> *The Start Date for principal photography of the Picture is October 14, 2006. Principal photography will end on October 31, 2006.*

7.   <u>**DIRECTOR**</u>: *NAME OF DIRECTOR.*

8.   <u>**NAME AND LIKENESS**</u>: *Artist hereby grants to Producer the right to use Artist's name, likeness and approved biography in connection with the production, exhibition, advertising and other exploitation of the Picture and all subsidiary and ancillary rights therein, in perpetuity, throughout the universe, in any and all media, whether now known or hereafter devised, including, without limitation, recordings (in any configuration) containing any material derived from the Picture, all or any part of the soundtrack of the Picture, and publications (including music folios); provided however, that in no event shall Artist be depicted as using or endorsing any product or service without Artist's prior written consent and provided, further, that Artist shall be portrayed only in the role played by Artist in the Picture.*

9.   <u>**PUBLICITY SERVICES**</u>: *After the photography of the Picture, Artist will, if so requested by Producer, reasonably cooperate with Producer in promoting and publicizing the Picture.*

10.   <u>**"MAKING OF" FILMS**</u>: *Artists agrees to cooperate with Producer in the creation of promotional "Making Of" films. Additionally, Artist agrees that Producer may use portions of the Picture and "behind the scenes" shots in said promotional "Making Of" films and may exploit said promotional "Making Of" films in any and all media whatsoever without the payment of any additional compensation whatsoever.*

11.   <u>**INDEMNITY**</u>: *Producer assumes liability for, and shall indemnify, defend, protect, save and hold harmless Artist (the "Indemnified Party") from and against any claims, actions, liabilities, losses, penalties, expenses or damages (including, without limitation, legal fees and expenses) of whatsoever kind and nature imposed on, incurred by or asserted against any of the Indemnified Party arising out of any breach by Producer of any representation, warranty or covenant made, or obligation assumed, by Producer pursuant to this Agreement or otherwise arising out of the development, production, distribution or exploitation of the Picture or any element thereof in any and all media now known or hereafter devised throughout the universe in perpetuity.*

12.   <u>**ARTIST'S REMEDIES:**</u> *In the event of any breach by Producer of this Agreement, Artist shall be limited to his remedy at law for damages, if any, and Artist*

FIGURE 8.3   *(Continued)*

shall not have the right to (a) terminate or rescind this Agreement or any of the rights granted to Producer hereunder, or to (b) enjoin, restrain or otherwise impair in any manner the production, distribution, advertising or other exploitation of the Picture, or any parts or elements thereof.

*13.   **DEFAULT, INCAPACITY, FORCE MAJEURE:** Producer may, upon written notice to Artist, terminate this Agreement if as a result of an event of force majeure lasting not less than six (6) weeks, Producer elects to abandon the Picture and all other above-the-line personnel are terminated. In the event of such termination, Producer will pay all accrued compensation up to the date of termination and no party shall have any further obligations to any other party pursuant to this Agreement; provided, however, that the representation and warranties and the indemnification and insurance obligations of the parties hereunder shall survive such termination. Producer shall have the right to suspend Artist's services and the accrual of compensation hereunder during all periods: (i) that Artist does not perform Artist's material obligations hereunder, as reasonably required by Producer, because of disability or default; and/or (ii) that production of the Picture is prevented or materially interrupted because of any event of force majeure. In such event, all dates herein set forth or provided for shall, at Producer's election, be postponed for a period equivalent to the period of such event and for such reasonable additional period of time thereafter as Producer requires to prepare for the recommencement of Artist's services, not to exceed two (2) weeks. If any disability of Artist shall exist for two (2) business days or more, or if any interruption of production as a result of force majeure event shall exist for one (1) week or more two (2) weeks or more for third party death, illness, incapacity or breach of contract, Producer or Artist may terminate this Agreement by written notice and be relieved of any further obligation to all other parties hereunder excepting as set forth above. In the event of a default by Artist, Artist shall have a period of five (5) business days, or in the case of principal photography, twenty-four (24) hours, following receipt of Producer's notice within which to cure such default. Artist may not be suspended for force majeure unless all above-the-line personnel are suspended. Producer shall not terminate a suspension and then re-suspend Artist as a result of the same event of force majeure. If suspended or terminated, Artist shall be reinstated if any above-the-line personnel is reinstated within eighteen (18) months of such suspension or termination and Artist shall be paid if any above-the-line personnel is paid within eighteen (18) months of such suspension or termination. Notwithstanding anything herein contained, if any suspension for a force majeure event shall continue for two (2) weeks or more, Artist may render services for Artist's own behalf or for others during the continuance of such suspension, subject to twenty-four (24) hour recall on the termination of such suspension.*

*14.   **PRODUCER'S BREACH:** No act or omission of Producer hereunder shall constitute an event of default or breach of this Agreement unless Artist shall first notify Producer in writing, setting forth such alleged breach or default and Producer shall not cure the same within five (5) business days after receipt of such notice, except that with respect to Producer's failure to make payment to Artist hereunder, the cure period shall be three (3) business days following Producer's actual receipt of such notice.*

*15.   **MISCELLANEOUS:**   a) Governing Law. This Agreement shall be governed by the laws of the State of California applicable to agreements executed and wholly performed therein and shall not be modified except by a written document executed by both parties hereto.*

FIGURE 8.3   *(Continued)*

b) Entire Agreement. This Agreement expresses the entire understanding of the parties hereto and replaces any and all former agreements or understandings, written or oral, relating to the subject matter hereof.

The screenplay is written by WRITER'S NAME. The Picture will be produced by YOUR NAME or YOUR COMPANY NAME, LLC, a WindChill Films Production.

Should you require any additional information, please do not hesitate to contact us. This offer is good until close of business, Friday, September 29, 2006.

("Producer")

FILM COMPANY NAME, LLC.

_____

Name: YOUR NAME

AGREED TO AND ACCEPTED THIS _____ DAY OF SEPTEMBER, 2006.

"Artist"

_____

ACTORS NAME

FIGURE 8.3   *(Continued)*

Number 1, *Term*, is pretty clear and straightforward. However, the wording will change slightly depending on whether it's guild or nonguild. The way it's worded in our example was for one of the lead SAG actors in *Portal*, so you will notice that it says "One (1) day for wardrobe fittings . . . plus one (1) day of post-production, including . . . ." However, for one of the non-SAG actors, it was worded as follows, "One (1) free day for wardrobe fittings . . . plus one (1) free day of post-production, including ADR." The word "free" is not used in the deal memo for the guild actors.

Another point to be aware of in this section is this sentence "plus four (4) nonconsecutive days of principal photography acting services." It is very important that at this budget level you use "nonconsecutive" even if it looks like your schedule is looking pretty solid by the time you send out the deal memo. Remember that this agreement is going to the agents nearly four weeks before principal photography, and a lot (*a lot*) can happen in that time. If things change and the actor ends up working two days and is not needed again until three days later, you don't want to have to pay the actor for the days in between. When it comes to bigger-name actors, that changes, but at this budget level, 99 percent of your actors will be working "nonconsecutive days," so reflect that on their deal memo even if their schedule ends up being consecutive days.

Number 2, *Guaranteed Compensation*, is pretty black and white as well: $100.00 (one hundred dollars) per day for four days. Both the SAG and non-SAG wording is identical here, except for the fact that on the non-SAG version, I exclude the last sentence. It's up to you if you want to include non-guild actors at a day rate, should they be required during the pickup day(s).

In item number 3, *Billing*, there are a few items to note. First of all, the wording is not just about whether the actor is guild or nonguild but refers to which actors are your leads and which will receive top billing. Usually, it's pretty obvious because it refers to the leads in your film, but may also be given to a supporting actor who has a name. In all of our low-budget films, there were between six and eight names in the main titles. Also, just in case you decide not to have main titles, it's important to make reference to that at this stage and include it in the deal memo. You don't want to promise something, sign off on it, and then change your mind and try to convince the agent or manager that you want to alter the deal – not a good business practice.

So, it reads, "On a separate card in the main titles (provided main titled credits are used and other cast member credits appear therein)." It also states that the artist will be included in all paid advertising where the billing block appears. Once again, your actor may not be affiliated with any guild but may be one of the leads or one of the main supporting roles, so you are including him or her in the main titles and wherever the billing block appears.

In addition, you may have plenty of guild actors on your film who have supporting or minor roles, and you will not be including them in the main titles. So here is how that would be worded in their deal memo: "3. Billing: Billing in the end titles only."

The deal memo is clear and concise and covers all the main areas, including something as basic as number 10, *"Making of" Films*. I noticed that some deal memos didn't have this section, so make sure to add it to yours. You want the actors to sign off on this item and agree that they are willing to be part of the "Making of" footage, even if you never use them or ever do a "Making of" film. Always cover your butt.

When you are doing the deal memo for your name actors, their agents may very well ask for a few additional items that are not listed here. For example, in *Séance*, Adrian Paul's deal memo included items such as a private office/dressing area while on location, approval of his still photographs, exclusive ground transportation and driver to and from the sets, back-end participation, and other things. There may be a few other items that you will need to add or alter when negotiating the deal memos for your name actors. However, you can always start with the basic deal memo and use it as your

**SCREEN ACTORS GUILD
EMPLOYMENT OF PERFORMER
FOR ULTRA LOW BUDGET FILM**

PRODUCTION COMPANY _____ DATE _____

PRODUCTION TITLE _____

PERFORMER'S NAME _____ START DATE _____

ADDRESS _____

ROLE _____ DAILY RATE $ _____

PERFORMER'S TELEPHONE NO. _____ NUMBER OF DAYS GUARANTEED: __

1. Subject to SAG approval, the following shall apply to this employment:

  a) Weekend premiums are waived.

  b) Consecutive employment requirement is waived provided scheduling of calls is subject to
      Performer's availability, except while on overnight locations.

  c) Daily overtime is payable at time and one-half. No work is permitted in excess of 12
      hours on any day.

2) The employment is subject to all of the provisions and conditions applicable to the employment of
   performers contained in or provided for in the Independent Producers' Ultra Low Budget Letter
   Agreement. Such Agreement is deemed incorporated herein.

3) Producer makes the material representation that either it is presently a signatory to the Screen Actors
   Guild collective bargaining agreement covering the employment contracted for herein, or, that the
   above referenced photoplay is covered by such collective bargaining agreement under the
   "Independent Production" provisions of the General Provisions of the Screen Actors Guild Codified
   Basic Agreement for Independent Producers.

4) Rights Granted. By payment of at least the minimum fees specified for this employment, Producer
   obtains all theatrical rights.

5) Employment status. The performer engaged by this contract is considered an employee, not an
   independent contractor. As such, the compensation due the performer is subject to income tax
   withholding, social security and disability deductions. The performer is entitled to Unemployment
   Insurance coverage.

PRODUCER _____   PERFORMER _____

BY _____   SOCIAL SECURITY # _____

THE PERFORMER MAY NOT WAIVE ANY PROVISION OF THIS CONTRACT WITHOUT THE
PRIOR WRITTEN CONSENT OF SCREEN ACTORS GUILD.

FIGURE 8.4

template, then make any additions. It is usually in a section that reads as follows: "MISCELLANEOUS: Artist shall be provided with the following . . . ."

As I have mentioned earlier, I am not a lawyer, so if you choose to use any portion of the example deal memo, you do so at your own risk. Please use your own counsel for anything contractual.

There are a couple of other agreements that you will need to deal with as well. If you are using a stunt performer, then you will be using a separate contract. Call your local actors' guild or go online and pull down the agreement for stunt performers. They are not $100 per day like the SAG ultra-low-budget actors. In fact, they are quite expensive, so be sure to keep their days to a minimum.

Also, if you have nudity in your film, you will have to keep that in mind when doing the deal memo for that actor. On the SAG ultra-low-budget agreement, the cost per day when we were shooting was $250. When we were shooting our films, part of the SAG ruling was that a SAG actor had the right to refuse to do the nude scene – even if he or she had originally agreed to do it. So please check and double-check the rules and regulations to be prepared for this type of situation.

In addition to the deal memo for your actors, if you are using SAG actors there is another agreement that needs to be signed before you begin principal photography. It is included in the SAG package, and although your line producer is responsible for making sure this is signed, I strongly suggest that you oversee this aspect.

On *Séance*, I asked Mike to bring all the agreements to the actors' table read, knowing that all the actors on the film were going to be there. Any agreements that were not yet signed were handled right there on the spot. Your line producer will need those when he or she creates the delivery book for SAG when the film is complete, and you really don't want to be dealing with any unsigned agreements at that time. In fact, I always double-check (just to be really sure) when the actor shows up for his or her first day on the set. Figure 8.4 shows a copy of the form.

Extras

There is a good chance that you will be using extras in your film. In our case, the investors and their families had a great time being extras. It was really a win/win situation because we didn't have to go searching for them. In the case of *Candy Stripers*, we had well over 100 extras, so that took some work. A friend of ours took on the job of getting the extras for us and set about calling the actors who didn't get cast in our film. In every case, they were thrilled. They knew they wouldn't be getting paid to be an extra in *Candy Stripers*, but they were thrilled to do it regardless. And why not? It's a great way to meet people, do some networking, and have a bit of fun at the same time. Figure 8.5 shows the simple release form that was used on our films.

EXTRAS RELEASE

PORTAL

PORTAL FILM, LLC 2321 W. OLIVE AVE., SUITE A BURBANK, CA 91056

I, the undersigned, hereby grant permission to PORTAL FILM, LLC to photograph me and to record my voice, performances, poses, acts, plays and appearances, and use my picture, photograph, silhouette and other reproductions of my physical likeness and sound as part of the FILM tentatively entitled PORTAL (the "Picture") and the unlimited distribution, advertising, promotion, exhibition and exploitation of the Picture by any method or device now known or hereafter devised in which the same may be used, and/or incorporated and/or exhibited and/or exploited.

I agree that I will not assert or maintain against you, your successors, assigns and licensees, any claim, action, suit or demand of any kind or nature whatsoever, including but not limited to, those grounded upon invasion of privacy, rights of publicity or other civil rights, or for any other reason in connection with your authorized use of my physical likeness and sound in the Picture as herein provided.

I hereby release you, your successors, assigns and licensees, and each of them, from and against any and all claims, liabilities, demands, actions, causes of action(s), costs and expenses whatsoever, at law or in equity, known or unknown, anticipated or unanticipated, which I ever had, now have, or may, shall or hereafter have by reason, matter, cause or thing arising out of your use as herein provided.

I affirm that neither I, nor anyone acting for me, gave or agreed to give anything of value to any of your employees or any representative of any television station, network or production entity for arranging my appearance on the Picture.

I agree that in the event of any default by Producer, my only remedy shall be an action law for damages, if any, actually suffered by me, and in no event shall I be entitled to rescind this contract or receive injunctive or equitable relief.

I have read the foregoing and fully understand the meaning and effect thereof and, intending to be legally bound, I have signed this release.

NAME (PLEASE PRINT)　　　　　　　*DATE*

_____　　　　_____

SIGNATURE　　　　　　　　　　　*PHONE NUMBER*

_____　　　　_____

SS#　　　　　　　　　　　　　　　*DATE*

_____　　　　_____

PRODUCER

_____

FIGURE 8.5

Chapter 9

Preproduction

It's three weeks before principal photography. My cast deal memos are complete, and the major locations have been found and deals drawn up. I have the company checkbook and credit card ready to start spending money and getting things pinned down.

PRODUCER VERSUS LINE PRODUCER

This is a fun three weeks for me because it's really the time for Mike – my line producer – to shine. He is going to have a million things to do and I want to be absolutely available for him. Because our films were low-budget, I used my Snowfall/WindChill office for preproduction to save money. Mike brought his production coordinator and his assistant. It was a little cramped, but hey, it's low budget!

I have responsibilities during these three weeks as well, but the major-ity of the duties fall on Mike's shoulders. I think some movies don't ever get made because people don't know the difference between a producer and a line producer, and as a producer, if you think you have to take on everything, you will get stopped. Of course, as the producer, I am still going to oversee quite a few of the areas that are Mike's responsibility, but that doesn't mean I have to know how to do each of his jobs. If I thought I had to do both jobs, I would go crazy! That is why it is so critically important that you hire a competent, accountable, brilliant, dedicated line producer.

Producer's Focus

My job during this time consisted of some of the following:

- Hire the Making-of producer.
- Hire the still photographer.
- Organize and schedule the cast table read/wardrobe fitting.
- Hire and write the deal memos for the editor and director of photography.
- Meet with the director and 1st AD to go over the storyboard and schedule.
- Be available to sit in on interviews for certain keys.
- Be available and ready for the crew table read.
- Sign off on last-minute locations.
- Update the investors and get the revised schedule to them.
- Make sure the actor's agents/managers get revised schedules.
- Be available to sign checks.

Line Producer's Focus

Mike's responsibilities included:

- Interview, hire, and create the deal memos for the keys (heads of departments).
- Negotiate and book all vendors, grip and electrical, camera package, catering, and other departments.
- Finalize the deals on the locations and any required city permits.
- Firm up the budget.
- Schedule the Humane Society (if animals are being used).
- Work with the director and 1st AD (assistant director) on the schedule.
- Work with the 2nd AD to create the Day Out of Days.
- Hire the company that will be doing the dailies.
- Create and sign off on all crew deal memos.
- Draw up the location map.
- Coordinate a detailed location list.
- Work with the 1st AD to schedule the table read with keys.
- Get the SAG performers' agreements signed.

Mike's job was to oversee and manage all the departments, making sure that departments are communicating with each other on all the details related to the script, while staying within budget. Mike believes that you do a production for a price. You set an amount for each department element in the budget and you find that vendor or crew who will give you the service or equipment at those fixed rates – never for a moment sacrificing quality. When one of my students asked Mike what a producer should look for in a line producer, he said, "Look for somebody that's actually going to be there every minute of every day. And somebody you can trust, so that you can leave things with them and you know that they're going to get it done."

The one thing that Mike was adamant about was the 12-hour work day. It was his firm promise to the crew that we would not go over the 12 hours, and on both *Séance* and *Portal* he followed that rule to the letter on our films – and we still came in on schedule. Another one of his strengths was finding great heads of departments. This is a big job, and there are a lot of keys to hire, no matter what size your budget is. In turn, the keys will hire their own crew, usually people with whom they've worked before, but if the keys are unable to find a crew, then Mike would hire the entire crew for that department.

Here is a list of keys:

Production coordinator
DP (usually the director will choose the DP)
1st assistant director
Key set PA (production assistant)
Script supervisor
Production designer (who will bring his or her own art director)
Prop master
Gaffer
Key grip
Editor
Costume designer
Key hair
Key make-up
Locations manager (if the budget allows)
Sound mixer
Special effects
Stunt coordinator
Casting director (if the budget allows)
Transportation

He was brilliant at finding the most fantastic vendors, as well. Our caterers were better on these low-budget films than some of the caterers I've had on my big international coproductions. Another area that Mike handled was the hiring of production assistants (PAs). At our budget, these PA positions are not paid positions; however, the key set PA usually gets a small (very small) salary.

A LOOK AT THE PRODUCER'S JOB

I think I know what you're thinking right now: "This is intense. There are a lot of jobs for me to do and a lot for me to oversee." Don't worry; you have three weeks, and I will give you all the details you need to make it effortless. Also, it is super important that you be organized. Clean your house, your closet, your car. Handle your taxes and any incompletions and out-of-integrities. You need to be focused, on purpose, centered, and clear. You will be setting the stage and setting the tone for how the production will unfold. You are in charge! There is no time for your own baggage here. The buck stops with you. It's your baby. Everything that happens from here on out is your overall responsibility. You don't get to blame anyone, you don't get to complain, and you don't get to find fault. This is a wonderful place to be – a great place to stand. With that in mind, let's take a look at some of your responsibilities during preproduction.

THE MAKING-OF PRODUCER AND STILLS PHOTOGRAPHER

At this budget level, there is a good chance that your making-of producer will also be your stills photographer. And there's a good chance that you are going to be working with someone who is fairly new with little experience. So to ensure that everything goes exactly as you want, you will need to do some micromanaging here. As I have said a few times now, you don't have to sacrifice quality just because your budget is low. You only have to watch a film like *Séance* to realize that. It was $200,000, and it looks amazing, and the making-of feature is excellent as well. So there is no excuse. It may just mean that you have to be more organized and do some additional overseeing.

You know from reading your delivery list that your sales agents and distributors will need from 60 to 75 still photos. Even if you don't go the traditional distribution route and you decide to self-distribute, you are still going to need quality stills. And that doesn't mean behind-the-scenes stills. What I am talking about here are photos that can be used for press packets, posters, website, EPK (electronic press kit) packets, film festival requirements and whatever else you or your sales agent may require.

Of course, you also want to have behind-the-scenes shots for your own purposes, but they are not part of the delivery. Chris Robbins was our stills and making-of producer and he took tons of behind-the-scenes shots, which we looped and used on the big-screen TV at our wrap parties. Everyone loved it. They're also fun to put on your own website. However, remember that your sales agent wants the money shots only. So it's your job to go through the script line by line, scene by scene with your yellow highlighter and flag all the areas that you think will make excellent stills and the areas that will be important for the making of footage as well. Then you can sit down with your stills photographer and making-of producer and go over everything with them.

Having this information will help you set up a schedule for your stills photographer and making-of producer. If you are shooting 14 to 16 days and paying them only a flat fee of $500 to $1,000 for the entire project, you can't expect them to be on set or location every day. By highlighting the shots and scenes you want, you will see very clearly the exact number of days that you will need them.

In addition, schedule specific times to interview your leads and any keys you may want to interview. With your highlighted script, you can now take your schedule and determine what days are best for your making-of producer to do the interviews. Chris and I brainstormed some basic questions. He was planning to come up with his own additional questions and be as creative and spontaneous as he wanted to be, but I, as the producer, wanted to make sure I had the basics covered. Here is a list of what was scheduled on *Séance* for both the cast schedule and some possible questions.

Still Photography and Making-of Cast Schedule

Here is the proposed schedule for selected still photography and for making-of interviews.

Making-of Interview Schedule

Chauntal Lewis on Thursday, May 26
Adrian Paul on Sunday, May 28
AJ Lamas on Thursday, June 1
Joel Geist on Thursday, June 1
Tori White on Thursday, June 1
Jack Hunter on Friday, June 2
Kandis Erickson on Friday, June 5 – early in the morning
Mark L. Smith, Suzanne Lyons, and Kate Robbins on Monday, June 5

Stills Photography Schedule

Adrian Paul on Sunday, May 28
Jack Hunter on Friday, June 2
Rest of cast on June 2nd and May 28

Key Days for Both Still Photography and Making-of Footage

Sunday, May 21 for stunts and practical effects
Monday, May 22 for stunts and practical effects
Tuesday, May 23 for stunts and practical effects
Sunday, May 28 for stunts and practical effects

Proposed Questions for Cast for the Making-of Feature

1. What motivated you to audition for the film?
2. What was the audition process like?
3. What attracted you to the script?
4. What about your role appealed to you?
5. How did you go about fleshing out your character?
6. Are you a horror film fan?
7. What was your favorite scene?
8. What's it like working with Mark?
9. What has it been like working with the other cast members?
10. How has this experience compared with your experiences on other films or TV?

We provided a small space for Chris to set up his interview chair, lights, and camera, and having this schedule prepared during preproduction made it easier for Chris and gave the actors lots of advance notice as well. There was no last-minute scrambling or chaos – and there doesn't have to be.

Something as simple as highlighting the script, creating a schedule, and sitting with your making-of producer/stills photographer during pre-production will keep you, the film's producer, sane during production. You will have other responsibilities during production, so you don't need to be thinking about the film stills or the making-of production. You have to learn to delegate! Of course, you'll be hiring some people who won't have the experience that you'll find on a big-budget film, but that doesn't mean they are not absolutely capable and creative. It just means they don't have a lot of experience yet. So you'll have to sit with them and tell them what you want and do a little micromanaging, but you'll also need to trust that they can do the job. If delegating is not yet your forte, then you'd better start practicing. It's something you want to get good at, so start now.

YOUR EDITOR

I had a director friend recently tell me that he was going to produce his own low-budget film and that one of the way in which he planned to save money was to not hire an editor until the film was shot. I nearly had a heart attack. That is not a good idea. Of course, in the low-budget world, we have to look at where we need to cut and save, but cutting back on the editor is not the place to do it. Your editor should start on day 2 of principal photography, and you want to start speaking with your editor now, in preproduction. In fact, if you can have him or her at your table read during soft prep, all the better. But certainly preproduction is the time when you want to sit down with your editor and really take a look at the script and discuss the project.

Your editor will be the one doing the assembly during production, so the editor knows better than anyone else what's missing and what's needed. There is always the possibility that you will need a pickup day, or better yet, a pick-up morning or afternoon. But that's it. If you are not in communication with your editor, you may end up having to shoot a number of pick-up days – and with a low-budget film, you can't afford that luxury. Start the conversation with the editor at this stage. For example, you don't want to find out after the film is shot that your editor doesn't have the transition shots that he or she needs. You can't go back and shoot that scene again. Find out during the shoot what additional shots the editor may need. Maybe it's as simple as a hand turning the doorknob. You will be amazed at the suggestions that you can get from your editor that will help give your movie that bigger budget look. Kate and I were blessed with a great editor, Greg Hobson, and when I asked him about getting the coverage he needed, he said, "If you're not getting it and you're on day 3 and you still haven't got those specific angles that you know the producer and director wanted, then you should talk to the producer about talking to the director because you're not getting anything to cut." With these types of low-budget films, you will often be using first-time directors who may be overwhelmed by the job. The director's job is gigantic during this time, and he or she may not be aware of all the different aspects that will be needed for editing the film. That's why it is so important to be in constant communication with your editor. He or she knows exactly what's missing and what's needed, and it's better to find this out now while you're still shooting the film.

Because you may not know at this stage if you will be going to a sales agent or self-distributing, I recommend that in your editor's deal memo you include the trailer of the film as part of his or her responsibilities. If you go the sales agent route, there is a good chance that they will use a professional company that does trailers, but I would still add that requirement to your editor's deal memo just in case. Regarding the editor's payment schedule, on our movies we agreed on a flat fee for his services, which was divided into two payments, one during production and one during postproduction.

On *Séance*, Greg began work on the second day of production and worked on the assembly of the film during production. He then completed the assembly the week following the shoot. Then the director joined him, and together they had two weeks to complete the director's cut version. Immediately following the completion of the director's cut, we scheduled an audience testing, and then, based on the notes from the testing and on notes from Kate and myself, the director and editor had a few days to go back and complete the editing. So, on *Séance*, Greg worked for six weeks.

I know producers who like to do two audience testings: one with the director's cut and one following the editing that has been done based on the first testing. Before you work out your deal with the editor, be clear about your own plan, because you don't want to confirm one deal and then later say you've changed your mind. Just another reminder here that this is a business and that your deal memos must reflect that.

YOUR DIRECTOR OF PHOTOGRAPHY

I said that your line producer will be doing the deals for your keys, but your DP is your responsibility. Ninety-nine percent of the time, he or she is chosen by the director and you want to be sure that you are absolutely overjoyed with his or her choices. Your DP is a vital part of your team. The look of your film depends on this decision. Also, in addition to wanting a DP who knows his or her stuff, you also have to keep in mind that your budget is low and that the DP will need to move quickly. So be sure to ask the right questions here. A DP from the studio world may have an impressive resume, but can he or she work on a low-budget film? When I saw the movie *The Undead*, I knew I had to meet Andy Strahorn, the DP on that film. What he had done at that low budget was amazing. DPs on these film have to move at lightning speed without sacrificing an ounce of quality. Andy did 650 setups in our 14-day shoot on *Portal*, and when I asked him about it, he said that what made this shoot more doable and enjoyable than other projects he'd worked on was this: "I already knew what I was walking into. This is it. It's 12 hours. We never break 12. It's a 14-day shoot. It's a 97-page script in 14 days. From my perspective, from a below-the-line perspective, the more up front you [producer/line-producer] are with your crew, the better."

In regard to his deal memo, all I did was take the crew deal memo that my line producer was using, and in the section titled Compensation, I typed in his salary and when and how he would be paid. That is all that was sent to his agent. Figure 9.1 shows an example of the crew deal memo that I used for our DP on *Portal*.

PORTAL
CREW DEAL MEMO

PRODUCING COMPANY: <u>Portal Film, LLC</u>   *DATE:* <u>9/14/06</u>

EMPLOYEE NAME: <u>Andy Strahorn</u>   *POSITION:* <u>Director of Photography</u>

ADDRESS: _____   *PHONE:* _____
_____   *ADDITIONAL CONTACT NUMBERS:*
_____   _____

EMAIL ADDRESS: _____

*LOANOUT CO. (IF APPLICABLE):*_____   *FEDERAL ID#:* _____

UNION AFFILIATION (IF ANY): _____   *S.S #:* _____

UNION/GUILD   ____*N/A*____

FLAT RATE: (In Town) $ _____   *to be paid in two increments:* $ _____
on the first day of principal photography _____   *and* $ _____
on the first day of week two of production

       (Distant Loc.)   ____*$ N/A*____   *PER DAY*

BOX RENTAL   ▓▓▓   *None   N/A*   *Per Day*
EQUIPMENT/VEHICLE RENTAL   *None   N/A*   *Per Day*
MILEAGE ALLOWANCE   *None   N/A*   *Per Day*

> **No Cellular Phone Calls**
> **Paid By Production Unless**
> **Authorized By UPM**

EQUIPMENT RENTALS* _____*N / A*_____

GAS ALLOWANCE/MILEAGE* ___*N / A*_____

PER DIEM _____*N / A*_____

NOTIFY IN EMERGENCY: _____*PHONE:* _____

1.   In accordance with the Immigration Reform and Control Act of 1986, any
offer of employment is conditioned upon satisfactory proof of Employee's identity and
legal ability to work in the United States (I-9 Form attached).

FIGURE 9.1

2.	Employment hereunder is of an "at will" nature and subject to termination without notice by either party. While employed hereunder, Employee's services shall be on an exclusive basis to Producer.

3.	Car allowance, Mileage, Box or Kit Rentals, Meal Money, Per Diems and Living Allowance will only be paid if agreed to in advance by the Unit Production Manager ("UPM"). All Box and Equipment Rentals begin and end with principal photography (unless otherwise approved by the UPM) and will be pro-rated to reflect actual days worked.

4.	No 7th day, holiday, or in-town 6th day will be paid unless authorized in advance by the UPM. No overtime prior to company call or after wrap may be worked, nor any forced call incurred without the UPM's prior approval.

5.	All provisions of this deal memo and all services rendered hereunder are subject to and must provide no less than the minimum of the applicable collective bargaining agreement, if any. To the extent that any of the provisions of this deal memo conflict with applicable law, applicable law shall prevail, but only to the minimum extent required to bring the provisions of this agreement in to compliance therewith.

6.	If a daily rate is indicated, services are for a minimum period of one day. Daily employees shall only be compensated for actual days worked; 6th or 7th days, idle days or holidays not worked shall not be paid. Nothing contained herein shall be construed as a guarantee of consecutive employment or employment beyond time actually worked. No premium compensation shall be payable for services rendered at night, or holidays. The start time will be determined by Employee's Supervisor. Wrap will be by department and approved by department head or designated by the Producer.

7.	This Agreement is subject to termination in the case of any suspension or postponement of production by reason of labor controversy, strike (or threat thereof), act of God, or any other customary "force majeure" reason.

8.	Producer shall be under no obligation to accord Employee credit on screen. In the event Producer desires to accord Employee credit on screen, Producer shall in its sole discretion determine such credit, including, without limitation, the size, style and placement of such credit. No casual or inadvertent failure to comply with the provisions of this paragraph shall constitute a breach of this agreement, nor give rise to any form of equitable relief, whatsoever.

9.	Any loss, theft or damage to Employee's personal property is the sole responsibility of the Employee.

10.	Employee agrees not to disclose any creative and/or material information whatsoever about this Agreement or the Picture (including giving interviews, taking photographs, copying written material, etc.) without Producer's prior written approval in each instance. Employee hereby grants Producer the right to use his/her name, likeness and voice in publicity related photographs, "behind the scene" films and "electronic press kit" video releases and in advertising or promoting the Picture.

11.	All results and proceeds of Employee's services pursuant to this agreement shall be deemed a "work for hire" and Producer shall own all rights thereto. If such results and proceeds are deemed not a "work for hire," Employee hereby assigns all rights, including copyrights, therein to Producer.

12.	Employee must clear any product placement or promotional activity with Producer.

FIGURE 9.1	(*Continued*)

13.　　　Any purchases or rentals must be by Purchase Orders approved in advance by the UPM. Petty cash expenses not accompanied by valid original receipts will not be reimbursed. Petty cash receipts must be submitted for reimbursement within 30 days of expenditure, and all submissions are subject to the approval of the UPM. Employee hereby expressly authorizes Producer to deduct any outstanding balance in Employee's petty cash advance fund or unsettled hotel incidentals from his payroll check if not cleared prior to termination.

14.　　　There will be no reimbursement of any cellular phone charges without prior approval of the UPM.

15.　　　Employee is responsible for all recoverable assets purchased or promoted on the production. Such items must be safeguarded, inventoried, and reconciled with accounting at wrap. No assets may be sold, traded or given away without written approval from Producer.

16.　　　The Production Office may assist Employee with certain personal matters such as travel, shipping of personal materials, etc., but any service will require payment in advance by check or credit card.

17.　　　Transportation to and from distant location will not be provided by Producer. Employee is to drive to a distant location. Any transportation costs and all travel days are unpaid.

18 .　　　Insurance coverage on items or vehicles rented from Employee is the responsibility of the Employee unless set out otherwise in a formal written agreement.

19.　　　Employee acknowledges that Producer has a strict policy prohibiting the use of alcohol or controlled substances on the job. Any Employee found in violation of a safety rule or guideline may be subject to disciplinary action, up to and including termination of employment.

20 .　　　Employee agrees that in the event of any default by Producer, Employee's only remedy shall be an action at law for damages, if any, actually suffered by employee, and in no event shall Employee be entitled to rescind this contract or receive injunctive or equitable relief.

21.　　　Producer may assign, transfer, license, delegate and/or grant all or any part of its rights, privileges and property hereunder to any person or entity. This Agreement shall be binding upon and shall inure to the benefit of the parties hereto and their respective heirs, executors, administrators, successors and assigns. This Agreement and Employee's rights and obligations hereunder may not be assigned by Employee.

22.　　　MAKING-OF FILMS: Employee agr ees to co-operate with Producer in the creation of promotional Making-of films. Additionally, Artist agrees that Producer may use portions of the Picture and "behind the scenes" shots in said promotional Making-Of films and may explo it said promotional Making-Of films in any and all media whatsoever without the payment of any additional compensation whatsoever.

23.　　　All notices hereunder shall be in writing and may be served personally or by certified or registered mail, telegraph, fax (faxes to be confirmed by mail) or cable sent to the addresses set forth herein.

_____

Director of Photography – Andy Strahorn or appointed represented

_____

PRODUCER – Suzanne Lyons

FIGURE 9.1 (_Continued_)

YOUR DIRECTOR

Be in constant communication with your director during this period. I know the director will be working with the 1st AD on revisions to the schedule and will be talking to various department heads about what he or she wants, meeting with some of the leads to discuss their roles and what he or she is looking for. And of course the director will be meeting with the DP to discuss the lighting and look of the film, not to mention a million other things that are on his or her mind. However, you want to set up meetings with the director and go over the storyboard, the schedule, his or her vision, the locations, and any last-minute script changes.

In many instances, with this budget level, you will have directors with little to no experience. In fact, often the writer is the director, so it's your job to make sure that he or she is okay. So stay in communication with them.

TABLE READ WITH YOUR KEYS

I've talked about a number of table reads. So let's get very clear about the ones that have taken place so far. We had one very early on in the development stage where we had actor friends do the read for us and we were able to hear the script out loud, giving us a real sense of what worked, what didn't, and what areas could be cut to suit our budget. Then, when we had a few more key people on board, we had another table read (also done with actor friends) with the purpose of people like your special effects expert, director, line producer, 1st AD, and so on being able to hear the script out loud and then discuss it at length after the reading. This third table read is organized for your entire group of keys.

This one is the responsibility of your 1st AD, but it's something that you want to fully participate in. This table read is usually scheduled for the week before principal photography begins, and it's best to hold it early that week so that when last-minute concerns, problems, or issues are spotted as a result of both the read and everyone being together in the same room, people still have time to handle it.

We held the table read in my office; my advice to you is to be fully awake and conscious the entire time. I know by this time you're ecstatic about getting started, thrilled that your whole team is together, and that you can barely contain yourself because you're about to make your movie! You already have a highlighted script that you have worked on with your making-of producer, so have that with you at this table read. It already has the "money shots" highlighted, and you can make notes beside anything else you want brought up or emphasized during this meeting. All the heads of departments are in one room, so it's a perfect opportunity to fix things. Here are a couple of things that happened on films as a result of me not stopping the table read and pointing out some of the items I should have discussed during this read.

These films were in the horror/thriller genre; in one particular case, I had underlined a number of spectacular shots (great money shots) that I knew were perfect for the trailer, the making-of video, and the stills. However, I never stopped the table read once to highlight them and ask, for example, what the costume designer had planned. We were going to be seeing lots of blood and because it was a horror film, seeing the blood was critical. As I have noted a number of times throughout this book, you don't have the luxury of going back the next day after seeing something in the dailies that you don't like. That set has been torn down and that actor isn't scheduled for today. Sorry, it's not going to happen!

So, I was watching the dailies and realized that there were two separate very important and excellent gory shots in which I couldn't see the blood. I couldn't believe it – the actors were wearing brown shirts, so you literally couldn't see the great bright red blood that would make the scene brilliant. I asked my costume designer about it, and he said that that color suited the actors' skin tone and really worked with the rest of their costume. I would love to blame him for this mistake, but I'm afraid I have to take all the blame. I was the producer on the film; I was responsible for overseeing everything. During the table read, I could have stopped the read several times to point out issues that were important.

Often, on lower-budget films, you are getting people who may have been the assistant costume designer or assistant make-up artist, and you will not have the big salary to offer them, but you can offer them the credit that they are looking to put on their bio. They get to move from assistant costume designer to costume designer. However, what that means to you as the producer is that you have to be even more awake than anyone else. The costume designer is not thinking of the money shots you need for the stills that you'll have to deliver to your sales agent six months from now. That's not their job. They are not as experienced as the bigger-budget keys, and they can't be expected to read your mind. In addition, they don't have six weeks or eight weeks on the set and six weeks of preproduction to prepare. Our shooting schedule was 14 days! The keys were crazed.

The costume/blood problem could have been totally averted if I had pointed out items like this. I could have just said, "Wow, this is a great shot – lots of action and lots of blood. As you're planning and purchasing your wardrobe for the actors, please just keep in mind that we need to be able to see the blood."

Here is another example of something that I noticed too late. I am always on the set. I believe the producer should be on the set all the time. Well, there were a few hours one day that I was not on set. I have only one fear in life, and that is a strange fear of heights related to cliffs. The shot that was happening was a fantastic money shot. Our hero and heroine had escaped the evil monster and were going to survive and be together. That kiss and embrace was important – really important. And there was no going back to get it. I was watching the dailies the next morning and was shocked. My beautiful blonde looked terrible.

I called the make-up artist and asked what happened. She said that of course she had to look that way; after all, in the story she'd been held prisoner for months with little food in dreadful surroundings. I realized at that moment that people read literally. Yes, that's how the script read, but this was my female lead, and I don't care what she'd been through; I want to see her looking gorgeous and glowing when she meets her hero and has that long-awaited embrace we've been dying to see. Once again, it is something that I could have addressed at the table read. So, please take responsibility here. Your 1st AD will schedule the table read and your line producer will make sure it all runs smoothly, but it's your job to have your highlighted script with you and to stay present, focused, and conscious.

CAST TABLE READ AND WARDROBE FITTING

One of your responsibilities during preproduction is scheduling and organizing the cast table read – which is the final table read! At this table read, we also did the final wardrobe fittings because the main actors were all there in one spot and the director was there to make final decisions on wardrobe. This is something we scheduled on the Friday before principal photography on each of the low-budget films. You will no doubt have access to a production assistant who will be working on the film, so you can have this PA book the room and make the calls to the agents. There is nothing wrong with delegating jobs like this. However, it is imperative that you be present at this table read – and I don't just mean showing up. I mean really be conscious.

For example, I was pretty proud of myself for asking the question, "Do any of you have any allergies?" They all said no, no allergies, no problem. I thought, "That's great," and moved on to the next question. However, it never occurred to me that when you say allergies, people automatically think "food." Well, guess where I spent the first night of the 14-day shoot sitting with my beautiful blond female lead who now had red blotches all over her body? You guessed it: the outpatient room at St. Joseph's Hospital.

As it turned out, she was allergic to laundry detergent. If I had asked the question a little differently – "Are any of you allergic to anything at all, food, any chemical, anything?" – this emergency would not have happened.

As it turned out, the doctor was able to give her some shots that worked within hours and cost us only $350, but it could have been a lot worse and cost a great deal more. So, once again, it's your responsibility. You have to stay calm and centered because almost everyone around you will be frantic, tired, and overworked.

PRODUCT PLACEMENT

Every so often, in the indie low-budget world, you hear that a producer is able to pull rabbits out of a hat and land an amazing product placement deal for his film, but those deals are few and far between. Even on our bigger-budget films like *Undertaking Betty* (also known as *Plots with a View*), which was a fun romantic comedy, we couldn't get money for product placement. We mentioned Princess Cruise Line a number of times throughout the film, and we mentioned it in a great fun way, but that didn't help get me any money for the film from that company. We got free footage that we needed from them for the film – but no money!

So, in the case of my low-budget films, which were genre movies where people were getting killed by aliens, monsters, and ghosts, I knew the chances of us getting a product placement deal were slim to none. What I really wanted were products we could have on set that were free. That was doable.

Sit down with your production designer and see what items they can get on set that will save you some money. Our production designer on each film was able to get soft drinks and water, and on the budget we had, every little bit helps.

Your make-up artist will be getting free make-up, but check to make sure he or she is on top of it. In one of the films I did, our make-up person was on set in Romania until a week before we started shooting, so I called him and asked if there was anything that I could do to help. Thank goodness I called, because he was so swamped with his job on his current film that he had not had time to call MAC cosmetics in Toronto and get the supplies he needed for our shoot. I put in the call to MAC, and they were fantastic. Within a week, we had everything we needed. It's always great for companies like MAC to get involved because they get a special thank-you and, if they want, their logo displayed in the end roll credits.

Once again, your job is to oversee and to speak with your line producer on an ongoing basis to see what is needed or missing. Because Kate and

I were in constant communication with Mike and available to step in and put out fires before they started, it made for an effortless production. On *Séance*, in preproduction we were still having problems finding an elevator shaft, so we – as the producers – worked through and brainstormed solutions with the line producer and director (include your location manager, if you have one). Kate happened to know someone who had a hotel in Hollywood, and we got our elevator shaft in time and for a great price.

UPDATE INVESTORS

Another one of your responsibilities during this period is keeping your investors updated. I started sending them weekly emails at the beginning of soft prep, but at this point, when the schedule is being locked down, you want to get your investors a copy so that they can book their time on set. Also, you want to make a point of suggesting the best days, as you want them coming to locations on days when there is some fun action happening. If you have a name actor, recommend days when he or she is on set so that your investors can have their picture taken with the actor.

On *Séance*, actor Adrian Paul was one of our leads, and the investors were very excited to get their pictures taken with him. I asked Adrian in advance, and he was more than happy to be available for photos with our investors. Also, a number of our investors wanted to be extras in the films, so it's very important that you give them lots of notice for the days they will be needed.

Regardless of whether your investors are coming to the set, continue your weekly emails informing them of what's happening. Preproduction is an exciting time with tons of activity: locking locations, hiring department heads, finalizing schedules, and lots of fun things that you can share with your investors. It is not a huge demand on your time at all, and it is well worth the effort to keep them involved. You wouldn't be in preproduction if it weren't for them, so please keep them informed and involved.

KEEP THE ACTORS AND THEIR AGENTS INFORMED

I know that the costume designer, director, and make-up artist are in communication with the actors during this preproduction period and that you are contacting them or their agents to set up the table read, but there is something else to be aware of here. Part of your deal memo states that you will be updating them with finalized schedules, and this is the time when the final touches are being made and the film schedule is being confirmed. So make sure to email copies of the finalized schedule to the agents.

Chapter 10

Principal Photography

NOW THE FUN BEGINS

This is my favorite part. I love being on location and having the hustle and bustle of production going on around me. All that work – developing the screenplay, raising the money, working with the director, organizing the table reads, doing the casting, working with the line producer on the budget and schedule, and all the other million details – was worth every minute to get to this moment. This is what it's all about. Being able to hire an entire crew and have incredible talented actors on the set is a dream come true. To be the one responsible for giving these creative people the chance to be fully self-expressed and have their own dreams come true is magical.

The schedule on these low-budget films was 14 days, so I needed to be in top form to stay a step ahead the entire time. I recommend that you really watch your diet during this time. Stay away from heavy foods and sugars. You really do need to be more alert and present than you've ever been, so there is no room for being tired or sluggish. I am about 70 percent raw vegan, but in the case of *Portal* – especially with a 6:00 p.m. to 6:00 a.m. schedule – I decided to do 100 percent raw. You don't have to be that strict, but do pay attention to your diet during this time.

Also, tell friends and family that you are on location and that unless there is an emergency, they should wait until the film wraps to contact you. Remember that you are the one setting the tone on set, so being relaxed, calm, and centered will be important. If you're anxious and stressed, it will show and will affect the space. You are going to have a number of responsibilities during principal photography, and you want to handle all of it with grace and ease. Are there going to be fires to be put out and breakdowns from time to time? Of course. But when you are centered and confident, you will handle the breakdowns effortlessly and with alacrity.

SÉANCE

CALL SHEET 5

THURSDAY 5/25/06

WINDCHILL FILMS

DIRECTOR: Mark L. Smith		SUNRISE: 5:45 SUNSET: 7:53
PRODUCER: Suzanne Lyons		WEATHER: Sunny H: 83 L: 54 0% precip
PRODUCER: Kate Robbins		SET PHONE: Mike Tarzian (818) 325-7346
LINE PRODUCER: Mike Tarzian	**8:00AM**	
COORD: Nikki Levine		**DATE: THURS. 5/25/06**
Production Q's? (317) 446 - 5070	CREW CALL @ LOC	DAY: 5 of 14
OFFICE: (818) 558 5005		CREW CALL: 8:00A
FAX: (818) 842 4112		SHOOTING CALL: 8:30A

ABSOLUTELY NO VISITORS or PETS without prior approval from PRODUCTION

NO SMOKING, EATING, DRINKING, OR CELL PHONE USE ON SET!

Breakfast is 7:30, so if you want to eat please come early

SET	SCENE	CAST	D/N	PGS	LOCATION
INT GIRLS DORM ROOM	45	1,3	N	6/8	Cheyenne Studios
Lauren sees Melina huddled on bed					27567 Fantastic Lane
					Castaic, CA, 91384-3313
INT GIRLS DORM ROOM	47	1,3	N	7/8	
Lauren & Mellina can't open door					PARKING
					On location
INT GIRLS DORM ROOM	51	1,3	N	3/8	
The door suddenly swings open					
INT GIRLS DORM ROOM	53	1,3	N	4/8	
Lauren & Mel wonder what's going on					
INT NINTH FLOOR HALLWAY 1960's	88	1,6,8	N	5/8	
Lauren sees Spence lead Cara to hall					
INT GIRLS DORM ROOM	66	1,3,4	N	1 7/8	EMERGENCY: 911
Diego bursts in looking for Alison					NEAREST HOSPITAL
					Henry Mayo Newhall Memorial
INT GIRLS DORM ROOM	81	1,2,3,4	N	1 4/8	(661) 253 8000
Grant & Diego argue over Alison					23845 McBean Parkway
					Valencia, CA 91355
INT GIRLS DORM ROOM	83	1,3,4	N	1 1/8	
Lauren suggests another Séance					

		TOTAL PAGE COUNT:		7 5/8	

#	CAST & DAY PLAYERS	PART OF	S-W-F	H/MU	SET	NOTES
1	Kandis Erickson	Lauren	W	7:30a	8:30a	
2	Joel Geist	Grant	W	1:00p	2:00p	
3	Tori White	Melina	W	7:30a	8:30a	
4	A.J. Lamas	Diego	W	11:00a	11:30a	
6	Adrian Paul	Spence	W	12:45p	1:00p	
8	Bridget Shergalis	Cara	W	12:30p	1:00p	

BG, STAND-INS, BITS, & OTHER INFO	CALL	SPECIAL INSTRUCTIONS
Adrian Paul to be picked-up @		
12:00p by Tracy Burns		**SET DRESSING/PROPS:** As per Eric J. Trowbridge
310 560 5395		1960's hallway, screwdriver, Diego's joint / lighter
		COSTUMES: As per Olivera Zemljak First call @ 7:30
Pick-up @ Whole Foods		1960's Spence & Cara
4520 N Sepulveda Blvd		**MAKE UP:** As per Andrew Baier First call @ 7:30
Sherman Oaks, CA, 91403		
1 1/2 blocks N of Ventura		**SFX:** As per Richard Miranda
Near exit of 405 Freeway		
		SOUND: As per Jerry Wolfe
		GRIP/ELEC: As per Jeff Siljenberg / Tari Segal
		CAMERA: As per Geoff Schaaf Shoot faster
		MISC:
		QUOTE OF THE DAY: "This is my Ed Wood nightmare..."
		Mark L. Smith

LINE PRODUCER
MIKE TARZIAN

1ST ASSISTANT DIRECTOR
PAUL HART-WILDEN

FIGURE 10.1

DATE: 5/25/2006　　　　　Seance Prod Office　　　　　　　　Crew Call:　　8:00a
DAY: 5 OF 14　　　　　　　2321 W. Olive Ave Suite A, Burbank, CA 91506

NO.	TITLE	RPT	CALL	
1	Director	Rpt@	7:30a	Mark L. Smith
1	Executive Producer	O/C	O/C	James Thorpe
1	Producer	O/C	O/C	Suzanne Lyons
1	Producer	O/C	O/C	Kate Robbins
1	Line Producer	O/C	O/C	Mike Tarzian
1	Production Coord.	O/C	O/C	Nikki Levine
1	APOC	O/C	O/C	Danielle Mandella
1	1st A.D.	Rpt@	8:00a	Paul Hart-Wilden
1	2nd A.D.	Rpt@	7:15a	Rob Bola
1	2nd 2nd A.D.	Rpt@	7:30a	Matthew McArdle
1	Key Set PA	Rpt@	7:30a	Russell Anderson
1	Production Assistant	Rpt@	TBD	Matthew Wright
1	Production Assistant	Rpt@	7:30a	Scott Hollenbeck
1	Production Assistant	Rpt@	TBD	Leigh Vega
1	Production Assistant	Rpt@	TBD	Deirdre Wagner
1	Production Assistant	Rpt@	11:30a	Tracy Burns
1	Production Assistant	Rpt@	11:00a	Liisa Kyle
1	Script Supervisor	Rpt@	8:15a	Erin Forrest
1	DP	Rpt@	8:00a	Geoff Schaaf
1	1st AC	Rpt@	8:00a	David Doko
1	Camera P.A.	Rpt@	8:00a	Andre Dos Santos
1	Still Photographer	Rpt@	8:30a	Chris Lenoir-Robbins
1	Gaffer	Rpt@	8:00a	Jeff Siljenberg
1	Best Boy Electric	Rpt@	8:00a	Brennan Maxwell
1	Key Grip	Rpt@	8:00a	Tari Segal
1	Best Boy Grip	Rpt@	8:00a	Ayako Ogawa
1	Dolly / Swing	Rpt@	8:00a	Henry Dhuy
1	Sound Mixer	Rpt@	8:15a	Jerry Wolfe
1	Boom Operator	Rpt@	8:15a	Doug Brandon

NO.	TITLE	RPT	CALL	
1	Costume Designer	Rpt@	7:30a	Olivera Zemljak
1	Wardrobe Assistant	Rpt@	7:30a	Penny Berman
1	Key Make-Up	Rpt@	7:30a	Andrew Baier
1	Key Hair	Rpt@	7:30a	Terry Akins
1	Assistant Hair	Rpt@	7:30a	Vanessa Garcia
1	Assistant Make-Up	Rpt@	7:30a	Joanne Jiang
1	Assistant Make-Up	Rpt@	N/A	Frances Muscio
1	Assistant Make-Up	Rpt@	N/A	Anastacia Mcpherson
1	Special F/X	Rpt@	N/A	Richard Miranda
1	Stunt Coordinator	Rpt@	N/A	Lynn Salvatori
1	Art Director	Rpt@	8:00a	Dustin Grabiner
1	Set Dresser / Props	Rpt@	8:00a	Eric J. Trowbridge
1	Leadman	Rpt@	8:00a	Samson Kellman
1	Location Manager	Rpt@	7:30a	Peter Abrahams
1	Breakfast ready to serve		7:30a	
1	Lunch ready to serve		2:00p	
	Caterer Contact:			
	Blue Tuesday			Gavin Glenn
1	Driver	Rpt@		Stefan Kollmuss
1	Driver	Rpt@		Leslie Lello
1	Driver	Rpt@	12:00p	Tracy Burns
				(See front page
				for pick-up
				directions)

ADVANCED SHOOTING SCHEDULE
FRIDAY MAY 26th, 2006

DATE	SET	SCENE	CAST	D/N	PAGES	LOCATIONS
5/26	INT TWENTIETH FLOOR RM	50	4,5	N	1 1/8	
5/26	INT TWENTIETH FLOOR RM	54	5,6	N	3/8	Cheyenne Studios
5/26	INT TWENTIETH FLOOR RM	57	5,6	N	6/8	27567 Fantastic Lane
5/26	INT TWENTIETH FLOOR RM	61	4	N	5/8	Castaic, CA, 91384-3313
5/26	INT 20th FLR HALLWAY	49	4,5	N	4/8	
5/26	INT 20th FLR HALLWAY	62	4,6	N	1	PARKING
5/26	INT 20th FLR HALLWAY	64	4	N	1/8	Parking on premises.
5/26	INT 20th FLR HALLWAY	68	1,2,3,4	N	3/8	
5/26	INT 20th FLR HALLWAY	72	1,2,3,4	N	1/8	
5/26	INT TWENTIETH FLOOR RM	69	1,2,3,4,6,7	N	3 3/8	
			SUNDAY MAY 28th, 2006			
5/28	INT GIRLS DORM ROOM	33	1,3,4,5,6	N	1 4/8	
5/28	INT GIRLS DORM ROOM	96	1,2,3,4,6	N	3 7/8	
5/28	INT GIRLS DORM BATHRM.	96A	1,2,3,4	N	4/8	

FIGURE 10.1 *(Continued)*

So let's get you prepared for principal photography. This chapter covers the areas that you, as the producer, need to focus on during this stage.

KNOW HOW TO READ YOUR CALL SHEETS, DAY OUT OF DAYS, AND SHOOTING SCHEDULE

I realize that creating the call sheets, Day Out of Days, and shooting schedule is not your responsibility, but you want to be able to understand them. If you don't know how to read these items, then have your line producer or 1st AD sit with you during preproduction (or even earlier) to go over them in detail. Basically, your call sheet is a daily schedule that is given to the cast and crew with all the details of where and when regarding the production. It also includes information like cast and crew contact info, the exact schedule for the day, which scenes will be shot, and more.

Take a look at the call sheet that I've included here for Seance (figure 10.1) and you will see the amount of detail it provides.

The Day Out of Days is pretty self-explanatory. It list the actors and gives each one a number and it clearly spells out the days in which each actor is working. Notice the SW, H, and WF in the headlines. The SW means start work, the H is hold (which means that the actor is not working that day), and the WF is work finish.

SHOOTING SCHEDULE

The shooting schedule is self-explanatory as well, but it is still wise to go over it with your 1st AD at this stage so you are clear on how to read it. Figure 10.3 shows a shooting schedule page from *Séance*.

It's important to understand that the date noted refers to the information above the date, not below it, as you would expect. So on the *Séance* schedule in Figure 10.3, when it refers to the 6 and 3/8 pages to be shot on Monday, May 22, it is referring to the scenes listed above the date: scenes 10, 15, 17, 22, 36, 38, 74, and 80. You'll notice that the page number of the script is noted to the left of the scene number. Also, the numbers in the right-hand column are the numbers that refer to the actors who are needed for that scene. So in scene 10, for example, the actors in that scene (as you will see from the *Séance* Day Out of Days, figure 10.2) are Lauren, Sid, and the Girl.

DAILIES

Watch the dailies! Let me say that again: watch the dailies. The dailies (or rushes as they are called in some countries) are the unedited footage that was shot yesterday and although you may be busy with lots of things to do, it is important to take some time in your first few hours on set to sit

May Select & Zoom PM			SEANCE - Day Out of Days Report for Cast Members												
Month/Day	05/21	05/22	05/23	05/24	05/25	05/26	05/27	05/28	05/29	05/30	05/31	06/01	06/02	06/03	06/04	06/05
Day of Week	Sun	Mon	Tue	Wed	Thu	Fri	Sat	Sun	Mon	Tue	Wed	Thu	Fri	Sat	Sun	Mon
Shooting Day	1	2	3	4	5	6		7	8	9	10	11	12		13	14
1. LAUREN	SW	W	W	W	W	W		W	W	W	W	W	W		W	WF
2. GRANT	SW		W	W	W	W		W		W		W	W		WF	
3. MELINA	SW	W	W	W	W	W		W	W	W	W	W	W		W	WF
4. DIEGO	SW	W		W	W	W		W		W	W	W	W		WF	
5. ALISON		SW	W			W		W		W	W	WF				
6. SPENCE	SW	W	W	W	W	W		WF								
7. SYD	SW	W				W										WF
8. CARA			SW	W	W				W	W		W	WF			
9. GIRL		SWF														
10. SECURITY GUARD				SW												WF
11. ROSA FURIA																SWF
12. COP																SWF
13. YOUNG ROSA				SWF												
14. PARAMEDIC																SWF

Day Out of Days Report for Cast Members

FIGURE 10.2

Scheduled						
SEANCE - revised shooting schedule - MAY 24th, 2006						
PLEASE DISREGARD ALL PREVIOUS SCHEDULES						
Universal Studios - Loading Dock & environs						
93	Sc: 92	INT	NINTH FLOOR STAIRWELL The group bounds screaming up the stairs	Night	1/8 pgs.	1, 2, 3, 4
72	Sc: 71	INT	NINETEENTH FLOOR STAIRWELL They go back up. Scared by the soccer ball.	Night	2/8 pgs	1, 2, 3, 4
74	Sc: 73	INT	TWENTIETH FLOOR STAIRWELL The soccer ball comes back	Night	4/8 pgs	1, 2, 3, 4
40	Sc: 39	INT	FOURTH FLOOR STAIRWELL Lauren races up the stairs. - hears whistling	Night	4/8 pgs.	1
71	Sc: 70	INT	FIFTEENTH FLOOR STAIRWELL The kids make their way down the stairs	Night	5/8 pgs.	1, 2, 3, 4
104	Sc: 103	INT	BASEMENT NEAR ELEVATOR Lauren and Melina follow after Grant	Night	1 1/8 pgs.	1, 2, 3
105	Sc: 104	INT	BASEMENT They find Syd. Spence attacks them	Night	2 4/8 pgs.	1, 2, 3, 6, 7
107	Sc: 106	INT	BASEMENT Spence attacks Melina. Lauren electrocutes him	Night	1 3/8 pgs.	1, 3, 6, 7
End of Day 1 -- Sunday, May 21, 2006 -- 7 pgs						
Cheyenne Studios - Stage 1						
11	Sc: 10	INT	CHELSEA HALL/LOBBY Lauren bumps into a Girl coming out of the elevator	Day	1 pgs.	1, 7, 9
16	Sc: 15	INT	CHELSEA HALL/LOBBY Syd sees Melina, shoots upright in his chair	Day	5/8 pgs.	3, 7
18	Sc: 17	INT	CHELSEA HALL/LOBBY Lauren and Alison break into Syd's desk	Day	4/8 pgs	1, 5
23	Sc: 22	INT	CHELSEA HALL/LOBBY Syd returns to his desk as Diego comes out of the shower	Day	3/8 pgs.	4, 7
37	Sc: 36	INT	CHELSEA HALL/LOBBY The kids ask Syd if the power went out downstairs	Night	1 4/8 pgs.	1, 3, 4, 6, 7
39	Sc: 38	INT	CHELSEA HALL/LOBBY The girls are unsure what they saw	Night	3/8 pgs.	1, 3, 5
75	Sc: 74	INT	CHELSEA HALL/LOBBY Syd hears someone in the shower room	Night	2/8 pgs.	7
81	Sc: 80	INT	CHELSEA HALL/LOBBY Syd calls for help. Gets attacked by Spence	Night	1 6/8 pgs.	6, 7
End of Day 2 -- Monday, May 22, 2006 -- 6 3/8 pgs						
Cheyenne Studios - Stage 1						
116	Sc: 114	INT	NINTH FLOOR HALLWAY Spence confronts Lauren	Night	5/8 pgs.	1, 6
119	Sc: 117	INT	NINTH FLOOR HALLWAY Lauren takes off down the hall. Spence races after her	Night	2/8 pgs.	1, 6
121	Sc: 119	INT	NINTH FLOOR HALLWAY Spence fights with Lauren. Grant comes to her aide	Night	1 pgs.	1, 6

FIGURE 10.3

down in a quiet room and watch the dailies. And be conscious while you're watching them. Look for potential problems so that you can catch them early in the shoot and early in the day. Also, you should pick a few great scenes to cue up to show investors when they arrive on the set.

On my first couple of films, I was so busy putting out fires and handling a ton of issues that I barely had time to watch the dailies, and, as it turned out, there were problems. But by the time we got to post, it was too late to rectify. It's your film, your baby; you are the one that is 100 percent responsible, so you have to be aware of exactly what is happening at all times, and that includes knowing what the shots you did yesterday actually look like on screen. How many takes does it look like you really have? Are they all consistent? Is the script supervisor doing his or her job? Is your director really getting enough transitional shots? Are you happy? You don't get to complain in post if you haven't taken the time during the shoot to sit down and watch the dailies. It's hard to know what's missing if you don't know what you have.

VIDEO VILLAGE

One of the most important (and fun) jobs for you during this time is being at video village. This is where the monitor is set up and where your director, DP, and script supervisor are situated during the shoot. Talk to your sound supervisor during preproduction and make sure that he or she has multiple headsets for you and for your visiting investors. Watching the monitor at video village is so important. I know it is a director's medium, especially during production, but as the producer, you should know exactly what is being shot. It's entirely your responsibility. You are the one who's going to be answering to your investors and your distributors.

I am not saying that you will be telling your director and DP what to do or how to shoot the film. I am just saying that you want to be aware of exactly what is being shot, so being at video village as much as possible is an important part of your job during this time. Even when you have to leave video village, have your headset turned on as much as you possibly can. You want to know what is happening on set, and you can't always be there, so having your headset on will certainly help keep you informed.

Also, as I mentioned in Chapter 9, make sure that your production designer has a number of director's chairs so that you will have your own chair and additional chairs for visiting investors. I know the budget is low, but it is important that you have these two items – headsets and director's chairs – planned and ordered well in advance. You don't want to be scrambling for chairs in front of the people who gave you money.

Another advantage to being at video village is getting to know your script supervisor. He or she is a critical player in the look of your film. When you get to the editing phase and realize that of those four takes, only two are usable – and they are the two that are your least favorite – the process is a lot more difficult. That is what happened to us on one particular film. The script supervisor was not great; for example, she didn't pick up on the fact that the actor waved with her left hand in two of the shots and her right in the other two shots. It becomes a nightmare for the editor and director – and eventually for you, the producer – because the look of your film suffers. I really didn't know just how important it was to have a fantastic script supervisor until I was sitting with the editor in post. Don't learn this the hard way. Be at video village, watching the monitor and getting to know your script supervisor and his or her ability to do the job.

KNOW YOUR SCRIPT

Know your script inside and out. There are times when you may need to make a quick decision about cutting a scene; at these times, you want to be thoroughly aware of what you can cut without affecting the flow and integrity of the story. Or you may be caught off guard and have extra time. When Kate and I were shooting *Candy Stripers*, we found out by surprise that the effects make-up schedule for the alien scene was going to take something like six hours! We assumed that it would take three. First lesson is to never assume. We should have asked our make-up effects artist well in advance. So here we were on the set with an additional three hours!

Kate, who was directing the project, got together with the DP and 1st AD and reworked that day's scheduled shots. They moved the scene with the monster make-up later in the day and proceeded to set up tracks along the hospital hallway and create some fantastic shots dollying the camera along the hallway, getting every possible angle; they also got some great close-ups for transitional shots that would be needed during editing. So know your script and be able to make decisions on a dime.

YOUR EDITOR

You have already had meetings with your editor during soft prep or preproduction. He or she starts work on day 2 of principal photography. Don't try and save money here. We've made that mistake before, and believe me, this is not the place to cut corners. You really want the editor there and beginning the assembly of the film. More than anyone, the editor will be aware of what is not working and – just as important – what's missing. Stay in communication with him or her throughout the entire production.

STAYING ON TIME: YOUR 1st AD

Our 1st AD on *Portal*, Frank Caridi, defines his job as "the master of the schedule. You have to have control over the set and you have to coordinate the action as it's happening. We made a commitment to 12-hour days and we have a monetary commitment to stay on budget, and a commitment to our actors. So as the 1st AD, I need to make sure that the director and the DP and everyone understand that what I'm saying isn't because I'm the bad guy, but rather I'm helping us coordinate our effort to meet that commitment." Also, Frank is a big advocate of preparation. He believes that "what you do in prep has a magnified exponential effect on what happens when you're shooting. Creative solutions are always good to find before you start shooting."

WRITING CHECKS

As I mentioned earlier, at this budget we couldn't afford a payroll company for the non-SAG actors or for the crew. So, at the end of each week, Mike would give me the list of people and their salary. I would sit in the production office we had on location (with my headset on) and write the checks. It took me about an hour. I gave them to Mike when they were complete and he hand-delivered them to everyone shortly before we left for the day.

STILLS AND PRESS RELEASE

From day 1 of principal, you will begin to have stills. And because a good deal of your time will be spent at video village and there will be plenty of downtime between scenes, I recommend that in the first few days of shooting, you write a press release. I had already created contacts when I sent off emails during preproduction inviting to the set the representatives from *Fangoria* magazine, fangoria.com, and other horror/thriller sites and magazines that were popular. As soon as I had some great stills and a press release, I sent them off to my contacts. Within days, we were on the front page of some of the top horror sites, and it looked fantastic. I continued to send a few stills and press updates as we went through production. It was great press for us and good press that I could use later when I was approaching sales agents. And, if I were shooting these films today, these are items that I would be including in my movies' website, You Tube channel, and other social media platforms.

Also, ask your cast if they have their own websites and who has their own publicist. In the case of *Séance*, we had a great international TV star, Adrian Paul, and he gave me the name of his publicist. I sent the press release to him, and within days he had taken the info and created an amazing press release of his own and posted it on Adrian's site. I copied that for my files. Of course, if you are thinking of self-distributing your film, this type of press is gold, and it's actually critical that you make a point of doing this. You will need as much exposure as possible to help facilitate sales of your movie when you're ready to deliver.

On one of our bigger films, we hired a publicist and she was on set with us quite a bit setting up interviews for our stars with the local radio, newspaper, and TV stations. It was all great stuff to have for the EPK and for film delivery, and of course it provided great footage for when those films came out. But in these lower-budget films, you will no doubt be the one writing the press release and getting it off to the proper sources.

Any time we received any press, I forwarded it to our investors right away. The feedback I got from them was lovely. It made investors – especially those who couldn't make it to the set – feel like they were involved in the production.

TREATS

I know what you're thinking. Treats! On this budget? I don't care what your budget is: you have to put some money aside for treats for your cast and crew. In fact, the lower the budget, the more important it is to treat and acknowledge people. Everyone is putting in more than 100 percent and working long hours. Please don't take that for granted. I am not saying that you have to spend a ton of money. I would keep it all in proportion to the fact that you are doing a low-budget indie film. Remember in Chapter 4, when I was explaining the different categories of the overall budget, how I broke it down into the film budget, operating expenses, executive producer fees, and delivery? Well, the treats come out of your operating expenses.

Be creative here and have some fun with this. During the shoot of *Candy Stripers*, it was extremely hot here in the San Fernando Valley. It was over 100 degrees every day of the shoot. So one day during lunch, we ran across the street to the Food for Less grocery store and bought a really big bucket, filled it with ice, and bought more than 100 ice cream drumsticks and popsicles. We brought them in just as everyone was finishing their lunch and put it on the table. A few people actually cried, they were so thrilled. Everyone thanked us a million times, saying how much it meant to them. It was a drumstick, for goodness' sake! But the point was that we had bought them a treat and that was what mattered. The whole thing cost around $50. It wasn't even about the treat itself – it was the fact that we were thinking about them and that's what was important.

We did a few more things during that shoot. One day we went back to the same store and they had all the pies on sale, so we bought a bunch of pies and jars of whipped cream. Once again, everyone was thrilled. On another day when we all knew we were going to go into overtime, my husband went to an office supply store and bought some color ink for his printer and some poster paper. He made everyone a copy of the *Candy Stripers* one-sheet poster that we had created for our business plan. We gave one to everyone (cast and crew) at the end of the night, and it was like giving them a big check. They loved it, and everyone started running around getting each other to sign their copies. Once again, the whole cost was low – around $100 – but the impact was gigantic.

One night, we planned for a bigger expense and ordered the Chinese food truck to arrive as a late-night treat. It was a great surprise, and people loved it. That was around $400, but once again, it was well worth it. People were working so hard and deserved these little bonuses.

On *Séance*, we had a friend who was an amazing massage therapist come in and set up her massage table. When people had breaks, they were welcome to have a free 10- to 15-minute massage. She wasn't at all expensive for us because it was a win/win situation: we had her on the set and she got to pass out her business cards to (very happy) future clients. This was a big hit!

One of the treats that I remember on *Portal* was Halloween candy. We were shooting in late October, so on a few of our late nights we went to the drugstore and bought Halloween candles, lanterns, buckets, and tons of candy. We decorated the tables before dinner and it was great fun.

During the filming of *Jericho Mansions* (a bigger-budget film), a couple of the people from the crew approached me with a request. We had had some lumber left over after all the sets were built; I could have returned it and gotten some money back, but a couple of the guys asked if they could have it. They were planning a surprise for the cast and crew and they wanted the lumber for that surprise. I could have said no and gotten a bit of extra money for the lumber, but this crew was amazing. I had never seen people work so hard, and they were all so committed to doing a great job. I said yes, and on Monday morning, when I got to the set, I saw that they had built what they called "The Grip-A-Go-Go Lounge." Everyone had brought their musical instruments, and every night from then on they all got together from 11:00pm (when we wrapped) for a couple of hours to jam and sing. The phenomenal talent among them was incredible and the morale and level of impeccability on set was outstanding every single day.

In addition to our own ideas for treats, we also made a point of noting cast and crew birthdays that might be happening during our shoot. We would be sure to pick up a cake and candles and surprise them during dinner. All of this means being conscious, considerate, appreciative, and thoughtful. Just because you may be crazed and putting out fires does not let you off the hook. This is all part of being a producer. It's your job.

PUTTING OUT FIRES

Speaking of putting our fires, let's talk for a bit about that topic. Am I preparing you for a smooth, fun, exciting shoot? Absolutely. However, even with all this great information on producing your indie film and even after learning from my mistakes, I guarantee that you will have a few fires to put out during your production. Hopefully, there will be 90 percent fewer fires because of this book . . . but a few nonetheless.

The trick is to be awake and aware enough to know there's a fire – and then to handle it immediately. On one of my earlier films, I had some pretty serious conflicts going on between the director, the line producer, and the DP. It was like oil and water, and it started in preproduction. At first I thought it would all get better when we started principal photography. Well, it got worse. And it created a lot of anxiety on the set. It affected the space so badly that everyone was affected, causing communication breakdowns through the entire crew. It spread like wildfire.

I had to make an executive decision quickly; I decided to take some of the money from the wrap party budget and planned a party for the end of our first week of shooting. The night was a huge success. I stayed away from the party for the first few hours, and by the time I walked in, everyone was having a ball. They were all dancing and having a great time like nothing had ever happened. That will not be the answer to every communication breakdown, but I knew in this case it needed something pretty special and it worked. Your job as producer has many titles: therapist, babysitter, creative genius, fairy godmother, acknowledgement maven, and more. Embrace them all and enjoy them all.

PLANNING YOUR WRAP PARTY

Another responsibility you will have during production is planning for your wrap party. This part is fun. Here are a few things to keep in mind to ensure that it goes smoothly, is a big hit, and doesn't cost much. As I mentioned earlier, I really don't think the wrap party should be included in your film budget. By opening the business savings account and putting all the investors' checks in that account until the money was needed on the first day of preproduction, I was able to make $835 in interest. That is where the money for the wrap party should come from. If you don't have the business savings account, take the money from the funds you set aside as operating expenses. That is what we did on *Portal*, and it worked fine.

Keep in mind that clubs and restaurants are often quiet on a Monday or Tuesday evening and would love to have you use their facilities. I like to book the wrap party immediately following production because people often have to move on to other projects, and I really want to have everyone enjoy the completion and acknowledgement that takes place at the party. I usually took care of booking the location for the party during week 1 of

FIGURE 10.4

principal photography. Once the place is confirmed, I have the invitations made up. In the case of *Candy Stripers*, I just used the poster we had created for the business plan, put the information on the poster, and had them printed in postcard size. Toward the middle of the second week (we were shooting for only 14 days!), I gave everyone the invitation and emailed the invitation to all of the investors as well. Figure 10.4 shows that invitation.

Kate and I made the decision to give everyone two drink coupons for wine and beer only. I didn't want to be responsible for or concerned about drinking and driving, so I decided to limit the amount of alcohol we provided. Also, I wanted to keep the budget for the party at a reasonable price. The club we chose was spacious, with both indoor and outdoor areas, which was perfect for the time of year we were shooting.

Kate and I dressed up, met people at the door as they arrived, and handed them an envelope that had their name typed on it and contained the drink coupons. When the investors arrived, we did the same but told them that if they (and their guest) wanted additional coupons, they had only to ask.

The club had multiple televisions, and our stills photographer had taken well over 500 stills, most of which were really fun behind-the-scenes shots of everyone. He made disks with the stills on a loop, and they played on the TVs the entire time. Everyone loved it. The club had an excellent sound system and people danced all night.

I had done some research looking for great restaurants in the area that catered; I choose a Thai restaurant that delivered some wonderful dishes in our price range. The food was a huge success. *Candy Stripers* had 33 speaking roles and a big crew and a surprising number of investors who wanted to attend the party, so I knew I would have to spend some money, but I was really careful about where it went. For example, the bartender worked very hard, and of course I would be expected to add the tip onto the bar bill at the end of the night when the coupons were added up. To help with that, we wanted our guests to be generous with tips as well, so we took the scariest still shots from the film and had them blown up to 8½ × 11 and put notes on them like "this could happen to you if you don't leave a tip" and placed a few different notes around the bar. It was really fun. I still left a big tip for the bartender, but I knew that others had chipped in as well.

Kate and I made a point of moving around the party and thanking and acknowledging people throughout the evening. The party went on until 2:00 a.m. – when they finally kicked us out – and then it moved to one of the actor's homes and went on until daylight.

GOING THE EXTRA MILE

By "going the extra mile," what I mean is simply this: you want everyone around you to go the distance – everyone working long hours, a crew that's brilliantly creative, and actors whose performance will win you accolades at the film festivals. You will need to remember that *you* are the one setting the stage, creating the tone, and specifying how high the bar should be raised. You demand 200 percent from them; you'd better be willing to do the same.

During the filming of *Undertaking Betty*, we had some pretty intense, difficult dance scenes for our leads. We had hired Peter Darling (*Billy*

Elliot) to do the choreography, but what is the point of great choreography if your two lead actors aren't exactly Fred and Ginger on the dance floor? Brenda Blethyn was fairly confident, but Alfred Molina needed some help (and he was the first to admit it). We were working six-day weeks, so the only time to schedule dance lessons was Sunday morning. It was their only day off each week during a six-week shoot. However, both of them jumped at the chance to have lessons to make sure the scenes were perfect (and watch the movie – the scenes *are* perfect!). Kate and I were exhausted. In fact, "exhausted" does not even begin to describe it. It was a long, tough shoot. Yet no one on set ever knew it. We never even used the word "tired." Not once. And early each Sunday morning, we were up and waiting for Brenda and Alfred to arrive for their dance lesson with Peter, and we stayed with them during the entire lesson.

One night, while we were shooting a scene on location in *Portal* that required mealworms (really gross-looking little worms that look like maggots), our line producer went beyond the call of duty. We needed to have these little worms wiggle around the floor to look really creepy. What we hadn't planned for and didn't know was that maggot-type worms don't wiggle on a cold floor. They just become totally still. Not a good thing in a horror film. So now that we'd learned that lesson, we needed more worms. Making the floor warmer was easy; getting more worms was a whole other story. It was 11:30 p.m., and we all started brainstorming ideas. One of our actors went online and found out that the local Walmart sold meal worms in their fishing department. Go figure! Kate, Mike, and I all looked at each other like, this is impossible, right? Just getting there before they closed at midnight was crazy, right? But everyone was looking to us to see what we were going to do. The scene was okay the way it was, but it was just okay. It wasn't perfect. So Mike said, "I'm going to Walmart to get the maggots." Everyone cheered, and he jumped on his motorcycle and off he went. He ended up getting stopped by a policeman for speeding, and after explaining our dilemma to the cop, even he got excited about us getting our gross little mealworms in time. So he let Mike go without a fine and gave him directions to Walmart. Mike got there at 11:55 p.m., bought the maggots, and returned to the set and to a standing ovation.

When I asked Kate what stood out for her regarding going the extra mile, here is what she wrote:

"You can't make this film!" *Those were the first words out of our line producer's mouth. Mike Tarzian is never negative. But when we told him we wanted to make our feature film, Portal, for under $200,000, he thought we were crazy.*

Not only did we have a feature film that takes place almost entirely at night, which requires a lot bigger grip and electric package than your typical low-budget film, but it takes place in a literal and figurative fog. The fog had to surround the motel, which was the main set; actors had to drive cars through it; a whole coven had to walk through it; and we had to fill rooms with it . . . all for less than $200,000, including the cast!

Mike was right, it was impossible without a much bigger budget and a soundstage. But we couldn't possibly afford a soundstage. We were going to have to shoot on location – but how?

The first order of business was to find a vintage motel that we could rent within our meager budget, or a building that we could dress as one. After a lot of looking at a ton of properties we found a small hotel in La Crescenta that was right out of the 1930s. It was the perfect look, and the price was right, but how to shoot the fog?

Digital fog was discussed for about a microsecond before being dismissed as impractical and, again, way too expensive. Then Mike had a stroke of genius: we'd tent the entire motel. It seemed crazy at first, but as we examined the areas that needed to be covered, he convinced us that we could do it. So we hit the phones looking for a tent.

"I have good news and bad news," Mike said. "The good news is that I can afford the frame for the tent; the bad news is that I can't afford the tent itself." A tent frame with no cover wasn't going to do us much good when it came to containing fog! What to do?

After a round of brainstorming, we came up with an alternative plan. We'd rent half of the frame and use the motel roof to support the other side. That was a tidy little savings. But what were we going to cover the frame with? We talked about renting a black tent (after all, we had saved some money on the frame), but even with our savings, that was still too costly. We ruled out fabric and landscaping fabric and finally ended up with black polyethylene. We knew it was a risky solution because it would take only a whisper of wind to blow the whole thing away. But we were low budget, and we didn't have much of a choice. Fortunately, we were lucky: the Santa Anna winds didn't blow.

Mike and his production coordinator worked all night on the roof of the hotel putting the tarp in place. Once it was in place, we filled the space with smoke, used black tape to cover the shine on the tent poles, and shot most of the film in the covered motel and parking lot in what anyone would have sworn was fog. Mike and what he did was the perfect example of what it looks like to go that extra mile.

CHILDREN AND ANIMALS

First of all, if you can avoid using them, please do so. Both are a bit of a problem, and at this budget level, you don't need the problems or the expenses that come with them. However, in many cases, there's no choice. It's part of the script – and it may be an important part of the script. In the case of *Séance*, the main focus of the story was our little girl ghost. And the script also called for a parrot. Thank goodness it wasn't a talking parrot.

In the case of children, it is very important to check with your local guild and get the guidelines on using children in film. The number of hours they can work will differ dramatically from those of the rest of your cast. That is why twins are so often cast. Also, you are required here in the United States to have a teacher on set with them every day, even if you're shooting in the summer. At the time we were filming *Séance*, that cost added an extra $250 per day.

When it comes to animals, it can be pretty scary. Is the animal going to behave like you want it to? You can't afford numerous takes in an already tight schedule. And they can be expensive as well. I asked Kate to share what she remembered about casting our parrot in *Séance*.

We were totally immersed in preproduction and running into budget concerns because we were shooting Séance on a soundstage and had to build all the sets, which is a huge expense at our budget level. When our line producer, Mike, got quotes for the parrot that is a character in the story, the quotes for a trained parrot came in at well over $1000 to do the shoot, which was just impossible for us. So Mike put his foot down and said we had to replace the parrot with another animal. One that we could buy at a pet store. One that was cheap. His idea was to use a bunny. Well, we were making a horror film, and there is nothing less scary than a little bunny. The idea was laughable – way too Monty Python. We really needed a parrot, because the bird is supposed to become possessed and a possessed animal with a big beak and claws is a scary idea. So I took on the task of finding a parrot for free. I called all of my friends who were obsessed with their pets and asked for help; I called pet stores and offered them a credit in the film if we could use one of their parrots; and at each turn, I struck out. Then I got the idea to call my dog groomer, Lisa, who is a dear friend. Sure enough, Lisa hooked me up with a wonderful woman who rescues birds. The director and I visited her at her home and she had an amazing aviary – worthy of a zoo. She recommended a particular parrot who was not inclined to squawk (something that I had failed to think of). His name was Johnny. And Johnny was worth about $1600. She and her daughter agreed to put Johnny in Séance for free. Johnny was a flawless performer. We gave Johnny his credit as well as our wonderful parrot wranglers. It was a win for everybody.

American Humane Association

Film & TV Unit

NO ANIMALS WERE HARMED®

July 6, 2006

Snowfalls Films/WindChill Films Productions
2321 W Olive Ave Ste A
Burbank, CA 91506-2663

RE: **Seance**

To Whom It May Concern:

It has come to the American Humane Association's attention that principal photography on **Seance** is nearing completion. In order for your project to qualify for our end credit disclaimer and/or rating, the Film & Television Unit must screen the finished product prior to its release. We make this requirement in order to substantiate the animal action depicted in the final cut as that which was monitored by our Certified Animal Safety Representatives during production. By doing so, American Humane can stand behind our "No Animals Were Harmed"® end credit, and, if necessary, defend your production from erroneous criticism.

The public looks to our organization for assurances of humane animal treatment, and for every monitored film production, American Humane publishes a review explaining how the animal action was accomplished. This enables our staff to respond to public inquiry throughout the entire life of your project. These reviews are posted on our Web site, www.americanhumane.org/film, and may be released to a variety of electronic and print media.

Please be aware that the American Humane logo and registered end credit language is tracked via a unique alpha-numeric code and cannot be transferred or reassigned from any other production. Also, we suggest you refrain from using any wording that speaks to the treatment of the animals, as this would constitute a dilution of American Humane's registered disclaimer and could be considered in violation of the Federal Trademark Dilution Act of 1996, as well as other applicable U.S. trademark laws.

If you are still in post production, please contact me as soon as you are ready for American Humane to screen locked picture. You may arrange a screening at your facilities, or submit a confidential VHS or DVD preview copy.

We appreciate your cooperation and look forward to hearing from you.

Sincerely,

Cheryl Kearney
Post Production Manager
Film & Television Unit
American Humane Association

15366 Dickens Street
Sherman Oaks, CA 91403
(818) 501-0123
(818) 501-8725
www.americanhumane.org/film

FIGURE 10.5

Also, having a parrot in our script meant contacting the American Humane Association well in advance of principal photography. We were required to send them the script for approval and get them a copy of the schedule so that they could plan to have a representative from their organization on the set during the days that we were shooting the parrot. Then, after the film was complete, we needed to get a letter from the American Humane Association saying that the parrot wasn't harmed during the shoot. That letter was required as one of our delivery items. Figure 10.5 shows the letter we received on *Séance* requesting a copy of the film so that they could verify and confirm that "no animals were harmed."

Once again, if you do your research and follow guidelines, all of this will be easy – a little more work and a little more costly, but pretty effortless when you know what you're doing.

INVESTORS

During preproduction, we invited our investors to come out during production. We sent them the schedule and suggested days that would be the most fun and entertaining. So now that we were in production, we needed to find out from them exactly if and when they were coming. There are a couple of things I did to made sure they felt involved and had some fun. Because I started my day watching the dailies from yesterday's shoot, I made a point of choosing some great scenes to set aside to show investors.

No matter how confined our location was, I made certain that there was a room set aside to show the dailies that was separate from any rooms used by the cast and crew. That way there was an opportunity for me to show the dailies to the investors and have some privacy to talk to them as well.

In addition, I had director's chairs set up for them at video village, which was always a big treat. I had their headsets ready and made sure that I introduced them to the director and DP as soon as they arrived so that they would be comfortable sitting at video village if that was something they wanted to do.

In some cases, the investors wanted to be an extra in the film, which was something we had worked out in advance. One of my investors lived in the area; he brought his son, and they are in multiple scenes in *Candy Stripers*. They had a blast and were on set quite a bit during the shoot. Another investor came out from Denver with her daughter, and while her daughter was an extra nearly every day on the film, our investor helped us out in the costume department. We put a lot of our investors to work, and they loved it.

Keep in mind also that if you have a name actor – as we did in *Séance* and in *Portal* – some of your investors will certainly want their picture taken with the actor. One of our investors came with his wife and sons from halfway across the country and got their picture taken with Adrian Paul. It was great fun.

Because we were shooting at a hospital on *Candy Stripers*, we asked the people in charge if we could use the huge welcome sign in front of the hospital to headline our investor's name. So when an investor was coming, we would find out what time their plane arrived and send one of the PAs to pick them up. When they arrived, we would send the PA, Chris, down to take their picture in front of the gigantic sign that now had their name on it. Within a few hours, the photo would be emailed to them. It was a lot of fun and they truly appreciated it – and it didn't cost a cent.

It's important to remember to email your investors a few great stills every couple of days. And when you get any of your press releases and stills posted on genre websites, be sure to forward them that information as well.

INTERVIEWS FOR POSTPRODUCTION POSITIONS

During production, I made a point of researching the postproduction positions. I knew that I would need a composer, a sound designer, and a color correction expert. Researching, interviewing, and choosing the postproduction team is the job of the producer, especially when you can't afford a postproduction supervisor. I didn't sign their deals at this stage, but I did start asking around and doing the research.

ACKNOWLEDGMENT

Acknowledgment is something that is sadly missing these days. I make a point of acknowledging people every day. It is so important. At these budget levels, your cast and crew are working crazy hours, putting their heart and soul into the job, and so often this hard work goes unnoticed. That's just not right. You, as the producer, need to be responsible for making sure this happens.

I know you're busy, and maybe it's your first film and you have enough to handle. Too bad. No excuses here. Make a note of it in your agenda if you have to, but do it – even if you just pick a different department each day and make a point of looking at the work they've been doing and acknowledging them for their talent and commitment.

Chapter 11

Wrap-Up and Postproduction

The 14-day shoot is over!! It was a great shoot, and – as much fun as it was to be on set and location – it's sure nice to be back in my office again. It's nice when all your hard work has paid off – especially when you know that you have everything you need to move on to postproduction and delivery. So let's take a look at all the areas that you will need to handle during this next stage.

WRAP PARTY

The first order of business is the wrap party. It is usually scheduled immediately following principal photography because the cast and crew are still available. And you want as many people as possible to be able to attend so that everyone can have a chance to enjoy themselves, be acknowledged, and do a little networking that they didn't have time for during the shoot. I went over all the logistics for the wrap party in Chapter 10, but I want to highlight a couple of points.

Kate and I made certain to greet as many people as possible and personally gave them their drink tickets. Throughout the evening, we made a point of acknowledging everyone for the great job they did on the film. We booked great spots for our parties, ordered excellent food, had hundreds of stills from the film running on a loop on all the TV sets available, and played great music. The last point I want to stress is that it's your party, too. So have fun, relax, and dance! You've worked hard – really hard – and it's your time to chill and have a ball. You've earned it!

LINE PRODUCER'S WRAP-UP

On the Monday after production Mike moved back into my office again. You will need your line producer for a full week after you wrap. Mike started immediately finishing up any final payments that were due. He made sure that he was in touch with the keys to ensure that any rentals were promptly returned. You don't want any surprises in that department. Those companies have your credit card number, and the fine for late returns is insane.

Another job that your line producer will be doing is working on the SAG delivery book. This task is pretty intense, as the delivery list includes all the SAG actor's contracts, production reports, call sheets, final cast list, final cost reports, signatory letters, and more. Make sure that you make a copy of the entire delivery book before you send it off to SAG, because if it happens to get lost or if they have questions about anything, then you have a copy at your fingertips. Also, you want to get your deposit back from SAG because you are moving into postproduction and you'll need that money. When they receive their delivery book, you should make the request for the refund of your deposit.

Another item that Mike was busy working on is the wrap book. I love this book. It includes the final version of the script, the shooting schedule, crew list, cast list, vendor list, location list, call sheets, and production reports. In fact, when you're interviewing line producers, make sure that they include a wrap book as part of their service. Mike made copies for me, Kate, and our director.

EDITOR'S ASSEMBLY

Also happening during the first week following production is your editor's assembly. Your editor is doing this continually during the shoot, but now he or she gets a full week to complete the assembly before the director joins him or her.

COPYRIGHT TRANSFER

If you didn't have time to do the copyright transfer during principal photography, now is the perfect time. You are back in your own office now with access to your files, your computer, and everything you need to do the transfer.

You can go online and pull down the copyright paperwork. There is nothing special or challenging about it. In fact, it's the same exact paperwork that the writer originally used when he or she did the copyright on the screenplay. The only difference now is that in the section asking who the author is, it will no longer be the writers (for instance, Kate Robbins and Jill Garson); it will be Candy Stripers, LLC. You have your short-form assignment that I talked about in Chapter 3, so you have the right to transfer the project from the writer to the company. As long as you have paid the writer the purchase price, which happened on the first day of principal photography or before, you are good to go.

This transfer is all part of the "chain of title," which you will need for delivery; put it in your schedule so that it happens at this time. It may take a year to get it back from the government, but don't worry about that. All you need for delivery is the proof that you have sent off the paperwork to the government copyright agency. Just remember this: no chain of title, no movie.

FILM WEBSITE

I didn't take full advantage of this opportunity. Today, the Internet is vital. It's how the world communicates. If you haven't put a website up yet, do so at this stage. You now have access to some great stills. You have your synopsis and possibly even a trailer and a press release.

HIRING FOR POSTPRODUCTION POSITIONS

In most budgets, you would have the luxury of having a postproduction supervisor, but at $200,000, I just couldn't justify it. Also, it was an area that I wanted to know more about. I wanted to save as much money as possible, yet have high-quality films to give our investors a better chance for a return on their investment. This seemed like a way that I could save.

During production, I started getting suggestions and asking around about great people for the post positions. I needed a sound designer, a composer, and a color correction expert: three very important positions. I wanted the best in the business, but I didn't have a lot of money for the jobs.

Sometimes you can find people who have held studio positions and are now opening their own company and are looking for new clients. They are far more inclined to lower their prices just to get the word of mouth started. Also, another way that we got quality people for a reasonable price was by saying that we were willing to extend the time period that they would have to complete the job; that way, they were able to take on their higher-paying clients and still fit us in during their off hours.

When it came to doing the spotting for our color correction, my director, my DP, and I were often called to come in and view the scenes at midnight. And Saturday morning was usually the time I did the spotting with the composer and sound designer. It was well worth it because I was able to cut thousands off their price.

Regarding deal memos: make sure to carefully review a list of delivery items (which you can get from a sales agent) before you type up any contracts. Even if you are planning to self-distribute, you will need to do this. You don't want to go back months later and say, "Oh, sorry, but I didn't know that I would need such and such, would you mind doing it?" Having everything that you will need to deliver your film in the deal memos for your sound designer, your color correction artist, and your composer will save you time and money and prevent embarrassment. In fact, in some of our composers' deal memos, we included music for the film trailer as part of the responsibilities. Ordinarily, your sales agent will handle the trailer, but if you want to cut down on the sales agent's expenses or if you plan on self-distributing your film, then I would certainly include the music for the trailer in your composer's deal memo.

Figure 11.1 shows a deal memo that was used for our composer on a couple of our films.

This Composer Agreement, dated as of _____ , is entered into between (the "Composer") _____ and _____, LLC (the "Producer") with respect to composing and packaging services to be performed by Composer for the motion picture currently entitled _____ (the "Picture").

1. Services

    (a) Composer, on a non-exclusive, first priority basis, shall write, compose, arrange, orchestrate, prepare, and submit to Producer, music (the "Score"), where such Score shall not exceed fifty-five (55) minutes in length;

    (b) Composer's Score shall be a virtual score. In the event Composer and Producer mutually agree or Producer requires Composer to augment the Score with musician(s), any and all costs related to the utilization of such musician(s) shall be borne by Producer;

    (c) Composer's Score shall be approved by a single designee of Producer, which approval shall not be unreasonable withheld;

    (d) Composer shall supervise music editing and dubbing of the recording of the Score in connection with the Picture

    (e) Composer shall deliver the Score to Producer in a form consistent with what is considered acceptable for a picture of this nature, or, in such form that is mutually acceptable to both Producer and Composer;

    (f) Composer shall prepare, and have the right to receive, a copy of the formal cue sheet for the Picture from the Producer when Picture is in final rendering; and,

    (g) Composer shall create a trailer for the Picture for promotional purposes, incorporating music from the Picture.

2. Compensation: Composer shall receive the sum of _____
                (the "Fee) for the composing and music packaging services as directly related to the Score for the Picture.

FIGURE 11.1

3. *Method of Payment:* *Payment of the Fee pursuant to Provision 2 above shall be made as follows:*

    (a) _____ *promptly upon commencement of services; and,*

    (b) _____ *promptly upon the completion of services and delivery of Score.*

4. *Costs Excluded:*

    The following costs are excluded in the recording and delivery of the score, and are not included in the services provided by the Composer:

    (a) Music Editor;
    (b) Musicians and related studios costs of recording said musicians;
    (c) Licensing of pre-existing music
    (d) Re-use, new use, supplemental market fees and any other residual type payments generated under the American Federation of Musicians (AFM) Agreement, with the understanding that the Producer shall be a signatory of the AFM should union musicians be employed;
    *(e) Any costs incurred resulting from the creative changes in the Picture, or, changes in the designated music direction occurring prior to the recording of the Score, where such changes would substantially alter the music **production** schedule and related expense;*
    (f) Re-scoring or re-recording costs solely for creative reasons after Composer's delivery of the Score, where such creative reasons are beyond the control of the Composer, with any additional costs and compensation of Composer being separately negotiated;
    (g) Payroll services costs; and,
    (h) Lyricist and vocal related expenses, if any.

5. *Term of Engagement:* *Composer shall perform its services within a mutually agreed period, with commencement of services on or about _____, and ending upon delivery of the Score on or about _____.*

6. *Screen Credit:* *The Composer shall be afforded full card screen credit on a separate card in the main titles of the Picture, of the same size, stature, style and duration afforded the writer, producer, and director, such credit reading: "Music by _____." Composer shall also be afforded credit in the end titles of the Picture reading, "Music Composed, Conducted, and Produced by_____" Producer shall also afford credit in the end titles of the Picture for the orchestrator, music recording engineer, music editor, and featured soloists, if any, provided that Composer furnishes Producer with such credit information in advance of the filming of the credits for the Picture.*

7. *Credit in Paid Advertising and Printed Material:* *Composer shall receive credit in all paid advertising (including, but not limited to, billboards, DVD cases, videocassette boxes and one-sheets), excluding award and congratulatory advertisements, that are under Producer's control and under the control of the distributor of the Picture, of the same size, stature, and style as that afforded the writer, producer and director of the Picture, in the following manner: "Music by _____."*

FIGURE 11.1 *(Continued)*

8. Publishing Rights and Royalties: Composer's publishers, (the "Publishers"), shall own all rights, including publishing rights, masters and copyright in the United States and throughout the world, in and to the Score resulting from Composer's services. Publishers grant to Producer and its successors and assigns, in perpetuity, the non-exclusive, irrevocable right, license, privilege and authority, throughout the universe, both known and unknown, to perform publicly, either for profit or non-profit, and to authorize others so to perform the Score only in synchronization or timed relationship to the Picture and promotional uses and, in all media now known or hereafter devised. Composer shall be entitled to receive 100% of the "writer's share" of public performance royalties directly from, (ASCAP/BMI) provided, however, that if, and in the event that, Producer is required to directly license public performing rights in and to the Score, Producer shall negotiate a reasonable fee for such direct license and Producer shall consult with Publishers in connection therewith.

9. Soundtrack Album: In the event Producer or Composer secures a recording company to record all or part of the Score for inclusion on a soundtrack album, Producer and Composer shall negotiate in good faith, the provisions for such soundtrack album. Notwithstanding the foregoing, Producer shall make best efforts to ensure that Composer shall be the designated music producer for any such soundtrack album.

10. Performing Rights Society: Composer is a member of ASCAP/BMI/Other.

11. Changes: Producer shall make best efforts to ensure that Composer shall have the first right to make any changes in the Score for the Picture for the initial release.

12. Errors and Omissions: Composer shall be named as additional insureds in the errors and omissions policy for the Picture, if and when Producers secure a Policy.

13. Copies of the Finished Picture: Composer shall receive two (2) DVD copies of the Picture at no charge, for personal, non-commercial and archival purposes only, at such time that the Picture is completed and in final rendering, and two (2) posters from the Picture, subject to a theatrical release.

14. Identification Number: Composer's Federal Identification Number is

_____

15. Notices: All notices, requests, demands and other communications under this Agreement shall be given in writing, and shall not be unreasonably withheld or delayed, and shall be served either personally, by facsimile (with the original forwarded in the following manner) or delivered by first class mail, registered or certified, return receipt requested, postage prepaid and properly addressed as follows:

Producer: $\qquad\qquad\qquad\qquad$ *Composer:*
Ms. Suzanne Lyons
Suite A
2321 West Olive Avenue
Burbank, California 91506-2603

A copy of all notices to Composer shall be sent contemporaneously to:

Agent

FIGURE 11.1 *(Continued)*

16. _Indemnifications:_

(a) _Composer shall defend and indemnify and otherwise hold Producer free and harmless from and against any and all liabilities, claims, demands, actions, damages, costs, penalties, and expenses (including, without limitation, reasonable attorney's fees and court costs) rising out of or resulting from any breach or claim of breach of Composer's agreements, representations or warranties hereunder reduced to judgment by a court or competent jurisdiction or settled with Composer's consent, which consent shall not be unreasonably withheld. Notwithstanding the foregoing, if Composer withholds consent to settlement which Producer is willing to make, the Composer promptly assumes all costs of defending against said claim; provided, however, that (i) the final control and disposition (by settlement, compromise or otherwise) of the defense shall continue to be controlled solely by Producer, and (ii) in the event Composer assumes said costs, Producer shall nonetheless have the right to settle such claim in its sole discretion without Composer's consent thereto, but in such event, Composer shall not be obligated to reimburse Producer for payments made by Producer in connection with such settlement. Composer shall reimburse Producer, on demand, for any payment made by Producer at any time with respect to such damage, liability, cost, loss or expense to which the foregoing indemnity applies. Pending the determination of any such claim, demand, action or proceeding, Producer shall have the right, at Producer's election, to withhold payment of any monies otherwise payable to Composer hereunder in an amount reasonably related to such claim._

(b) _Producer shall defend and indemnify and otherwise hold Composer free and harmless from and against any and all liabilities, claims, demands, actions, damages, costs, penalties, and expenses (including, without limitation, reasonable attorney's fees and court costs) arising out of or resulting from any breach or claim of breach of Producer's agreements, representations or warranties hereunder reduced to judgment by a court or competent jurisdiction or settled by Producer._

17. _Representation and Warranties:_

(a) _Composer represents and warrants that: (i) Composer is not subject to any obligation or disability which could interfere with or impair the full performance by Composer of Composer's services hereunder; (ii) Composer has not done or made, nor shall Composer do or make, any act or grant of rights which could interfere with or impair the full performance by Composer or Composer's services, obligations and all rights granted by Composer to the Producer pursuant to this Agreement; and, (iii) that portion of the Score delivered hereunder by Composer (excluding portions of the Score consisting of pre-existing musical compositions or sound recordings composed and/or created by third parties and specifically requested or provided by Producer to be included in the Score) shall be wholly original with Composer, not copied in whole or in part from any other literary, musical or other work, and the use thereof by Producer shall not infringe upon or violate any common law or statutory rights of any person, firm or corporation, including, without limitation, contractual rights, copyrights and rights of privacy;_

(b) _Producer represents and warrants that: (i) Producer is not subject to any obligation or disability which could interfere with or impair the full performance by Producer or Producer's obligations hereunder; and, (ii) that portion, if any, of the Score added by Producer to the picture delivered hereunder by Composer, and any_

FIGURE 11.1 _(Continued)_

portions of the Score specifically requested or provided by Producer to be in included in the Picture, shall be duly licensed or owned by Producer or in the public domain, and not copied in whole or in part from any other literary, musical or other work, and the use thereof by Producer shall not infringe upon or violate any common law or statutory rights of any person, firm or corporation, including, without limitation, contractual rights, copyrights and rights of privacy.

18. Governing Law: This Agreement shall be construed in accordance with the laws of the State of California and of the United States applicable to contracts entirely made and and to be performed in California. The state and federal courts of Los Angeles County, California, shall have exclusive jurisdiction of any claim, dispute or disagreement with respect to this Agreement.

In the event of any dispute arising out of this Agreement, whether based in contract or tort theory, the prevailing party shall be entitled to its costs and all reasonable attorney fees incurred. For the purposes of this Agreement, prevailing party shall include a party in whose favor a voluntary dismissal is entered.

19. Other Terms: All of the customary terms and conditions favorable to producers customarily included in agreements of this type are hereby incorporated by reference. The parties agree upon the request of either party to negotiate with respect to a long form agreement containing the above terms and other terms customary in the industry. However, until such agreement is entered into, and if such agreement is never entered into, the foregoing Agreement shall be deemed the entire agreement between the parties, superseding all prior agreements written and oral, and cannot be amended or changed orally.

IN WITNESS WHEREOF, the parties have executed this Agreement on the date first above written.

AGREED TO AND ACCEPTED:

_____   _____
NAME of Composer   *Date*

_____   _____
NAME of Producer   *Date*

SPECIAL THANK YOU: My thanks to Otto Vavrin II, SMC Artists, for his assistance in generating this document.

FIGURE 11.1 (*Continued*)

I have known producers who have joined ASCAP (American Society of Composers, Authors, and Publishers) or BMI (Broadcast Music Incorporated) in order to receive money when their film is played, by either owning the rights to the score and/or songs or sharing in the rights. I think if you are using a new composer, he or she may be more willing to include this in the deal with you. But in our case, we were using an experienced composer, and we were getting him at a great price, so I really didn't feel it was at all fair to take a percentage of his future earnings.

Here are the items from our sound designer's deal memo on both *Séance* and *Portal*:

Re-recording mix & sound designer
Foley
ADR includes one 5-hour session; after the one 5-hour session, ADR will cost $65.00 per hour.
Reel Changes (new Picture) there will be a new $200.00 per-hour charge for resyncing audio to new picture.
Delivery:
1. 5.1& Lt/Rt Feature & Trailer English Language Printmaster
2. 5.1 & Lt/Rt Feature & Trailer M&E
3. D/M&E (Dialog, Music & Effect Stems) Feature & Trailer – Stereo Parallel Tracks
The audio on the DVD is SDII format, continuous multiple mono files at 48k, 24 bit. They include Head Tones and 2-pops.
Payment Schedule – Sound Rage Recordings:
First Payment: Due at signing of this agreement
Second Payment: Due on 9/15/06 (completion of sound design)

As with so many of our cast and crew on our films, Kate and I were blessed with an amazing sound designer, Marcus Blanchard. What we learned from Marcus was to be extremely aware of noise. Our hotel in *Portal* was fantastic in many ways, but it was right on the highway, and even with the night shoots, the noise from the trucks was constant. Our editor brought this to our attention a number of times as well. The ADR on *Portal* was double the cost of *Candy Stripers* and *Séance* combined. In *Candy Stripers*, we had a problem with the shoes that our candy stripers wore. The shoes were constantly squeaking, and that had to be fixed in post. When you need to duplicate sounds it's very costly.

Here are the items that were included in our deal with our color correction artist:

Inclusive:
HD Conform to 24P
HD Color Correction @ 40 hours
Layoff to D5
DVD Screener Master
Client provides the following:
24fps EDL & 24fps offline reference

Main & End Titles (Adobe Illustrator and/or pre-build 24p QuickTime/Video Element)

Production Representative for color and conform sign-off

HD Services Terms:

Full Primary and Secondary color-correction is inclusive in price

Client will provide "off-line" reference for picture, titles, etc.

Client must provide an accurate EDL for conforming

Payment Schedule: in advance to secure discounted rate

Color Correction beyond 40 hours will be billed @ $350/hour

VFX outside included elements will be bid accordingly

Editorial changes beyond the scope of the offline/EDL will be billed @ $250/hour

Any questions or items that you may wish to negotiate, please contact Cranium Filmworks L.A.

As I've mentioned, make sure that you check out a current detailed delivery list and be certain to include in the deal memos any and all requirements on that list that are related to the composer, sound designer, and color correction expert.

DIRECTOR'S CUT

Once the editor has his or her week to finish up the assembly, he or she is ready for the director to join him or her in the editing suite. At this budget level, our director had two weeks to complete the director's cut. On my bigger-budget films, it varied drastically, but two weeks is absolutely fine in the ultra-low-budget world. As the producer, you stay away from the editing suite at this time. The editor had a week to do the final assembly, and now the director has two weeks, so you get to do all the other items that need seeing to. During the director's cut, the editor will use what is called temp music so that you will get a true feel for how the final project will look.

AUDIENCE TESTING

While the director and editor are working together, you get to plan and book the theatre for the audience testing. I wanted to hold it immediately after the director's cut was complete because I had only an additional week or so with the editor. So I booked it for late Monday afternoon, and I sent out the email invitations early the week before. I booked a theater that held 35 people and I wanted at least 15 or 20 of them to be the perfect demographic for the film. I wanted the rest of the people to be from different areas of the entertainment industry. I thought that would be a good mix of people to get an honest account of what worked and what didn't about the film.

In some cases, during the audience testing, we just gave people the forms with a pen and then gave them a certain amount of time at the end to fill them out. Then we collected them and that was it. In other situations, we asked people to stay after we had collected the forms to discuss certain aspects of the film that we wanted to get further information on. We had a prepared list of questions ready. It just depends on your film and how close you feel it is to being ready. If it's close, then the form is enough, but if you know that there are problems, be sure to plan for a discussion with your audience at the end of the testing. Here is the information that was in the email that went out about the *Portal* audience testing screening:

Dear Friends:

We are holding the Audience Testing for Portal on Monday, February 5ʰ at Raleigh Studios in the Mary Pickford Screening Room (Raleigh Studios) from 4:00 to 6:00 p.m.

We are looking to fill seats with our target audience, which is aged 18–30 years old and has seen three out of six of the following films:

The Undead
The Hills Have Eyes
Saw
Dawn of the Dead (remake)
Dark Water
Boo

If you or someone you know fits this demographic and would be available to come to the Audience Testing, we'd love to have you.

We have limited seating, so if you would like to attend, please call me (Kate) by January 29 to put your name on the list. My direct line is (310) 555-5555.

The address is 5300 Melrose Avenue, Los Angeles, 90038. There is free parking on the street for a two-hour period or at meters, which go up to four hours. Parking is also available in the Raleigh Studios garage for a fee of $5.00.

Thanks for your help. Hope to see you there.

Yours as always,

Kate Robbins and Suzanne Lyons
WindChill Films

As you may have noticed on the invitation, we made a point of mentioning our target audience. We wanted a number of people to be between 18 and 30 years old because we felt that this age range was our demographic. Also, we wanted to make sure that we had people in the audience who were true fans of this genre. That is why we mentioned six films that were similar in nature and requested that they should accept our invitation only if they had seen at least three of these films.

Our audience testing form is the result of a few different forms I have seen over the years. We took the best of each one and created our own. Feel free to use it for your own films. Figure 11.2 shows a copy of the form we used.

SÉANCE Preview Card

Please take a moment to tell us how you feel about the movie you just saw

1) What was your reaction to this movie overall? (Check one)

☐ Excellent
☐ Very Good
☐ Good
☐ Fair
☐ Poor

2) Would you recommend this movie to your friends? (Check one)

☐ Yes, definitely
☐ Yes, probably
☐ No, probably not
☐ No, definitely not

3) How would you describe this movie to your friends?

_____
_____
_____

4) What did you **like most** and what did you **like least** about this movie?

LIKED MOST	LIKED LEAST

5) Please list the scenes and moments you **liked most** and **liked least**, if any. (Please be as specific as possible)

SCENES LIKED MOST	SCENES LIKED LEAST

6) How would you rate the following performances and elements of the movie? (Please check one answer for each item)

	EXCELLENT	VERY GOOD	GOOD	FAIR	POOR
LAUREN	☐	☐	☐	☐	☐
MELINA	☐	☐	☐	☐	☐
GRANT	☐	☐	☐	☐	☐
DIEGO	☐	☐	☐	☐	☐
SPENCE	☐	☐	☐	☐	☐
The story	☐	☐	☐	☐	☐
The scares	☐	☐	☐	☐	☐
The effects	☐	☐	☐	☐	☐
The pace	☐	☐	☐	☐	☐
The title, SÉANCE	☐	☐	☐	☐	☐
The ending	☐	☐	☐	☐	☐
The beginning	☐	☐	☐	☐	☐

Who was your favorite character?_____

(PLEASE TURN CARD OVER)

FIGURE 11.2

7) What are your feelings about the **end** of the movie? (Please be as specific as possible)
_____
_____

8) What are your feelings about the **beginning** of the movie? (Please be as specific as possible)
_____
_____

9) What are your feelings about the **length** of the movie? (Please check one answer)
☐ Just right   ☐ Too short   ☐ Too long

10a) What are your feelings about the **pace** of the movie? (Please check **one** answer)
☐ Moved just right   ☐ Moved too quickly   ☐ Generally OK, but dragged in spots   ☐ Moved too slowly

10b) If you thought the film moved too quickly, too slowly or dragged in spots; in which scenes or parts did you feel this way?

MOVED TOO QUICKLY	MOVED TOO SLOWLY/DRAGGED
_____	_____
_____	_____

11) Please check all of the following terms that you feel describe the movie.

1 ☐	Entertaining	6 ☐	Scary
2 ☐	Boring at times	7 ☐	Interesting characters
3 ☐	Different/original	8 ☐	Well acted
4 ☐	Nothing new/done before	9 ☐	Too dark
5 ☐	Suspenseful	10 ☐	Unbelieveable

12) Did you find anything confusing, hard to follow, unclear or not fully explained in the movie?   ☐ Yes   ☐ No
    If **yes**, please explain:
_____
_____
_____

13) Please indicate your gender: ☐ Male   ☐ Female
14) Please indicate your age: ☐ 17-20   ☐ 21-24   ☐ 25-29   ☐ 30-34   ☐ 35-44   ☐ 45-54   ☐ 55 and over
15) Please check which of the following films you have seen and note the venue in which you FIRST saw them:

	Movie Theater	Rental	Purchased DVD/Video
THE UNDEAD	☐	☐	☐
THE HILLS HAVE EYES (REMAKE)	☐	☐	☐
DAWN OF THE DEAD (REMAKE)	☐	☐	☐
JEEPERS CREEPERS	☐	☐	☐
DARK WATER	☐	☐	☐
BOO	☐	☐	☐
SAW	☐	☐	☐

THANK YOU. PLEASE GIVE THIS COMPLETED SURVEY TO THE PEOPLE COLLECTING THEM AT THE EXIT.

FIGURE 11.2   (*Continued*)

PICK-UP DAY

Pick-up day is something that you want to be sure to include in your budget. When you have a shoot as limited as 14 days there's a chance that something may be missed. Sometimes it as simple as needing a few transition shots, like a hand turning a door knob. Or in the case of my film, Undertaking Betty, the audience testing revealed a question about the relationship between Betty and her husband. To fix the problem we had to book a full day and call back one of the actors. If you end up not needing a pick-up day, that's excellent, but plan for it just to be safe. In the case of *Candy Stripers*, we needed a full day. On *Séance*, we didn't need one at all, and on *Portal*, we required only a half day of shooting.

On *Portal*, we were especially lucky because we were able to use our director's office for the shoot. Geoff Schaaf was our director, and he had a great office space – and the best part is that it was free! When we picked up the camera we had used for the shoot, the gentleman in charge at Sim Video said that there was no charge. Amazing. The few shots we needed were done in less than four hours. Quick and easy.

As soon as we finished, I called Sim Video and asked the assistant what her boss's favorite drink was. She gave me the name of his favorite scotch and I headed to Trader Joe's and bought the scotch with a nice box for it and a thank-you card. I dropped it off at his office, and by the time I got back to my office, there was a message from him on my machine that was amazing. He was so moved by the fact that I had bought and dropped off a gift. His message nearly brought me to tears. He had saved us a day's rental on the camera, and I thought it was important to acknowledge his kindness.

I know that when you are in the middle of producing your movie, you may feel that there are a ton of details to handle, but it's important to stay conscious and present and remember to thank and acknowledge people on a constant basis.

LOCK PICTURE

After the audience testing, it's great to sit down with your editor and director and discuss the responses you've received. Once you are all in agreement, the director goes back into editing for a few days to make the changes.

I remember that with *Séance*, there were only a few changes suggested, but everyone (I mean everyone) had the same thought: to get rid of the two emotional scenes toward the end of the film. I was so upset. Those scenes were fantastic. Award-winning! I had a really hard time agreeing. But if everyone was saying the same thing – "it slowed down the fantastic action adventure scenes where the killer ghost was chasing the girls through the dark creepy tunnels" – I had to surrender. My director and editor went back in to make the changes. Looking back, I wish I had set those scenes aside and had them-color corrected and saved them to put on the DVD as deleted scenes.

When you are happy and totally satisfied with the film, you do what's called "lock picture." The final editing is complete and it's time to move on to your next phase of post: working with your composer, color correction artist, and sound designer.

SALES AGENTS AND FIRST ROUND OF FESTIVALS

If you have time to wait for all aspects of post to be complete before you start sending it off to sales agents (if you are going that route) and festivals, that would be excellent. However, we don't always have that luxury. With *Candy Stripers* and *Séance*, we were so close to AFM and to some of the deadlines for the horror/thriller festivals that we had no choice. We had to send in the DVD from our locked picture. It had temp music, so it gave the feel of a completed film, even though it didn't have the color correction and sound design.

In our attached letter to the festivals and to sales agents, we explained this fact and said that the moment we had the competed film, we would be forwarding it to them. Anyone running those companies is absolutely fine with that, and as it turned out, we had sales agents competing for our films. We also got into and won a number of film festivals. Our final version of the film was ready in time for our sales agent to take it to the market and in time to screen at the festivals in which we had been accepted.

We used WithoutABox.com to gather information for submissions to the festivals. Figure 11.3 is a list from a few of the festival where we submitted *Séance*.

Withoutabox.com: Submission Status

Your audience is waiting.

Logged in as
snowfallfilmsk@cs.com | 2 projects,
12 submissions

14-Aug-2006
3:19pm PDT

BrigitFest: The International Film Festival Submission System

?

ACCOUNT HOME

Submission Status

Create New Project

Find a Festival

Watch List

Short List

Message Boards

Transactions

Preferences

Support

LOGOUT

Select a Project
| Séance |

Current | History

You have **5** current submission for this project.
After a fest is over, the record moves into your
status history.

⊚ **2006 Eerie Horror Film Festival**
3 Annual from October 04, 2006 to October 08,
2006

Tracking	**Entry Fee**: 65.00
ID: 3398	65.00 Rec'd via online 27-jul-2006
Categories:	65.00 Rec'd via online 27-jul-2006
Horror	-65.00 Rec'd via online
Feature	27-jul-2006
Entry date:	
July 27,	**Press Kit**
2006	Rec'd via WAB
Notify date:	**Judging Copy**
15-Sep-2006	Rec'd via Mail 01-aug-2006

View
Confirmation
Page

⊚ **ShockerFest International Film Festival**
4 Annual from October 06, 2006 to October 07,
2006

Tracking	**Entry Fee**: 65.00
ID: SF1114	65.00 Rec'd via online 27-jul-2006
Categories:	
Feature	**Press Kit**
Horror	Rec'd via WAB
Entry date:	
July 27,	**Judging Copy**
2006	Rec'd via Mail 05-aug-2006
Notify date:	
01-Sep-2006	

View
Confirmation
Page

⊚ **International Horror & Sci-Fi Film Festival**
2 Annual from October 13, 2006 to October 15,
2006

FIGURE 11.3

Withoutabox.com: Submission Status

Tracking ID: 3378
Categories: Horror Feature
Entry date: July 27, 2006
Notify date: 01-Sep-2006

Entry Fee: 65.00
65.00 Rec'd via online 27-jul-2006

Press Kit
Not required-do not send

Judging Copy
Rec'd via Mail 02-aug-2006

View Confirmation Page

○ **Eureka Springs Digital Film Festival**
7 Annual from November 07, 2006 to November 12, 2006

Tracking ID: 1100
Categories: Call For Entries
Entry date: July 27, 2006
Notify date: 31-Oct-2006

Entry Fee: 50.00
50.00 Rec'd via online 27-jul-2006

Press Kit
Rec'd via WAB

Judging Copy
Rec'd via Mail 03-aug-2006

View Confirmation Page

● **Chicago Horror Festival**
Annual from October 06, 2006 to October 09, 2006

Tracking ID: Fall06-1592
Categories: Feature Film
Entry date: July 27, 2006
Notify date: 15-Aug-2006

Entry Fee: 50.00
50.00 Rec'd via online 27-jul-2006

Press Kit
Rec'd via WAB

Judging Copy
-Not Yet Received-

View Confirmation Page

ABOUT YOUR SUBMISSION STATUS

● = SUBMITTED Awaiting acknowledgement or receipt of materials
○ = ACKNOWLEDGED Partially satisfied, not yet in consideration
◎ = IN CONSIDERATION All submission requirements satisfied
● = DELETED Submission withdrawn or reversed

If your submission is not showing as IN CONSIDERATION (Green Dot), it is possible that:

FIGURE 11.3   (*Continued*)

MUSIC SCORE, SOUND DESIGNING, COLOR CORRECTION, SPOTTING, AND ADR

If your deal memos are complete by the time you do your audience testing, I would invite your composer, sound designer, and color correction artist to the screening. That way, they will get a sense of the project; better yet, they will also get to meet each other. In fact, I think it's extremely important that your composer and sound designer communicate. I had a situation once where the composer was designing some of the sound effects as part of his score. It ended up conflicting with the effects that the sound designer was inserting. It's very important that they are talking to each other.

As I mentioned earlier, in order to get a better rate, I gave them far more time to do the project, and often they were doing it in their off hours. So when it came to spotting, I was often sitting in a dark theater with my director and DP at midnight viewing the color-corrected scenes or checking up on the music or sound on the film early on a Saturday morning.

With ADR, you certainly don't have to be there. But when it came to any of the lead roles, I made certain that I was there. On some of my bigger-budget films, I really made a point to be at ADR because, as the producer, I felt it was important for me to be available.

In the paperwork that your line producer receives from SAG, there is a sheet where you list any SAG actors who are doing ADR and how much they have been paid. They are paid the same rate that they were paid per day during the shoot. Usually, ADR is only a couple of hours (or less), but they are still paid for the day, which in our case was $100. When complete, this form should be mailed into SAG. In regard to your non-SAG actors, as you will remember from the cast deal memo, ADR (like the table read/wardrobe fitting) was included as part of their overall package.

ADDITIONAL SONGS

Kate and I had some great songs for our end-roll credits in all of our films. We had no money in the budget to pay for the rights to songs, but we were lucky in that we had people write songs that we could use during our end-roll credits or in some cases, allow us to use their existing songs. They would be paid through ASCAP and BMI as the films aired around the world. There was no paperwork to do with ASCAP or BMI. So the only paperwork necessary was the deal memo with the artist. Figure 11.4 shows one of the deal memos used for our wonderful singer, Laurie Foxx, who also happened to be one of our actors on *Portal*.

"PORTAL"

PUBLISHING, MASTER USE & SYNCHRONIZATION LICENSE

April 3, 2007

Laurie Foxx

Dear Ms. Foxx:

This letter shall serve as the agreement between Laurie Foxx ("Licensor") and Portal Film, LLC, 2321 W. Olive Avenue, Suite A, Burbank, CA 91506 (and its licensees or assignees) (collectively referred to as "Licensee") with respect to the Master Use & Publishing Synchronization License granted in connection with the use of the recording "Curiosity Killed The Cat" ("Recording") and the composition embodied therein in the theatrical motion picture entitled "Portal" (which, together with all trailers (including, without limitation, video trailers), advertisements and clips therefrom, shall herein be collectively referred to as the "Picture").

MASTER:	That Master recording, "Curiosity Killed The Cat" performed by the artist professionally known as Inside Sharks.
WRITER:	Laurie Foxx
PUBLISHER(S):	Laurie Foxx
PERFORMING RIGHTS SOCIETY:	ASCAP
ADMINSTRATIVE SHARE:	100%
TERRITORY:	The World
TERM:	In Perpetuity
USAGE:	Multiple uses not to exceed 10:00 minutes

CREDIT   Provided that the Recording is included in the Picture as commercially released, credit will be accorded in the end titles of the Picture in the following form:

"Curiosity Killed The Cat"
Written by Laurie Foxx
Produced by Laurie Foxx and Derek Freeman
Performed by Inside Sharks
©1996 Laurie Foxx
ASCAP

LICENSED USE:	In, and in connection with, the soundtrack of the Picture on a buy-out basis, the non-exclusive, unrestricted and irrevocable right to use and perform the Recording and the Composition

FIGURE 11.4

embodied therein in any manner in and in connection with the Picture, in any and all media and by all means of transmission now known or hereafter devised (including but not limited to theatrical, non-theatrical, free, pay, subscription, toll, direct broadcast, cable and closed circuit television and other transmissions to home monitors, on-line uses, videodiscs, videocassettes, laser discs, DVD, DIVX, CD-ROM, videotape and any other form of audiovisual device) throughout the Territory ("Licensed Use").

LICENSE FEES: For the Licensed Use, Licensee agrees to pay Licensor a combined master use & publishing synchronization fee. No further amounts shall be payable by Licensee to Licensor in connection with the Licensed Use other than applicable ASCAP/BMI royalties associated with any exploitation of the Picture.

SOUNDTRACK ALBUM: In the event that Licensee secures a soundtrack album distributor and the Recording is selected for inclusion on the soundtrack album, Licensee and Licensor shall enter into a good faith negotiation to determine the license fee for such use. Notwithstanding anything herein to the contrary, any such use shall be on a non-exclusive basis.

REPRESENTATIONS

AND WARRANTIES: Licensor represents and warrants that it owns, controls and administers the rights necessary to enter into and fully perform this license and that Licensee's use of the Recording and the Composition embodied therein in accordance with the provisions hereof will not violate the rights of any person or entity. Licensor will indemnify and hold Licensee harmless from any and all claims, liabilities, issues, damages and expenses arising from any breach or alleged breach of Licensor's warranties or representations under this license. Licensor warrants and represents that it has obtained all requisite consents and permissions from the copyright owners of the Master Recording, if applicable, and further represents that it has the permission of the Writer and the applicable publisher(s) of the Composition that it represents for the rights granted in this license, and that Licensor controls 100% of all rights in and to the Composition (including 100% of the copyright thereof) and that Writer shall look solely to Licensor for any remuneration resulting from this license.

MISCELLANEOUS: Licensee is proceeding in reliance on the terms of this license as such terms are specified above. Licensee shall have no obligation hereunder in the event that the Recording is not included in the Picture as generally commercially released other than payment of any and all License Fees under the terms described above. Licensee will not authorize or permit any use of the Recording not set forth herein, all rights not granted herein being reserved to the Licensor.

FIGURE 11.4   (*Continued*)

Please return two fully executed copies of this agreement to: Suzanne Lyons, Portal Film, LLC, 2321 W. Olive Ave., Suite A, Burbank, CA 91506.

Sincerely,

Suzanne Lyons
Portal Film, LLC

Agreed to and Accepted this 4ᵗʰ day of April, 2007.

Social Sec./Tax ID .#:

Laurie Foxx

FIGURE 11.4   (*Continued*)

FRONT-ROLL CREDITS (MAIN TITLES)

Chris Robbins, our "making of" producer and stills photographer, did the style design for the front-roll credits for *Candy Stripers*, *Séance*, and *Portal*. Unbelievable work! Really excellent. We didn't have a lot of money, but we did have time, and that is what worked for us. Like the rest of the postproduction experts, we gave him the time to work on his off hours. So instead of two to three weeks, which would be the norm, everyone had two months.

Regarding the actual credits, Kate came up with a brilliant idea. To be absolutely safe, she went back to each of the lead actor's deal memos and cut and pasted the section that said what order their name was to be placed in, then put all the information on one page. That way, you could see clearly exactly the order and placement of our cast in the front-roll credits. It was so easy. We also gave Chris the list and order of the other names and titles that would be needed for the front-roll credits.

Please be sure to check all the deal memos on all the actors just in case you've made any mistakes. When I was going over the list on *Séance*, I realized that I had used the wrong deal memo for one of the actors, who literally had one line in the movie. She is in the front-roll credits because in her deal memo it says, "Billing on a separate card in the mail titles (provided main titled credits are used and other cast member credits appear therein). Advertising Billing: Artist will be included in all paid advertising where the billing block appears." Please take time and double- and triple-check your deal memos before they go out.

It was my fault, and I am so happy that I caught it before the credits were locked in. Also, just make sure that the way that the actors have signed their deal memos is in fact the way they want their names to appear in the credits. We have had to go back more than once because the actor, director, DP, or someone else has said, "I really want to use my middle initial" or "I really want you to use my nickname." I try to get all that handled as people are signing off on their deal memo during soft prep and preproduction. But it's always safe to do a double check.

Speaking of double-checking, as the producer, when the main titles are complete, be sure to look over the spelling, the placement, and the number of seconds each name is on screen and also check that all names are inside the required aspect ratio. Better to check now than to have a sales agent or distributor call and say that there are problems with the aspect ratio and therefore the titles are not acceptable. That would not only be painful – it would be costly.

In *Candy Stripers*, we chose not to do front-roll credits. The film had a really scary scene right off the bat and we thought it would diminish the impact to lay credits over that scene.

Here is the order for the main titles for *Portal*:

Windchill Films Presents

> *PORTAL*
> Lead actors' names
> Line Producer
> Costume Designer
> Production Designer
> Music By
> Editor
> Director of Photography
> Executive Producers (on a shared card)
> Executive Producers (on a single card)
> Produced By
> Screenplay By
> Directed By

END-ROLL CREDITS

If you think making your movie might be stressful, believe me, it's nothing compared to the end-roll credits. Okay, maybe I'm exaggerating a bit – but not by much. This job may very well fall on your shoulders at this budget level, and it's a job you want to take seriously, because people are very fussy about getting the credit they deserve – and rightly so. Everyone wants their name spelled correctly.

I think Kate and I spent a week just double-checking people's names. Remember that in the investors' subscription agreement, I had added a section where they printed exactly how they wanted their name in the credits. Be sure to do that with every deal memo. In fact, I suggest you have a special area where you ask specifically how they want their name spelled and then have them initial it.

If I am sounding a bit tense about this, it's because I have reason to be. Until I learned to do this, I just assumed that the way people signed their deal memos and agreements was how they wanted to be listed in the credits. Never assume! You don't have the money to keep going back to make changes, so know up front exactly what you need.

Also, be sure to include everyone. For example, our composer had outsourced some of the work to friends of his who were musicians in Switzerland. I had forgotten all about this until I was double-checking and going through every single deal memo and agreement related to the film.

Something to keep in mind is the list of people you want or need to place in the thank-you section. I start working on that list in preproduction because I want to be extra careful here. People want to be acknowledged, and people should be acknowledged – especially at this budget level, where a lot of people may be jumping in to help.

Another item to add to the end-roll credits is a thank-you for – or in some cases the logo of – any companies that have been involved in the film. In *Séance*, the Humane Society's logo was required. Also, we wanted to thank MAC Cosmetics for their contribution of make-up during the shoot. Or, if you were able to get free water or soda, you may be required to do a thank-you or use that company's logo. If you are doing a SAG film, you will need to get the SAG logo as well. Go over every deal memo very carefully. In fact, make a point of highlighting this area in each deal memo as they come into your office, starting as early as soft prep. That will make your life so much easier when it comes to creating the end-roll credits.

On *Candy Stripers*, *Séance*, and *Portal*, we had a lot of songs that we wanted to use in the end-roll credits. Remember, we had promised our investors that we would use songs they or someone in their family had written and performed. So we became very creative and used amazing stills from the film throughout the titles. I think it looks fantastic.

Finally, please don't forget to put the disclaimer at the end of your credits. I just looked at other films and duplicated what others had done. It reads like this:

The characters, events, and places depicted in this film are fictitious. Any similarities to actual persons, living or dead, or actual entities is purely coincidental.

MAKING OF

Like the composer, color correction artist, and sound designer, our "making of" producer was given a longer time period than usual to create the "making of" for the film. During this time, I did spot checking, like I did with music, color, and sound. Chris had already explained how he planned to create the 15-minute production, but I wanted to see it as it progressed. On one of our earlier films, it turned out that the "making of" producer had taken on another job and never delivered one minute. If I had been doing my spot checking, that never would have happened. I would have caught the problem early on, and we could have hired someone else to step in. Spot checking is not only important: it's part of your job.

INVESTORS

Just because I've moved on to postproduction doesn't mean I forget my investors. During this period, I continue to send out my weekly email update as to what Kate and I were doing. I kept them informed throughout the entire process.

Chapter 12

Delivery and Sales Agents

Now that postproduction is complete and you've got your DVD with the burn ("For Viewing Purposes Only"), it's time to go back and look at the festivals where you've sent your initial version of the film. Remember, that version had no color correction, sound design, composer's score, or final main or end credits. So it's time to get the fresh completed DVD off to them. Because pirating has become so frequent, you may want to consider placing your burn a little higher on the screen. Our sales agents have recommended that we do this on our last few films. It's a bit more distracting, but it does discourage pirating.

It's also time to replace the old DVD that went off to your selected sales agents. Get them the new copy and if any newsworthy items have happened during these two to three months, send that news along as well – for example, if you've been accepted into any of the film festivals, if you have a new press release that went out, or one of your cast or anyone else involved in the film has won an award or been cast in a studio movie or TV show. Be sure to include anything new, fun and exciting.

PUT THE HORSE BEFORE THE CART

In the early chapters of this book, I mentioned the importance of being aware of all the elements related to delivering your film long before you ever shoot your first frame. Throughout the entire book, I've been trying to take you through the producing process one tiny step at a time. My goal has been to make film producing look easy because it *is* easy when you break it into small doable pieces. It's no different from anything else in life.

However, although I've been encouraging you to start at the beginning and go step by step, the one area where you must focus on the end before beginning is delivery. I know delivery is one of the final pieces, but it is the one piece that you have to get acquainted with up front. In fact, I would have to say that of the hundreds and hundreds of producers I have talked with over the years, the biggest mistake we've made – and we've all made it – is that we've waited until we're ready to deliver the film before learning about delivery requirements.

There are items in that list that you will need to know about as early in the film making process as the script stage. Kate and I shot *Undertaking Betty* in the fall of 2001, and a year later we got a call from our sales agent saying that she needed our script clearance report to send to the company that was providing our E&O insurance. By the way, no E&O insurance means no domestic delivery of our film! We didn't even know what a script clearance report was, so needless to say, we didn't have one.

A script clearance report is a report done by a company that gives you a list of the areas you need to address long before you shoot your film. Here's an example of something we overlooked that could have kept the film from ever being released. In our romantic comedy *Undertaking Betty*, the mother-in-law chokes on some chocolates and the box of chocolates is sitting on her lap with the name of the company clearly displayed. This would have been fine if it had been a fictitious company or even if an original box had been greeked (obscured) in some way to make the company name look fictitious. However, neither had been done, so it was the real chocolate company's name on the box. We had no letter from the chocolate company granting us permission because we didn't know we needed it.

I have producer friends whose movies have never and will never see the light of day because of these types of problems. One of my students in my low-budget workshop told us how his first film (which cost $300,000 to make!) will never be seen because he had Coke cans through the film, cars with visible license plates, full names that were never cleared for some of his evil characters, and a ton of other products completely visible – yet no permission letter. He just didn't know he needed the rights to use them. As I mentioned in my introduction, I have a friend whose movie will never be released because he failed to get the option agreement signed and now has no chain of title, one of the most critical items on the delivery list. Remember, if you can't deliver the items on the delivery list, you don't get to deliver your movie. No delivery, no money!

Luckily, Kate and I got a break. We called the chocolate company and explained what happened, and they said that they would gladly give us a letter granting us permission. They were incredibly gracious – and we were very, very lucky. I know what some of you are thinking: "If I made that mistake, I would just go in and do a little CGI surgery to clean it up." Sorry, the film is done. Going back in will cost money – a lot of money. Money you probably don't have. A script clearance company will alert you to every possible potential issue long before you ever shoot your film. Handle those items now, not when your film is complete.

MISTAKES CAN BE EXPENSIVE

I hope I have scared you sufficiently to get you to look over a film delivery list well in advance of production. After learning a few of these lessons the hard way, my advice to you is to start working on delivery as early as possible. If you have time during preproduction, principal photography, or postproduction, look at your list and see what you can complete. Kate and I did that during the production of *Portal*, and by the time we had to deliver, 80 percent of it was already done.

Call sales agents and get their lists. Figure 12.1 shows the list we got from one of our sales agents. It is the longest list I've ever received, but I encourage you to use this as your template. Keep in mind that some of the items may be outdated, as technology changes rapidly.

I realize that this list looks daunting, but if it is something you have access to well in advance – which you now do – then you can begin getting prepared in advance.

EXHIBIT "A"

A.   *VIDEO MATERIALS*

1.   *Printmasters:* Access to the original and delivery on DA-88 tapes or Protools Data Files
     of a digital clone of the two-track stereo and/or the six-track 5.1 printmaster
     and, if applicable, any stereo or 5.1 digital printmaster(s) (i.e. the MO Disk)
     from which the Optical Sound Track Negative was made and shall run in
     complete synchronization with the Digital Video masters (item 7 below).

2.   *Music and Effects Mix:* Access to the original and delivery of a DA-88 tapes
     or Protools Data Files containing the 6-track 5.1 or 8-track 6+2 DA-88
     combined mixed music tracks and the 100% fully filled effects track where
     the effects track contains all effects including any effects recorded on the
     dialogue track. This M&E Track shall also include a separate dialogue
     guide track. There shall be no English dialogue in the M&E tracks with the
     exception of English lyrics performed in the songs. If any dialogue is
     treated or used as a sound effect, an additional sweater channel is to be
     used containing said dialogue. If the Picture is to be released with digital
     sound, an additional multi-channel 100% fully filled M&E Track, minus any
     English dialogue or narration, shall be delivered in order to recreate the
     appropriate digital format. This M&E track shall run in complete
     synchronization with the Digital Video masters (item 12 below)

FIGURE 12.1

3. _Dialogue, Music and Effects stems:_ Access to the original and delivery of a DA-88 tapes Protools Date Files containing the 6-track dialogue stems, music stems and sound effects stems, which shall run in complete synchronization with the Digital Video masters (item 6 below).

4. _DAT/CD Music Tracks:_ Access to the original and delivery of (1) Digital Audio Tape ("DAT) or CD copy of original source music which Distributor can utilize in connection with creating trailers or other recordings for the Picture.

5. _Trims and Outs:_ Access during the Term to all digital picture cutouts, trims, lifts, unused outtakes, plus matching soundtrack cutouts (including "dailies", looped dialogue, wild tracks, sound effects tracks, music tracks) on CD, DAT, or AVID back-up and all takes made for the purpose of making the Picture suitable for television exhibition).

6. _Digital Feature Video Masters:_ If available, three (3) Digital Beta video masters of the picture individually manufactured (conversions not acceptable) in the NTSC format and Three (3) in the PAL format as follows: (a) 4x3 standard TV full frame pan and scan; (b) 16x9 format with a 1.78 letterbox hard-matte, matching the aspect ratio of the theatrical check print; and (c) 16x9 format with a 2.35 letterbox hard-matte, matching the aspect ratio of the theatrical check print. Each video master shall be made from the inter-positive of the feature or high definition master. All video masters shall contain stereo audio on Channels 1&2 and stereo M&E on Channels 3&4. The Textless backgrounds shall be attached to the tail of the video masters, 30 seconds after the end of the Picture. The transfer process from film to videotape shall not cause any coloration when a pure white, gray or black scene is reproduced. For full frame or panned and scanned versions, all transfers done from widescreen or anamorphic film elements to tape must be panned and scanned so as to make them acceptable for television framing. In the case of 1.85.1 or 1.66.1 elements, frame lines in the picture (letterboxing) are not acceptable. (White or colored titles in a black field need not be wiped). Main and end credits must fall within title safe. Additionally, manipulation of the video master(s), except with respect to standard color correction, will not be acceptable (i.e. speed-ups, slow downs, squeezes, etc.) without the prior written approval of Fabrication. If not available, Distributor shall manufacture from the Feature High Definition Video Masters and recoup the costs as a Delivery Expense.

7. _Digital Trailer Video Masters:_ Intentionally Deleted.

8. _Feature High Definition Masters:_ Access to, and delivery of two (2) clones, of the original D5 high definition masters full assembled with main and end titles and sound synchronized to image, formatted as follows: (a) 4x3 standard TV full frame pan and scan , stereo audio on channels 1&2 and M&E on channels 3&4; and (b) 16x9 format with a 2.35 letterbox hard-matte, matching the aspect ratio of the theatrical check print, stereo audio on channels 1&2 and M&E on channels 3&4. Each video master shall be made from the inter-positive of the feature or high definition master. The Textless background(s) shall be attached to the tail of the video masters,

FIGURE 12.1 _(Continued)_

30 seconds after the end of the Picture. The transfer process from film to videotape shall not cause any coloration when a pure white, gray or black scene is reproduced. For full frame or panned and scanned versions, all transfers done from widescreen or anamorphic film elements to tape must panned and scanned so as to make them acceptable for television framing. In the case of 1.85.1 or 1.66.1 elements, frame lines in the picture (letter boxing) are not acceptable. (White or colored titles in a black field need not be wiped). Main and end credits must fall within title safe. Additionally, manipulation of the video master(s), except with respect to standard color correction, will not be acceptable (i.e. speed-ups, slow downs, squeezes, etc.) without the prior written approval of Fabrication.

B.   PUBLICITY:

1.   _Color Slides:_ Fifty (50) production Digital color stills on CD_ROM (with minimum 600 dpi) depicting key scenes in the Picture with members of the cast (including principals) appearing therein, and specifically not including pictures of the crew or production equipment. Distributor shall have irrevocable access during the Term to all original photography. Any and all approvals or other authorizations that may be required in connection with the use of said photographs shall be secured prior to delivery.

2.   _Advertising/Publicity Materials:_ A minimum of one (1) hard copy of all advertisements, paper accessories and other advertising materials, if any prepared by the Producer o by any other party in connection with the Picture, including samples of one-sheet posters and individual advertising art elements and transparencies necessary to make proofs thereof. Whenever possible, this material shall also be provided in layered files on a CD Rom.

3.   _Billing Block:_ Two (2) copies of the approved and final billing block to be used in paid advertising of the Picture. One copy shall be provided on hard copy, the other on CD Rom, which must include all required logos.

4.   _Press Kits:_ Two (2) press kits which include a one-page synopsis, production notes, biographies of principal cast and crew members, complete cast and crew list, running time and copyright notice. One copy shall be provided as a hard copy, the other on an IBM word compatible disk.

5.   _Video Trailer:_ Intentionally Deleted.

6.   _Electronic Press Kit:_ If available, one (1) Digital Beta NTSC Beta SP and one (1) PAL Beta SP of the Electronic Press Kit ("EPK") created using 35mm film or broadcast quality videotape. The EPK shall contain interviews with the principal cast, the director and producer as well as behind the scenes footage, production footage, outtakes and deleted scenes. The EPK shall have four-track discreet audio with the voice-over and/or narration on one track, the dialogue on a separate track, the music on a separate track and the effects on a separate track. Any and all approvals and other authorizations that may be required in connection with the use of the EPK shall be secured prior to delivery.

FIGURE 12.1   (_Continued_)

7. *Commentary Tracks:* If available, (1) DA88, DAT or Protools Files of Director, Producer and/or Actor commentary tracks for the Picture.

C. DOCUMENTATION

The following items are to be delivered in 3-ring binders with tab dividers. The first page shall be a table of contents indicating what can be found in that binder. The tab dividers shall reference the numbers for each item indicated below.

1. *Laboratory Access Letter:* Laboratory Access Letters in a form acceptable to Distributor granting Distributor irrevocable access during the Term to all delivery items.

2. *Dialogue Continuity and Spotting List:* One (1) copy in the English language of a detailed, final combined dialogue and action continuity list (delivered on paper and on IBM word compatible disk) with all opening titles and complete end credits appearing in the Picture and the Trailer. One (1) copy in the English language of a spotting list (delivered on paper and on IBM word compatible disk) containing all spotted dialogue, narration, sound vocals, all opening titles and complete end credits appearing in the Picture and the Trailer, as well as cut-by-cut description of the action of the Picture in its final form, with time code in and time code out and the total duration of each line of dialogue.

3. *Shooting Script:* The final shooting script of the Picture, on paper and on IBM word compatible disk.

4. *Contractual Obligations and Restrictions:* A statement, on paper and on IBM word compatible disk, summarizing the following contractual credit obligations and restrictions, in a format to be provided by Distributor:

a. Main and end screen credits;

b. Paid advertising credits;

c. Dubbing of any player's voice into another language;

d. Use of the likeness of any talent in any advertising, promotions, etc;

e. Talent travel; and

f. Editing and post-production (timing of the picture, video transfers, television editing, etc.).

The statement shall also include all talent approval rights as they apply to stills, artistic renderings, biographies, credits, merchandising and tie-ins, and any related matters. If there is no contractual obligation to accord credit, which has been accorded in the billing block, the "obligation" should be stated as "Producer's Discretion."

5. *Cast/Talent/Personnel Agreements:* Copies of fully-executed Agreements for the writer, director, producer, composer and principal cast members, as well as all other cast members, talent and personnel who are afforded credit on-screen in the main titles or the billing block.

FIGURE 12.1 (*Continued*)

6. *Affidavit:* An affidavit sworn to by an officer of the production company stating that all costs of production have been paid for and there are no liens, encumbrances or claims as of the date of such Affidavit.

7. *Releases:* Signed releases from all persons identified by name or likeness in the Picture who do not have signed contracts.

8. *Other Agreements:* All product placement Agreements and clip licenses. Access to all other Agreements and documents relating to the Picture (employment Agreements, clearances, releases, location Agreements, and evidence of payment in full respect thereto) as may be reasonably required.

9. *Music Cue Sheet:* Three (3) copies of a Music Cue Sheet stating for each composition in the Picture the title, the composers, publishers, copyright owners, usage, performing rights society, as well as the film footage and running time.

10. *Music Licenses:* Fully-executed synchronization and master use licenses on an all media full worldwide buy-out basis, inclusive of advertising and publicity rights, in perpetuity, for each item of licensed music used in the Picture; fully-executed Agreements for each obligations); and evidence of payment under each synchronization and master use license and composer Agreement.

11. *Producer's Errors and Omissions Insurance:* One (1) copy of the policy and one (1) Certificate of standard producer's Errors & Omissions Liability Insurance under a standalone policy with minimum coverage of US $1,000,000 per claim and US $3,000,000 in the aggregate with no restrictions, with a deductible amount not more than US $10,000 providing coverage for Distributor, its parent, subsidiary, and related entities, its distributors, licensees, sub-distributors, affiliates and assigns, and their respective officers, directors, shareholders, employees, and agents of the foregoing as "Additional Insureds", with evidence showing that the premium for such policy has been paid in full for 3 years from the date of delivery and a guarantee of at least 60 days written notice of cancellation or other material change to the policy. For the avoidance of doubt, so-called "Rights Endorsement Policies" are not acceptable. One (1) letter to the carrier of said policy authorizing Distributor to order certificates and endorsements naming its licensees/designees as Additional Insureds when necessary at no charge to Distributor. Distributor hereby acknowledges that it shall provide coverage through its Distributor's E&O coverage and recoup as a Delivery Expense.

12. *Chain of Title:* Complete chain of title materials filed with the United States Library of Congress and reasonably suitable to Distributor's insurance carrier and /or primary lender evidencing Producer's ownership and each step towards Producer's ownership of the Picture and all underlying property and the Producer's right, title and authority to grant the rights being granted hereunder. The chain of title shall include a cover sheet summary of the chain, including name and significance of each document in the Chain of Title.

FIGURE 12.1 *(Continued)*

13.   *Certificate of Authorship:*   One (1) original Certificates of Authorship.

14.   *Certificate of Origin:*   Ten (10) original notarized Certificates of Origin of the Picture certifying that the Picture was produced in the United States and is a Picture of the United States origin and that Distributor is the exclusive distributor of the Picture in the Territory, as defined in the Agreement.

15.   *Copyright Registration Certificates:*   One (1) filed U.S. Copyright Registration Certificate/Form PA) for the screenplay and one (1) filed U.S. Copyright Registration Certificate/Form PA for the Picture. If the certificate (Form PA) has not yet been returned, Producer shall deliver a copy of the certificate (Form PA) to the Copyright Office. Producer agrees to deliver one (1) copy of each of the Copyright Registration Certificates to Distributor when received.

16.   *Title Report:*   One (1) title report with a clean legal opinion from a recognized source (e.g. Dennis Angel or Thomson & Thomson) which researches prior uses of the same or similar titles, showing that the title of the Picture is available for use without infringing any other person or entity's rights. If the title of the Picture has insurance coverage, a copy of the Title Report submitted to Producer's insurance carrier shall suffice.

17.   *Copyright Research Report:*   One (1) copyright research report from a recognized source (e.g. Thomson & Thomson), showing that Producer has good clear title to the picture and all underlying rights.

18.   *Copyright Mortgage and Assignment:*   One (1) original mortgage of copyright and assignment, fully executed and notarized by Producer, granting Distributor a security interest in and to the Picture and the rights granted to Distributor under the Agreement. Distributor shall prepare such documents for Producer's review and execution.

19.   *Short Form Assignment/Instrument of Transfer (notarized):*   Three (3) original notarized assignments of the rights granted Distributor in and to the Picture under the Agreement. Distributor shall prepare the document for Producer's review and execution.

20.   *Dolby or Ultra Stereo License:*   Film is not Dolby or Ultra Stereo, intentionally deleted.

21.   *Author's Confirmation:*   A notarized Author's confirmation certifying that said author(s) has been paid in full for his services and has no claims against the story, the screenplay, or the Picture of any kind whatsoever, which statement has been signed by the author(s).

22.   *Director's Confirmation:*   A notarized Director's confirmation certifying that said director(s) has been paid in full for his services and has no claims against the story, the screenplay or the Picture of any kind whatsoever, which statement has been signed by the director(s).

23.   *DGA letter:*   If the Picture is DGA, a copy of a letter from the DGA approving the main and end credits, a copy of all documents required by the DGA for residual payments and all DGA deal memos. If the Picture is not DGA, a letter from the Producer stating the film is not DGA.

FIGURE 12.1   *(Continued)*

24.	*WGA letter:* If the Picture is WGA, a copy of a letter from the WGA approving the main and end credits. If the Picture is not WGA, a letter from the Producer stating the film is not WGA.
25.	*SAG letter:* If the Picture is SAG, the final SAG cast list and all SAG deal memos. If the Picture is not SAG, a letter from the Producer stating the film is not SAG.
26.	*IATSE letter:* If the Picture is IATSE, a copy of the IATSE Agreement for the Picture and a letter from Producer confirming that all requirements of IATSE have been met. If the Picture is not IATSE, a letter from the Producer stating the film is not IATSE.
27.	*Credits:* A copy of the title's house's final main and end credits on paper, as they appear in the Picture.
28.	*Cast and Crew List:* The final production cast and crew lists.
29.	*MPAA:* Intentionally deleted.
30.	*English:* All documents delivered hereunder shall be in English; the Picture as originally photographed shall be in English language and not dubbed.

FIGURE 12.1   (*Continued*)

THE COST OF DELIVERY

You can see from some of the items on the example list how important it is to raise the money for delivery while you are raising funding for the film. Why people don't do that is a complete mystery to me. We estimated at our budget that we would need an additional $20,000 for delivery costs. Another way to come up with the amount would be to go through the list and make some calls to get estimates. See what you might want to take on yourself that could cut down on the costs. For example, when we checked on the price for the dialog spotting list, we realized that it was pretty expensive at nearly $2,000, so Kate said she would learn how to do it and we would save that money. It took her two weeks to complete the dialog spotting and it was a pretty grueling experience, as she had to go through the time-coded DVD line by line and create the dialog spotting. But saving $2,000 was worth it.

ITEMS TO WATCH FOR

A pan-and-scan is one thing to watch for. It is a method of printing films for presentation on television that modifies the rectangular theater image by trimming the sides and focusing on significant action within the newly truncated image. When it comes to the pan-and-scan of your film, I suggest that you or your director be present during this process. Otherwise, if it is left to the distributor, you may very well end up with a film that you're not happy with. When we saw the pan-and-scan that the distributor had done on one of our films, we realized that they had not taken the time to include all the great stuff that was happening on the periphery of the screen, so we had it redone. Because we had the money in our delivery items to pay for it, it was worth it to have it done correctly. When you or your director is in the suite sitting with the pan-and-scan technician, you can make sure that he or she is including all the action that is happening on every corner of the screen.

A couple of other important items are the title report and the copyright report. These are items that are part of the delivery list. The title report is needed to show that there are no other films using the identical name that you are using as your film's title. Kate and I used Dennis Angel's company on all of our films. Dennis Angel's company provides legal chain of title opinions. They review all the full documents and give an opinion as to who owns the various rights in the property. Figure 12.2 shows the title report we got back on *Séance*.

The Law Offices of
Dennis Angel
1075 Central Park Avenue, Suite 306
Scarsdale, New York 10583

Telephone: (914) 472-0820
            (212) 239-4225
Fax: (914) 472-0826
Email: DANGELESQ@AOL.COM

Of Counsel:
Robert Angel
Washington, D.C.

June 23, 2006

Via Mail and Facsimile

Ms. Kate Robbins
Windchill Films
2321 West Olive Avenue, Suite A
Burbank, CA 91506

Request: **TITLE REPORT AND OPINION**
Re: **SÉANCE**

Dear Kate:

You have advised us that Windchill Films wishes to use the above title for a motion picture.

The following compilations, indices and records have been checked for possible uses of the above title:

o   Works registered for United States copyright from 1946 to date, including motion pictures, television, books, periodicals and contributions, screenplays, teleplays, scripts, plays, music, artwork and other works;

o   The United States Patent and Trademark Office records for all classes of marks, currently registered or pending;

o   Professional and Industry subscription sources, indices and collections compiled in our own library as well as The Library of Congress for the following: motion pictures, television, video (all formats), plays, radio, literature, music, etc.; and

o   Various Internet search engines for website references and domain name registrations.

The search discloses:

• No use of this exact title for a registered trademark.

FIGURE 12.2

MOTION PICTURES

SÉANCE: completed motion picture from Windchill Films and Snow Falls Films, produced by Suzanne Lyons and Kate Robbins, written and directed by Mark L. Smith, starring Kandice Erickson, Ruby Garson, and Joel Geist (according to Studiosystem.com updated June 23, 2006).

Of interest are the following:

1. **SÉANCE**: 2004 short from the Netherlands, written and directed by Tamer Avkapan, starring Herald Adolfs and Peter Faber.

2. **SÉANCE**: motion picture from Harbourside Pictures and Beyond Films, with producer Bryan Lowe and director Richard Franklin that was reportedly in development (according to Studiosystem.com updated August 27, 2003).

TELEVISION

1. **SÉANCE**: 2002 30-minute television drama produced by Gil Adler, with executive producers Richard Donner, Robert Zemeckis, and others, directed by Gary Fleder, written by Harry Anderson, starring Ben Cross, Cathy Moriarty-Gentile, and John Vernon, broadcast over HBO as a presentation of the anthology series "Tales From The Crypt."

2. **SÉANCE**: 2001 television motion picture from 4 Lane Productions, produced by Lyle Howry and Shelly Kirwood, directed by John Preston, starring Corey Feldman, Shannon Malone, and Adam West, offered for television worldwide by Kismetic Productions, Inc.

3. **SÉANCE**: English title for the 2000 Japanese television motion picture "Korei" from Kansai Telecasting Corp. and Twins Japan, directed by Kiyoshi Kurosawa, based on the novel "Séance On A Wet Afternoon" by Mark McShane, starring Koji Yakusho and Jun Fubuki, offered on DVD by Home Vision.

Of interest is the following:

"Derren Brown: SÉANCE": 2004 British television special from Objective Productions, directed by Stefan Stuckert, featuring host/illusionist Derren Brown, broadcast over Channel 4 (UK).

LITERATURE

1. **SÉANCE**: book edited by Christine Wertheim and Matias Viegener published by Make Now Press in 2005.

FIGURE 12.2   (*Continued*)

2. SÉANCE: book by Jo Gibson published by Kensington Publishing Corporation in 1996.

3. **SÉANCE: A Guide For Living**: book by Suzane Northrop with Kate McLoughlin published by Alliance Pub. Co. (Brooklyn, NY) in 1994 and distributed by National Book Network.

4. SÉANCE: magazine first published quarterly in Fall 1988.

5. **The SÉANCE**: book by Joan Lowery Nixon published by Harcourt Brace Jovanovich (New York) in 1980 and in paperback by Harcourt Children's Books in 2004.

6. **The SÉANCE And Other Stories**: book by Isaac Bashevis Singer published by Farrar, Straus & Giroux (New York) in 1968 and in paperback by Random House Publishing Group in 1980.

7. **SÉANCE**: book by Mark McShane published for the Crime Club by Doubleday (Garden City, NY) in 1962; first published in 1961 under the title "Séance On A Wet Afternoon."

There is other literature with the title **SÉANCE**.

MUSIC

1. **SÉANCE**: song performed by Nicholas Payton on the Warner Bros. Records CD "Sonic Trance" released in 2003.

2. **SÉANCE**: song performed by Joe Stump on the Leviathan CDs "Conquer & Divide" released in 2002 and "Shredology" released in 2005.

3. **SÉANCE**: song performed by Possessed on the album "Beyond The Gates" from 1988, released on CD in 1999 by Relativity.

4. **The SÉANCE**: song by Hampton Hawes performed by the Hampton Hawes Trio on the album **The SÉANCE** from 1966, released on CD by Original Jazz Classics in 1991.

There is other music titled **SÉANCE**.

COPYRIGHTED WORKS

A search of the United States Copyright Office records under the title **SÉANCE** discloses registrations for several of the above-mentioned works as well as an unpublished video directed by Debbie Meyer from 1988, unpublished screenplays,

FIGURE 12.2 (*Continued*)

television episodes, other literature, songs, sound recordings, artwork, and other unpublished works.

INTERNET

A limited search of various Internet search engines discloses domain name registrations for **SÉANCE** as well as website references. Enclosed are sample pages from our search.

Of possible interest are the following:

1. "Séance On A Wet Afternoon": 1964 motion picture written and directed by Bryan Forbes, based on the novel of the same title by Mark McShane, starring Kim Stanley and Richard Attenborough, offered for television in North America by Janus Films, offered on DVD by Home Vision.

2. A search of the United States Patent and Trademark Office records discloses the enclosed trademark under the title "The Official Houdini Séance."

Titles of possible interest include "Sunday Séance" (2004 British short), etc.

OPINION

You will note that our search of the above categories discloses several uses of the title **SÉANCE** including for your completed motion picture. As our search fails to disclose any other use of this title for a recent full-length theatrical motion picture and in view of the descriptive nature of the title, in my opinion it would be safe for Windchill Films to use the title **SÉANCE** for its above-mentioned motion picture.

Sincerely,

Dennis Angel

DA:ks

FIGURE 12.2 (*Continued*)

In addition, you will be required to obtain a copyright report. I realize we talked about copyrights way back in Chapter 3 and again in Chapter 11, but this is a little different. This report proves that you have done the copyright paperwork for you film. Figure 12.3 shows the one we got back from Dennis Angel on *Séance*.

The Law Offices of
Dennis Angel
1075 Central Park Avenue, Suite 306
Scarsdale, New York 10583

Telephone: (914) 472-0820
(212) 239-4225
Fax: (914) 472-0826
Email: dangelesq@aol.com
www.dangelesq.com

Of Counsel:
Robert Angel
Washington, D.C.

December 14, 2006

Via Mail and E-mail

Ms. Suzanne Lyons
Séance, LLC
2321 West Olive Avenue, Suite A
Burbank, CA 91506

Request: **COPYRIGHT REPORT**
Re: **SÉANCE**

Dear Suzanne:

The motion picture **SÉANCE** from Windchill Films and Snow Falls Films, produced by Suzanne Lyons and Kate Robbins, written and directed by Mark L. Smith, starring Kandis Erickson, Ruby Garson, and Joel Geist, is reportedly completed (according to Studiosystem.com updated June 23, 2006).

According to IMDb.com, this motion picture was executive produced by Ronald P. Bova, Jason Eaton, Mike Kimmel, Ron Nicynski, Terry Smith, and James Thorpe, and was the winner of "Best Picture" at Shockerfest 2006.

A search of the United States Copyright Office records fails to disclose any copyright registration for this motion picture, as yet.

A screenplay **SÉANCE** was registered for United States copyright as an unpublished work in the name of Mark L. Smith on May 20, 2005 under entry PAu-2-953-878.

A search of the Assignment and Related Documents Indices and Document Index of the Copyright Office and the Copyright Office Automated Documents Catalog fails to disclose any recorded document relating to this motion picture, as yet.

There are many documents recorded in the Copyright Office under the title "Séance" none of which appear to relate to the above-mentioned motion picture.

Please let me know if you have any questions with respect to this Report.

Sincerely,

Dennis Angel

DA:ks

FIGURE 12.3

I am showing you this report because, as you can see, even though Kate and I had sent the copyright registration form and payment to Washington months prior, the copyright office had not yet processed our forms. So attached to this report, we included a copy of the forms we had submitted, along with a copy of the check showing that we had paid the registration fee.

SALES AGENT OR NOT?

If you choose to self-distribute, you won't need to worry about the next piece, but I still think it's wise to know the details about getting a sales agent. You may change your mind at some point and decide that you do want to go for the sales agent, so it's always good to have the knowledge.

THE TABLES ARE TURNING

Things have changed quite dramatically in the past few years. The fact that many producers are looking to self-distribute, the alarming rate of increase in pirating, and the downturn in the economy (which affects the amounts territories are willing to pay) have caused havoc for sales agents and distributors. And of course the digital camera has made it possible for thousands more producers to make their films under amazingly low budgets, causing a glut of product. For the first time in history, the tables are turning, and many sales agents are being forced to close up shop.

The Internet, in particular, has created a new way of doing business, and producers are taking full advantage of this. In the next chapter, I interview a few people who are enjoying the independence and potential financial benefits of self-distribution.

PROBLEMS WITH THE OLD MODEL

Only a few years ago, when we were doing our deals on *Candy Stripers*, *Séance*, and *Portal*, we were very much at the mercy of whatever deal our sales agent would bring to us from the distributor. Unless there was big competition for the film, there was no negotiating with the distributors. Take it or leave it! And trying to get any back end was difficult. Getting a back end return is important not necessarily because of the money (you'll probably never see any of it) but because it would be great to have the quarterly records so that if your film is doing well, you can use that information to raise money for your next film. Even if you have a great sales agent or producer's rep, they can push only so hard to get you the best deal with the distributors.

BUY-OUTS

Another difficult element for the producer is the fact that the distributor in each territory does what is called a "buy-out." In other words, they pay a flat fee for the film for a specified number of years. Because of this, it is extremely important that you tell your sales agent that you want the term of the deal to be as short as possible. It is imperative that you ask for this option specifically, because your sales agent really doesn't care, and if the distributor in that territory says they want 15 or 20 years, your sales agent will agree. So be sure to have a conversation with them about this and request that they keep the number of years to five or seven for foreign territories. You want to be able to have the opportunity to resell the film in each territory, and more important, you want to get your films back for your own library down the road. The domestic sale is the most difficult in terms of the number of years, so try to get it down to 15 years if possible.

CHANGES ARE HAPPENING

The good news is that distributors, including domestic distributors, are far more open to negotiating deals today. They are even doing split rights deals. Producers are able to maintain the rights to sell DVDs (and VODs) on their own websites, keep the right to create and sell merchandise related to their film, and a ton of other options that were not even open for discussion just a few years ago.

YOUR DEAL WITH A SALES AGENT: DO YOUR RESEARCH!

When it comes to doing your deal with the sales agent who will be taking your film to the markets, be sure to do your due diligence. When Kate and I first started Snowfall Films, we made the decision to go to AFM, and we met nearly every sales agent at that market. We had done our homework in advance and researched who was focusing on the types of films we were looking to produce. We read the bumper issues (weekly issues) of the *Hollywood Reporter* that highlighted the previous year's film markets. The trades list not only each sales agent but also what films they are selling so you can get a fairly good sense of who is doing what.

In addition, we started asking our mentors and other producers whom they would recommend. So even if you can't get to a market, when you are looking to choose a particular sales agent, contact other producers who have worked with them to find out what their experience was.

Hopefully, you will have healthy competition with more than one company wanting your film. That way the power is in your hands when it comes to doing the deal. However, even if you have only one sales agent interested in selling your project, there are certain items to be aware of when it comes to making your deal with them. Here are eleven points to consider while doing your deal.

Expenses

For years, sales agents have had a fixed amount they put in their deals for their expenses. It was $50,000 to $75,000, and on the low-budget films, that's crazy. With the amount of money we are now getting per territory, $50,000 to $75,000 for expenses is just way too high. I know they are going to be doing a trailer, getting posters and one-sheets, and of course attending multiple markets. All of that costs money, but you are not their only film. I have done a deal at $15,000 and one at $25,000 for their expenses. Even if it means you have to do your own trailer, it's worth bringing the cost of their expenses down. The way it works is that their expenses come off the first money in, so please keep that in mind when you are telling your investors about the first sale. *Please note:* If you do end up having to do your own trailer, be sure to ask for their advice and suggestions before you produce it. The trailer can make or break a deal, and sales agents have been selling films to international buyers for years; they know what makes a great and marketable trailer.

Commission

When you are dealing with sales agents' commissions, I would agree to do no more than a 20 percent commission. In fact, what Kate and I have done on a few of our films is offer a two-tier deal. Until we reached the amount where our investors would be paid back, our sales agent would get a 15 percent commission on foreign territory sales, and the minute we had reached that amount, they would begin to get a 20 percent commission. It was fair and it created an incentive at the same time. If your sales agent is planning to handle your domestic sale, the norm for a domestic sale is a 10 percent commission.

Get a Copy of Each Territory Deal

Getting a copy of each territory deal sounds like something you would assume – of course you would be privy to the contracts done with the territories on *your* film. We assumed it, and in two different cases when I called to say that I had received the quarterly report and the check but had not received the territory deal memos, I was told that we had no right to them. Years from now, how am I supposed to renew the sales? That sales agent will be long gone, and I will need to renew those territory sales. It is crazy that I don't have a copy of the original contracts. In fact, we are dealing with that very issue right now on one of our first films. We are in the process of renewing nine different territories, and I can't imagine what that would be like if we weren't able to refer to their original deal. So please make a note of this point, and although it sounds like common sense, make certain to put it in your contract with your sales agent.

Keep the Number of Years Low and Get Back-End Deals

Talk to your sales agent before every market and remind them that when they are doing each territory sale, you want them to keep the term (number of years) to a minimum. You want to be able to resell to those territories in a reasonable number of years. For foreign territories, try to keep the terms of a deal to no more than five to seven years. Of course, this is more difficult to demand when it comes to the domestic sales, because the norm is often 15 years or longer. Try to get it down to 10 or 12, but certainly no more than 15. In addition, have your sales agent push for back-end deals, especially if they are handling your domestic sale. As I mentioned earlier, it's not so much about the money as it is about having the quarterly reports that will let you know how your film is selling. If it's doing well, it's great ammunition for your next business plan.

Money Goes Into *Your* Bank Account

Having the money go into your bank account may be an issue for some sales agents, but I would fight for this one. Kate and I have done this in the past, and it makes everything so easy. You don't have to wait until the quarterly or semiannual report from your sales agent to see your money on territory sales that were done months and months before. And in many cases (we've had a few), you don't have to be hounding the sales agents to send you the check. It should go directly into your account, and then you pay the money owed to the sales agent for their commission and expenses. After all, it's your money. That way there is no waiting and you can get it directly back to your investors.

If they have a concern about your paying them their commission promptly, all you have to do is state in your deal with them that you will mail (or messenger) their check to them within 24 hours of the money going into your film's bank account. It is simple, fast, and a win/win for everyone. Otherwise, when your money goes into their account first, you run the risk of getting it late – or worse, not at all. We have had two different situations over the years in which our sales agent literally took the money and used it, in one case to pay off debts on bigger projects, and in another case just took it and left the industry – and the country. It's your money, and it should go directly into your account.

Have Them Check With You if the Amount Is Below the Estimate

This point is fairly standard, but just be certain that it is in your deal. You might want to remind your sales agent prior to each market just so they are conscious and will remember to call you if they get an offer that comes in below their estimated amounts.

Which Territory Sold?

Knowing which territory sold may sound like common sense as well, but we had one situation where we would get a quarterly report with a check included, but there would be no way of knowing which territory it was from. This was the company that refused to give us the territory contracts. I wanted to know so that I could not only keep track but also inform the investors. So be aware of this issue and include it in your deal memo with your sales agent.

Do They Have an E&O Umbrella?

Often, your sales agent who is doing your foreign territory sales will handle your domestic sale as well. You will need to purchase E&O insurance if you get a domestic sale, and if your sales agent has an existing E&O umbrella policy, it may be cheaper for you to purchase it under their policy. We have always had to buy our own E&O insurance, but I would ask your sales agent before you purchase your own.

Get a Box Of Dvds

Okay, this sounds downright silly. You would think that if the domestic sale includes a DVD release, you would automatically get a box to give to your investors, your lead actors, and your director. I have never thought to put it in the deal with our sales agent. It was always something that we just assumed. Well as I have said before: never assume. Put it in the sales agent's deal so that they can put it in the deal they do with the domestic distributor. If you use a producer's rep or someone else to do your domestic sale, mention it to them. I have had to fight to get even a handful of DVDs in each case – and on some films, we've received none.

If They are Doing Your Domestic Sale, be at That Meeting

If your sales agent is doing your domestic deal and you are in the same city, I strongly suggest you be at those meetings. The domestic sale is extremely important, and these days, the domestic distributors are far more open to split rights deals. This is your baby; given that the domestic deal demands a longer term, it's important that you know exactly what you're entering into. If you aren't at these meetings, make absolutely certain that you speak with your sales agent or producers rep before they do the deal and go over exactly what you want with them. In addition, make certain that you get copies of the contract and go over it line by line until you are happy with every detail.

Exit Clause

When you are doing your deal with your sales agent, be sure to put an exit clause in their contract. For example, if they have not sold a certain number of territories that total a specific amount of money by a specified date, then you get the project back from them free and clear. That way you are able to go to another sales agent and begin again. I think in one of our deals, we specified that if they didn't bring in a minimum of $375,000 within 24 months from delivery (which would give them time to attend the three major markets twice), then we got our film back and were free to shop for a new sales agent, should we choose to. The major markets are the AFM, Berlin, and Cannes. By the time your sales agent has attended each one at least two times, they have usually exhausted the possibility of a sale, and they have most likely lost interest in your film.

Chapter 13

Distribution Alternatives and Film Exposure: Guest Interviews

Today, we have access to so many ways to find our audience and get our movies out to them. The Internet has had an impact on the world, touching every facet of our lives, and the film industry is no exception. It has provided filmmakers with a venue to create buzz, enroll an audience, and offer a platform from which to sell and market our films.

Distribution consultant Peter Broderick suggests that film producers should be more proactive in their distribution strategy. In Rebort's article "Rethinking Film Distribution" (www.iofilm.co.uk), he asked Peter about the opportunities now available. Broderick said,

The filmmakers that are doing the best are the ones that have chosen some kind of hybrid strategy. Service deals, for example, can be a very effective way to go. In a service deal, the filmmaker fronts the bill for prints and advertising costs and hires a company to provide distribution services, from promoting the film to collecting revenues from exhibitors. The filmmaker is in effect renting the distribution system for theatrical release, but pays less for the distribution fee. The producer is risking his or her own money, but retains control over the film and continues to have final say in the promotion and cost. New technology continues to offer unprecedented distribution opportunities and digital downloads are becoming more common.

In a *New York Times* article, "No Film Distributor? Then D.I.Y.," John Anderson cautions film producers who are considering self-distribution to learn how the marketplace works. In the case of *Bottle Shock*, Anderson says that

by going their own way, the director and producer retained the DVD and other rights to their film. They also were able to control how their movie was rolled out and marketed. That didn't mean that they didn't hire professionals to help make it all happen. To navigate the treacherous world of film distribution, Randall Miller and Jody Savin hired a consultant, a company to handle the physical distribution, and a publicist.

The site www.youmakemedia.com featured an article by Chris Van Patten, "Indies Paving a Self-Distribution Trail." He talks about the film *Four-Eyed Monsters* by Arin Crumley and Susan Buice and how they found success using the self-distribution path:

Through a massively successful video podcast and their connection to fans via social tools, they were able to garner enough support to set up a self-distribution platform. Fans could go to the movie website and request a screening. If enough people requested a screening in a certain area, the pair would call local theatres and set up a time and date."

I've become a big fan of Ellen Pittleman's blog (www.baselineintel. com). I spoke with Ellen, who really is a wealth of information for the indie film producer. Her article "What Are the Latest Online Self-Distribution Options for Filmmakers?" is invaluable. Although she warns that online self-distribution is not making film producers tons of money, it is early in the game and the future may hold a lot of surprises. She explains that

certain sites download movies onto one's hard drive or onto a physical device, while other sites stream films, keeping the intellectual property on the licensor's server so that it never rests with the consumer. The digital download of films, download to own or electronic sell through, as it's often called, is frequently defined as a home entertainment right and the kind of model that companies like Amazon and Apple initially used. Streaming of films is typically a VOD right so it's important that a producer understand which rights they're granting to a licensor if they're splitting a grant of right across platforms.

Some indie producers who don't have access to theatrical exhibition or TV channels; Pittleman thinks that these producers should take advantage of the digital model:

User-generated services like YouTube provide a platform, and with more than 600 million active users, Facebook could also become a serious competitor to film/ TV-centric digital distribution companies such as Netflix and Hulu.

In the same article, Pittleman suggests several sites that offer platforms and toolkits for self-distribution, each with their own approach to monetization:

SnagFilm and Open Film, for example, sell ad space and share the revenue with the licensee. MoPix is the newest addition to the self-distribution world and it's an app-based platform for content. Filmmakers or distributors can upload all content they would put on a deluxe DVD. One sets his/her own prices and makes the film available for viewing through the app and/or can use the app merely as a marketing tool for the film. Egg Up is an online media distribution application that facilitates both film rentals and sales by enabling a filmmaker to distribute films on multiple platforms and websites with creation of what they're calling the "egg." The "egg" is a secured film file that contains your film, images, trailers, and extras. A filmmaker is able to distribute the film on his or her own website and other online retailers without any set-up fees.

Pittleman cautions us that even though as film producers we now have these amazing opportunities to self-distribute our films worldwide, if we want to be successful at doing so, we must be brilliant at marketing our films and driving traffic to our sites.

I was so excited about all the new opportunities available to us. As a film producer, I chose a variety of producers, directors, and even a distribution expert and spoke with them about the power of self-distribution, self-marketing, the advantages of film festivals, and the impact that the Internet is having on our industry. I've asked for their suggestions and advice regarding this new terrain that we are now about to explore.

Marc Rosenbush

Film Producer and Founder of the Company Internet Marketing for Filmmakers

What prompted you as a film producer to get involved in Internet marketing?

I came to Los Angeles as naïve as anybody else. I'm going to move to LA, I'm going to make my first movie, I'm going to go to Sundance, Harvey Weinstein's going to buy it, and I'm going to get a three-picture deal and be rich. We all want to believe that the fairy princess is going to come down and wave the wand and it's going to happen. That is a myth. Luckily, while I was making my first movie, I paid my bills as an Internet marketing strategist outside the film industry. And I soon realized that there were marketing techniques available that no one in the industry was using.

The digital revolution democratized making films, so anyone with a camera and Final Cut Pro can make a movie. Getting noticed has gotten harder and harder and harder. There are thousands and thousands of movies being made, so I thought Internet marketing would be a way to give me an edge, and forming Internet Marketing for Filmmakers is allowing me to share that knowledge with other producers.

Do you feel that sales agents and distributors are aware of the impact that the Internet is having?

No, I don't think so. Even the distributors that are doing the digital distribution for you for the most part don't know the Internet marking world, so they don't know how to market it except in the old way. A few of them are ahead of the curve, and they understand that this digital stuff is the key to the universe but they have no idea how to do it.

What about producers today? Do you feel that we are really awake to the possibilities regarding the Internet?
The concept of Internet marketing is still a little bit alien to filmmakers, but the concept of social media they get now, and they get that they have to do it. At the same time, filmmakers really have no idea what they're doing. They think that, "Okay, I have a Facebook page and I have a website, so why am I not getting rich?" They don't understand that there is a methodology. There are principles at work of leveraging an audience, of building a relationship with an audience. In fact, my new mantra is "Audience first, movie second."

Here's the number one thing – *it is about identifying an audience, a specific audience*. I talk a lot about this in my workshops since I believe that there's a big difference between demographics and psychographics. Demographics, for example, are "males, 18–24." That is such a broad category that unless you have a $20 million to $30 million studio marketing budget, you're not going to get their attention because there's too many things going on. On the other hand, a psychographic is more like a niche. I like the term "psychographic" because what it refers to is the way they think and what their interests are.

This is new to me. Can you give me an example?
Yes, I'll do better than that, I'll give you an example from the movie I'm working on now. It's a vampire movie based on a graphic novel published by DC Comics. Vampire movies are popular, that's great. Lots of people like vampire movies, that's a good niche, but it's still a really big niche. There are the people who like *Twilight*, which is one kind of vampire movie, sort of the teenage girl's vampire movie, and there's the people that like *True Blood*, which is a different type of vampire project. What I've got is a sort of a David Lynch–y surreal vampire project with Eastern philosophy under the surface. So it's sort of an interesting cerebral kind of movie. At the same time, on the surface, it's got all the sex and violence to be marketable.

So I start thinking, okay, forget about the word "vampire" for a moment. What is the psychographic, what is a niche culture that would be interested in this movie? I started thinking about it and the word that came to mind is "goth." I went, okay, goths by and large are interested in vampire stuff but they also tend to have an intellectual vibe going on. You know they're readers but they may also have a dark spiritual vibe going on. Goth culture grew up and became intimately associated with Neil Gaiman and *The Sandman*. Okay, so that's interesting, but would the psychographic of "Sandman" fans be right for my movie? Those fans that are likely to have a goth component?

That all sounds great, but how do you get to those fans – that group of people?
Start with social media. Run a search on Facebook. Facebook has an advertising tool; even if you're not running an ad, you can just run a search on their advertising tool and just put in a key phrase. And what you want is for these people to like your page. Profiles of individual's pages are for products and entities. And the reason – and this is very important in terms of marketing for the long term because you're only allowed to have 5,000 friends max and you're limited in terms of the way that you can market to your friends – *pages* were developed as a marketing tool whereas *profiles* were developed as an interactive communication tool. Big difference.

So, for example, I could run a Facebook ad campaign targeted at Neil Gaiman fans. In fact, I did this a week ago. I set up the parameters and I spent $25 a day and for $25 a day, it was costing me less than a dollar per acquisition of links. And I wasn't selling them anything. The ad just said, hey, if you like Neil Gaiman, you'll like this movie. And they went and they checked it out. So I got 150 new followers in a few days. And that was just a test. So remember it's important to have the money in your budget to put into Facebook advertising just to build a fan base.

So this is important to literally put in your budget?
I would say for any new film, if you don't have a line item for the Internet, then you don't have a budget.

Do you mean separate from possible P&A money or potential four-wall money in the budget? In fact, before you answer, let me tell our readers what I am referring to here. P&A *money means prints and advertising and* four-walling a film *means that you rent the theatre and show the movie yourself. Usually the theatre keeps the concessions.*
No, I am not referring to either of those things. This is a marketing item that exists before the film does. This is not P&A. This is in the production budget. You can create the frenzy before you have the funding. Let me ask you a question: you're a producer, but let's say you're a studio or let's say you're an investor, if somebody comes to you with this little film, and says, "Okay, I want to make this for $800,000," they're going to look at you and say, "Well, what have you done before and why should I listen to you?" But then you say, "Oh, and by the way, I have 70,000 people who already are interested," you've just done their work for them.

The Internet is a numbers game. You need volume. For example, I am interested in creating an audience on YouTube that has the potential to grow to 40,000–50,000 a year and beyond. Now you can go to investors, or even if you're past the investor stage, and in production, at the end of the day, you can go to a distributor and say, "Oh, look, I've got 40,000–50,000 people." You just did their job for them. If you've got 40,000–50,000 people or if you've got 200,000 people, you don't even need a distributor!

My goal for my vampire movie is a million people in my social sphere or targeted fans of the movie and I don't just want them on Facebook. I want their email address and I want their zip code so I know where they live so I know whether to do a theatrical first, and if so, where to do it. And if so, how much to spend in each of those locations, and if I'm lucky possibly to not spend anything in those locations because I have their email addresses. We'll also have an iPhone, iPad, and Android app, so we'll get their information that way as well. I'll be able to text them, email them, so if I've got 30,000 people in Atlanta and I've got their email addresses, they've already made a commitment to the film by giving me their email address and zip code, that means they've already invested in a sense. Then all I need to do is four-wall, send them an email, and what's the worst that can happen? As long as I get enough of them to pay for the four-wall, I haven't lost any money.

Okay, if you've got 30,000 people in Atlanta, let's say, 300,000 in Chicago and 30,000 in LA, why four-wall? Why make the little bit that comes out of theatre? Why wouldn't you just sell those downloads for $15 and make $15 times 90,000 without having to leave your office?

That's one of those questions that the answer depends on the movie. You have to get your ego out of the way and decide, is this a theatrical movie? And you have to get your ego out of the way and decide, does this movie have international potential? Because if it has real international potential and you can get it into theatres and make money, you will do well overseas.

I was just curious, where can you make the money?

If you get 500 out of 30,000 to show up, you just paid for the theatre.

Yes, but where is the big money?

Well, it all depends on the size of the network that you build, and at a certain point it's going to depend upon whether the movie is good enough and theatrical enough. Your goal is to get those 500 people in the door, but then your goal is to have a good enough experience for them that they go out and talk about it to everybody.

And then Disney or Warner Bros come calling because the word of mouth is spreading? Is that part of the plan?

That is a possibility, but this may not be for everybody. That's something that could conceivably work for my movie if I get a million people on the list. But not necessarily for every movie.

Let's say, that if I were just going out to raise the funds for Séance with Adrian Paul attached, what would you suggest?

Today with the Internet, I would get the hardcore *Highlander* fans involved – I don't know how big those numbers are – my impression is it's pretty big. I'm guessing that's hundreds of thousands of people if not millions.

So would you suggest self-distributing by making it available to the Highlander fans through downloads on the Internet?

I realize that six years ago we didn't have the tools on the Internet to do it with any safety, but I'm not even talking about delivering the movie that way at the moment. I'm just talking about spreading the word. One of the big issues in this whole arena that I don't think anybody realizes is that distribution and marketing are two different things. *Distribution is delivery, marketing is awareness building.* CreateSpace, for example, will say, "let us distribute your film." You're not going to get an audience from them. All they're going to give you is a mechanism for taking the money and they will mail a DVD or do a digital download. Nobody's going to find you through CreateSpace. Because CreateSpace is part of Amazon, if somebody does a search on your topic under Amazon, even on the Amazon search page, it's going to come in order of how popular the searches are. Why? Because the stuff that's showing up on the first page is the stuff that's making Amazon money right now. On the other hand, if I built a social network, get 20,000 people, or even 5,000 people who are really seriously interested in what I'm doing, and I can send them a message on Facebook, or even better send them an email and text them and I can communicate with them, assuming I've built a relationship and they like and trust me, then if I want to put the movie on Amazon and CreateSpace, CreateSpace will do the delivery for me but I do the marketing.

Going back to what I said before, identify the audience that's specific to the niche of your film and the psychographic, understand their buying habits, locate them on Facebook, on YouTube, find out where they hang out. Because really 80 percent of what the Internet is used for, is for like-minded people to hang out together and talk to each other. So all you need to do is fall down in front of the right group of people. All you need to do is find the person or organization that already has a relationship with those people.

Marc, this has been fantastic. Thank you. Any final words of wisdom?
The problem is it's such a massive topic that I can barely scratch the surface, but what I want to get at is that the root of social media is building a relationship with the right people and who is right for your film. Actually, the phrase that I use that I think is in my video online is *building a relationship with people who are already predisposed to being interested in your film*. Building a relationship that feels personal. Building a human relationship doesn't have to be difficult; it could come through in a variety of ways, from baring your soul to humor.

Actually, the number one thing you can do more than anything else is *engage your audience*. Don't talk at them but invite them to talk to you. It's the first rule in sales. I've tested this and it works. Everybody wants to be heard. Everybody wants to feel significant and they want to feel listened to.

Okay, here is my final word: if there's a single value to the Internet for marketing, you can get to more people, more quickly for less money than any other form of marketing in human history. By the way, you'll also see on my video, YouTube, Facebook, and Twitter statistics that will blow your mind. You know, I was a theatre director in Chicago before I moved here and I remember standing in front of a 40-seat rat-infested theatre passing out flyers on a Saturday night hoping I'd get audience members. There's a moment on the Internet where you realize, oh, okay, the amount of energy it takes, the amount of time and energy and money it takes to get and print the flyer to 500 people for the same time and energy and money and actually less, I can get to 500,000 people. *It's a massive paradigm shift.*

I think if you're not using the Internet today then you have no chance. If it's not at least part of your strategy, if not the main part – in my philosophy – especially for a $1 million or lower movie, the Internet should be the primary means of getting your word out.

Check out Marc's website at www.Internetmarketingforfilmmakers. com. On his first $125,000-budget film, Marc made $40,000 in DVD sales in the first two days by marketing and creating a buzz on the Internet. He knows what he's talking about because he has literally done it himself.

Stacey Parks

Author of The Insider's Guide to Independent Film Distribution

What have you noticed from your years of experience in the traditional film distribution arena to the transition to the current trends toward self-distribution?

I've noticed that self-distribution has gone from being an "alternative" form of distribution to really very common. In fact, it's gone from being Plan B to Plan A, and I feel everyone should have self-distribution as part of their overall distribution strategy.

For anyone who is about to launch into producing their low-budget film, what is your advice regarding the direction they should take with distribution? And at what point should they begin thinking about the distribution of their film?

A producer always needs to be thinking about distribution from the beginning – in fact, the script stage of a project – because this will inform all sorts of decisions from casting, to genre, to target audience. Again, I think everyone should always shoot for the stars, but be realistic and keep self-distribution in mind as part of your overall distribution strategy.

While we were raising money to produce our films, we included in the total amount we were raising the money for our delivery costs. And once we delivered to the sales agent, the rest was in their hands. Now with the possibility of self-distribution, should we be raising additional monies? And do you have any ideas as to how much we should raise for this possible self-distribution?

Yes, you definitely want to budget for self-distribution from the beginning. As a general rule of thumb, take 25 to 50 percent of your budget and allocate it toward self-distribution. Of course, this will depend on what type of self-distribution you are planning to do – for example, doing a self-theatrical release is much more costly than just doing a self-distributed DVD. So let's say your production budget is $100,000, then I would actually raise an additional $25,000–$50,000 to cover self-distribution, depending on whether part of your self-distribution strategy includes theatrical screenings (which is expensive to execute).

I'm not sure what self-distribution really is. Is it mostly about selling your film as a downloadable product on the Internet? And is that safe as yet? Or is the risk of pirating too great for producers to even be considering this form of self-distribution?

Self-distribution entails distribution on most of the big platforms, specifically theatrical, DVD, and Internet. Honestly, pirating is a risk for all films, even at the studio level. So if a producer is self-distributing their work, then realize it's not just they that need to be concerned – everyone is concerned!

Should we just be focusing on using the Internet as a way to promote and market our film well in advance of producing it? Or does that work only when we have a film with a particular niche market audience?

Everyone should work on building an audience for their work even before making their film. However, I will admit this can be a challenge at such an early stage, so the idea is that you lay the foundation of audience building during pre-production (website, social media pages) and get started with it, but realize that it's a marathon, not a sprint, and it can take months if not years to effectively build an audience for your film.

I hear that domestic distributors are being more flexible with their deals these days. Split right's deals are something that are now becoming common practice. Can you tell us more about that and what we should be asking for in those deals?
Yes, good news for filmmakers is that traditional distributors are starting to agree to split rights deals with filmmakers. For example, if you are making a deal with a traditional DVD distributor, you should be prepared to ask to retain the rights to self-distribute your DVD off your own website and have them carve these rights out for you on the contract. Then you will be able to sell the DVD directly to your audience (remember all the audience building you've been doing?). This is where that will come in handy!

You can learn more about Stacey by going to her website at www .filmspecific.com.

Becky Smith

Writer/Director/Producer "16 to Life"

I know you are the queen of film festivals, with over 50 festivals to your credit on your film 16 to Life. *Was this something that you had planned from the get-go? And what was your experience starting out on the festival circuit?*
We thought we would try the festival route. The festival "how-to" books and the media hype a select few festivals – the obvious big ones, Sundance, Toronto, Berlin, and maybe Cannes. However, I think that conventional wisdom pays off for a tiny percentage of independent features. Even if your indie feature is one of the very small number of independent films that get into Sundance, the chance of getting a big sale –or any sale – is remote. It's not going to be an effective strategy for the majority of films.

We submitted *16 to Life* to those festivals – I guess it's worth a shot! But when we didn't get in, I had to reevaluate. My film is a small coming-of-age romantic comedy, which, I think, is not the most likely material for Sundance or Berlin. We needed to come up with a new strategy. I had no relationships with programmers, no track record as an indie feature director. My cast was young television actors and an adult actress who is an esteemed film actress. But I didn't have a "star." So I developed a new strategy based on the question, who does this film appeal to? Let's go back and look at the festival circuit again, and let's not use the conventional wisdom of Sundance and Toronto (highly unlikely for 99 percent of indie films). I felt that we needed to focus more on "Who is the appropriate audience for this film?"

There were some obvious selling points. First, the film was shot regionally, on the Mississippi River in a rural, beautiful community. Second, it was about teenagers. Third, a young girl is the protagonist. I started applying to regional festivals. I approached festivals that focused on women and/or supported small, regional films. I also looked at international festivals (there are a number of "youth festivals"). International youth festivals are more edgy and more open to exploration of teenagers in terms of darker themes and sexuality than American festivals. If you see an American film festival that is touted as a youth festival, you are going to get films for children. In Europe and Asia, when they say youth festival, they're talking about anything that explores issues of young people, i.e., much edgier films. I used Without a Box – because it's simple and efficient.

Did you have money in the budget? Because this isn't something you thought of before you made your movie. It sounds like you knew you were going to approach the big ones, but not the whole gamut of festivals you ended up submitting to.
I always thought I'd try for ten festivals. But I initially thought they'd be festivals like Sundance and Slamdance. I had a bit of money and I was aware that we had to have a killer website. We developed the website from the get-go.

Was that useful?
Oh yes, the website became profoundly important with festivals. I know that many festivals have gone to my website to check out the film. I add great quotes when we get them; I add awards we've won; I list the festivals we are attending.

Did you have a trailer up there, too?
I had a trailer, a music video, blurbs on all of the actors in the film. I have stills from production, a cast list. We have music – a wonderful soundtrack – you can see the music that's in the film. One strategic thing I held onto was that when we got into our first festival – whatever festival we first got into – we needed to make a huge splash with that festival. It had to be a festival carefully selected. The first festival we got into was a festival in Los Angeles called the Method Fest. You have to be what I describe as "pleasantly aggressive." You need to be brave in terms of calling programmers, though not obnoxious. If you don't get on the phone, I think your chances are diminished. I think it's important to talk to the programmers at the festival to let them know who you are. Not to be pushy, but to be proud of what you've done and articulate why it might be a good fit for the festival. We ended up getting a great screening time for our premiere at the Method Fest.

So even before you got accepted, you called to create a relationship?
Yes, I think it's a good idea to call the person – you probably won't talk to the head of the festival, they're too busy – but talk to the programmers: would this be a good fit for you? Would you look out for this film when it comes in? I think it's helpful, especially if you have something unique about the film to present to the programmer. Your film could get lost in the shuffle. There are an enormous numbers of films submitted to every festival. So with our first festival – the next smart thing we did – was we hired a social media/PR person. We said no matter what, we are going to fill this theatre. She immediately went to Facebook and Twitter and found ways to engage a broad cross-section of people. We made sure that we put great effort into getting people into that theatre. That night, not only were we the only sellout in the history of that festival, but we turned away 75 people at the door. Absolutely packed – people sitting in the aisles. They called the fire department to say we had to move some people out of there. That led to several nominations for awards in that festival and we won the audience award and Best Supporting Actress.

Had you discussed that fact with the programmer, that you had somebody who was a social media expert who was going to be getting the word out about the uniqueness of the film?
That's a good question. When they accepted our film into the festival, we introduced them to our social media/PR person. It's pretty divided – you're either

social media or you're PR these days – but three years ago she did both. I've heard that you have to be very patient in terms of the festival circuit; it's a slow process. It started very slow for us, then built and built – and we are still being invited to festivals, two years later!

What I found out was that success leads to success. From the moment that we got into the festival, won the audience award and Best Supporting Actress award, and filled the theatre – once we had those accolades plus many nominations for other awards – we were able to capitalize on them with other festivals. Here's my truth: there are many festivals around the country, including small festivals, medium-size festivals, big prestigious festivals. And all of these festivals are run by passionate people who love film. There are many older actors, wonderful actors, who are celebrated at small regional festivals. There are great directors and cinematographers who are celebrated at regional festivals. These festivals have appreciative audiences and they're wonderful places to submit, to go to, and to meet audiences and other filmmakers. We had a wonderful time at the Kansas International Film Festival and won both the audience and best of festival awards. We won the Mississippi International Film Festival, the Asheville International film festival in North Carolina – we went to as many festivals as possible and did Q&As.

Did they pay for any of this or was this out of your budget?
You always negotiate when you are invited to a festival; sometimes they pay, sometimes they don't. Sometimes they'll give you a hotel room, sometimes they'll pay your airfare. When I got to these festivals, I found that I was on panels with wonderful people. I was sitting in on workshops with amazing award-winning cinematographers.

The audiences were enthusiastic and vibrant and they filled the theatres. They were knowledgeable about film and – the good news is we kept winning festivals, which was astounding to me. I think now we've won a total of nine festivals and/or audience awards. We've won two Best Actress awards, two Best Supporting Actress award, and one Best Cinematographer award. It was a one-year journey, but even now as I sit and talk to you, we're in three new festivals: Russia, Armenia, and Spain. They just keep coming. They call me; we are no longer applying because we have distribution. And we would *not* have gotten distribution without these festival wins – and the great write-ups in newspapers about the film.

So how many total festivals do you think?
I may have lost count but I think we've been in some 40 festivals. I am convinced that the sale of the film to Warner Bros. Digital, for television, direct download, video on demand, Amazon, and Netflix would never have happened without the festivals wins – proof that we had a broad responsive audience.

Did you go after Warner Bros. or did you have a sales agent who went after them?
My sales agent submitted the film to distributors. It was a long and rather discouraging road – especially because we started the process before we got into a single festival. In hindsight, I think that's a choice you have to make, but I think an independent film needs some kind of credibility. A coming-of-age story is not always easy to sell. When I had to change gears and rethink the festival strategy because we didn't get into the top five, our decision to focus on getting attention

for the film and building an audience for it paid off. I don't think Warner Bros. would have picked up the film otherwise. Now they've come back to us with interest in selling foreign rights, but we'd already made a deal for foreign rights before we got the US rights.

With your deal with Warner Bros Digital, were you able to keep any rights for your film?
One thing that's happening now with independent features is that rights are often broken up. People tend not to sell all rights to one distributor. I think filmmakers are leery, and rightfully so, that they will have a hard time seeing a return. One thing I think indie film producers should consider is retaining the rights to sell DVDs themselves – unless they get a great offer.

If you had to go back in time and do it again, would you have not gotten the sales agent and just done the festival route and then been able to go directly to a domestic distributor like Warner Bros.?
I would love to say that I would not have used a sales agent, I would've loved not to have that middleman. But you have to ask yourself, do I know how or want to learn how to get to distributors? As first-time indie producers, we don't have credibility, so I don't know how we can bypass a relationship with a sales agent.

Is there anything you would do differently if you could go back to the beginning?
I would do a micro-budget feature. I believe you must make a very low-budget feature right now to have a realistic chance of getting your money back. Also, I would have thought more about trying to engage people at festivals in a personal way. I learned that as I went along.

I want to reiterate that there is so much hype around the top five festivals and the top ten festivals. But the odds are very much against the indie filmmaker getting into those festivals – or making a sale at those festivals. If you aren't one of the lucky few, be creative and think outside the box. Realize that there are many festivals that have film devotees and reviewers. They will treat you well, provide you a forum for Q&As, and you may get reviewed, win awards; plus, you will meet other filmmakers. For example, we were invited to Tunisia this year. Five famous French actresses were on the festival jury; one of them is Charlie Chaplin's granddaughter.

At the festival, the big announcement was the Best Actress award. My actress and I came running in from the beach wearing jeans and T-shirts and were shocked to hear the announcement. We were up against several films that ended up being the Oscar submissions from various European countries. Again, by American festival wisdom, who would have thought that by going to a festival in Tunisia we would end up meeting well-known producers, directors, and actresses and that we would win one of the top awards? Rethink what festivals are about, why you go to them, and what you do there. Getting sucked into this idea that it's just Sundance or nothing is harmful to independent film. Find your film lover, find the people who appreciate what you're doing, and remember that every single win or recognition or nomination goes back to your website. It becomes your press release.

What about your investors, did you keep them informed?
We send them an investors' newsletter twice a year. And many of them attended various festivals. We had a small theatrical release. We did it in conjunction with

private theatre owners and with AMC theatres. We opened in nearly 20 theatres. In almost every case, we beat out whatever Hollywood films were in the theatres in terms of audience attendance.

Did you do this to try to make money?
No, it wasn't about making money, since I knew through my research that films can't make money on theatrical anymore. I wanted to break even and get more buzz for the film. And we were selective. We kept going to where our audience was. We did well in about ten cities in Iowa, Wisconsin, Kansas, Nebraska, and Arizona. We wanted reviews. Every review, whether it's online or a small-town newspaper or a larger newspaper, can be added to your website and your poster. We have about 30 nice quotes at this point.

Was this before the Warner Bros. deal?
Yes, absolutely. Going the festival circuit, doing a small release, putting out press releases, and getting people to review the film – all those things helped us make our sell. Now our poster for the film has a *Variety* review. *It's thinking smartly, not giving up, and having patience.*

Any final thoughts you have for film producers?
Yes, your poster. You have to have a poster that encapsulates your story, that's engaging and makes your film sound intriguing. That gets to the core of your film in a smart way. You need to think about how to get people to see the film at festivals, how to engage programmers. It's a lot of follow-through. You can't just direct the film and think that's all, that you can walk away and someone else will be as passionate as you are about it – and nurture it to distribution. Nobody will care about it as much as you do. There's just too much noise in this day and age. Too many people with cameras who can go to Final Cut Pro and make a really low-budget film. You have to draw attention through having a quality product and knowing how to market it.

In addition to being a writer, director, and producer, Becky is also a professor in the master's program in Directing in the UCLA school of Theatre, Film, and Television. For more information on Becky's film, go to www.16tolifethemovie.org.

Jim Pasternak
Director, Certifiably Jonathan

Richard Marshall
Producer, Certifiably Jonathan

When you were raising the money to do your film, was your goal at the time to self-distribute?
RM: No, it actually came about as we were going through the process of making the film. We attended seminars and conferences, and we went to one called "How to Distribute Your Film Without Getting Screwed."
JP: And the irony of that was that one of the speakers on the distributors' panel said, "Well, you know the reality is that we will screw you, but you will love it

because we will get your film out there, you just won't see any money from it." Richard and I looked at one another and we knew that that was not what we were going to do. We were determined to repay our investors, and this is part of what drives us. But the most exciting person there was a gentleman named Peter Broderick, who in essence said that the studio system is a dinosaur, and as film-makers with access to the new technology and with the Internet, there was no reason that we shouldn't be distributing and marketing our own films. That gave us the inspiration to take it out to theatres ourselves.

How many theatres did you do?
RM: So far, we've done 48 theatres in a whole gamut of cities and all at independent theatres across the country. Probably our biggest strategy that we ended up at was to do some Internet marketing. Because our demographic is basically 45–50 and over, a couple years ago that demographic was harder to reach on the Internet. Right now, they're not. We set up a Facebook page and it's been very successful.

JP: We did the key cities: New York, Chicago, and LA. Everyone was telling us that you have to do those cities in order to be considered legitimate.

So I take it that the point was not so much about getting the money back from the theatres, but more to be seen, to entice and excite a domestic distributor?
RM: Yes, and what happened was that the combination of our Facebook page – which in 14 weeks has almost *89,000 fans* – and the fact that we had and were continuing to set up theatrical screenings brought Gravitas to us, and Gravitas is a digital aggregator. They are an aggregator of on-demand and digital rights.

JP: And they were an aggregator for Warner Bros. We ended up getting a deal through Gravitas with Warner Bros. for a VOD (video on demand) release. And now our film is going to be in 100 million homes in North America.

So do you get to keep the other remaining rights?
RM: Yes, Warner Bros. has exclusive VOD; however, it does not include Internet VOD, which is separate from cable VOD. So because we have signed on with Gravitas, they will make the deals for us with Netflix, Netflix streaming, Amazon streaming, and possibly Google streaming. They will make the Internet deals.

JP: After we've done our theatrical releases, we then start selling the DVDs on our website, because we have maintained those rights. And we're hoping that by then we'll have 100,000 fans on Facebook and those 100,000 fans will be a sort of tipping point for us to multiply our customers and sell our DVDs.

RM: We're not only selling DVDs of the film, but we're actually working on two additional DVDs at the same time of the additional footage we have. We're also setting up a store right now to sell T-shirts, hats, and posters and other related items of the film along with our premium DVD. And then we are planning a third DVD, collections of scenes with Jonathan and some other comedians.

You mentioned your Facebook page earlier. The numbers are amazing. Did it cost money to get involved in social media and what have you learned about that whole arena?
JP: Yes, so important to have enough money to market your film on the Internet – having enough money to promote it in such a way that you can sell the film yourself. And what that does to investors is that it says to them that this film is going to get made and it's going to be seen, because if a traditional distributor

doesn't want it, these filmmakers have thought ahead about how to get this film out into the world. The biggest problem is that people make films and they don't get seen. So what we're saying to our investors is, if we make this movie, it's going to get seen. And that's important. But it costs money to get a good website. It costs money to keep the Facebook page going. It costs money to enter into film festivals.

RM: I have to interject here. Making a film is easy compared to getting a film distributed.

That's a good line. I love that. Now, let's talk for a bit about theatrical. Do you feel it was worth the time, effort, and money?

JP: Yes, because what it did is it made us legitimate to other ancillary venues like VOD, and I think it helped drive our Facebook campaign. It's all very intertwined in a way that you can get the word out and create a profile for your movie that makes you legitimate.

RM: That just brings up another point. We spent a substantial amount of money on a publicist in one of those cities. The most important thing that we did with the theatrical was in Chicago. We were able to get one of our cast members to do publicity, and she did a half dozen television and print interviews and we had the best turnout in Chicago.

That's fantastic. Did you do the four-walling in these cities or did you hire a company to help you?

RM: We only four-walled once. We only four-walled in New York. We made a deal with Emerging Cinemas; they've been taking it out all over the country and what happens is we're getting requests through our Facebook page and our website from independent theatres to do screenings as well. The thing about Emerging Cinemas is that they are all digital projection, so we just have to make one digital master and send it to them. They send it out and take care of it.

Did you do the deal with Emerging Cinemas?

JP: No, we hired a broker, Richard Abramowitz and Kirt Eftekhar, at Area 23a. They set up the deal with Emerging Cinemas, and Emerging Cinemas is a company that goes in and they have their own digital equipment that they install in independent theatres all over the country. Theatres like the Laemmle and Landmark. It's a fairly new concept.

RM: So what Area 23a did is they contacted theatres, sent screeners, got commitments, made sure that they got all the posters, got all the deliverables. They collect the box office receipts for us.

Do they take a percentage?

RM: No, we pay them a flat fee to do the whole thing for a certain number of months.

For a flat fee they'll just get your film into as many theatres as they can and help you strategize how to get into theatres. The other thing I want to point out here is that you can't just send your film out and expect theatres to book you. They want to know that there is a certain amount of marketing and muscle behind your film because the last thing they want is a film in their theatres that nobody knows about and they're not making any money from.

JP: So, having the Facebook page really helped. And of course, opening in New York gave us certain legitimacy with other theatres in the country.

So you guys did that on purpose – you did the four-walling yourself in New York to help Area 23a have that credibility to take you to more theatres across the country.

RM: Exactly, we opened in New York to get the reviews, and we bought some advertising in New York, we did press in New York. And when other theatre owners see that you've opened in New York, and you've opened in Chicago and they knew we were opening in LA, then they go, "Okay, that's a legitimate film, we'll book that film."

JP: And I think it helped us get Area 23a. Once they knew we were going to open in New York, they were a lot more willing to take a chance and open in Chicago a week later. And knowing that we had a celebrity in Chicago – Nora Dunn is a fairly big celebrity there – they had the confidence to book us in one of the best art theatres there. And the great thing about Chicago is that we had a week-long run there and then we got a call from the Winnetka Theatre outside of Chicago, and they ended up booking the film because we did so well in Chicago. So it really is about building a momentum and then other independent theatre owners start to see what you're doing and then they actually start to request your film.

What about film festivals? Were you and are you actively doing the festival circuit?

RM: I have to say that the festival is sort of the perfect, ideal place to show a movie. I would advise filmmakers to use the festivals as a theatrical in a sense. I know there are companies popping up that actually get you booked in the festivals and to use the festivals to start to build momentum for a film. Because you've got a captive audience, they are there to watch films, and they're not as critical as the LA, New York audiences are, so it's kind of a perfect environment to view your film. So I think it's really important to do the festival thing.

How many festivals have you been in to date?

RM: We've done 18 festivals.

JP: When you're making a film or when you're trying to go out and raise money for a film, from this point on, I would never think of raising money for the film without raising the marketing money at the same time. And this includes festivals. If you want your film seen, it's important that you have a sense of the marketplace and you have a sense of what your core demographic is; you have an idea of who your audience is and you have that in mind from the beginning. You're thinking about what kind of campaign that you can have on the Internet and create interest and controversy and enroll an audience to see your film. Yes, before you make the film.

RM: I totally agree. You really have to understand this aspect. It's never been so clear to either one of us until we made a film and had to market it.

JP: And there really is no template. We were lucky. We were lucky that we had a comic icon like Jonathan Winters. Because we had Jonathan Winters, and all of the activities that were involved in making the film, we were able to get Jim Carrey to participate in the project. We were able to get Robin Williams, Sarah Silverman, Jimmy Kimmel, and Tim Conway. We have a cast! So for a relatively low-budget film, we have a big-budget cast! And that has made it much easier for us to get the attention of people in the distribution mechanism and our investors as well. We were able to finance the film because we had what everybody felt was a marketable film.

RM: If you're going to self-distribute, you still have to have names in your film. It still comes down to names. And the names change constantly.

Any final words of wisdom?

JP: I think it's very important for filmmakers to always work with people who know more about what they do than you do. It's better to be collaborative and build a team of people than it is to try to do it all yourself. Because when you try to do it all yourself, not only is it exhausting and not fun, but you have limitations and you need to have good arguments and playful conversations and people who are better at finance than you are or people who are better salesmen than you are or have a better sense of color than you have.

Or marketing experts or Internet experts . . .

JP: Exactly. So what you try to do is you try to develop a project that has a strong enough collective vision to attract the people you want to work with. And I think you have to be constantly thinking about marketing materials while you're making the film. And I think directors have to think like producers.

RM: Even beyond thinking like a producer, as a producer you have to be thinking like a distributor, and that's the reality of making independent films. There's no way around it any more. If you're going to be an independent filmmaker, you literally have to be a distributor at the same time. You have to understand that world so thoroughly that if you're lucky enough to get a distributor, it doesn't end there. You still have to be involved in the distribution because if you leave it up to a distributor, there's a good chance they won't get it right, because frankly, the reality of a sales agent/distributor is that they have 12 films they have to get out that year or 20 films that year and they only have so much time for each film. They can only put so much effort into each film and so many people to put on that film. They're not going to push your film as hard as you are. So you have to be willing and able and smart enough to be involved in that as much as if you were in producing your film.

For more information about Jim and Richard's comedy mockumentary *Certifiably Jonathan*, go to www.certifiablyjonathan.com.

Jerome Courshon

Award-Winning Producer, Distribution Expert, and Founder of Three-Day Distribution School

Jerome, I know you talked about democratization in reference to distribution on your video series "The Secrets To Distribution." Could you speak a little about that?
Yes, I think democratization has finally come to distribution. It's come to filmmaking and now it's come to distribution. Everybody now has the potential to actually make money these days by self-distributing. And there are some people who are doing it. The challenge is that it's hard work and most film producers don't want to spend their time doing that. Many just want to make movies and let someone else handle the distribution so they can move on to the next film.

For those who are considering self-distribution, what is your advice?

I think it's important that filmmakers really focus on what they want and *what their goal is*. What is your goal and what are you trying to achieve? If you know you're dead set on some theatrical deal, then you need to learn how to position your film and play the game to go after that. If you just want a home video deal, or VOD, etc., then you tailor your approach to the marketplace from that standpoint. Also, it's important to *build a pedigree* for your film (unless you've already got that with a name cast). This is essential. You build a pedigree to set yourself apart and show the world, not only distributors but potential customers as well, that your film is really good and that they should spend their money.

How did you do that with your first film, God, Sex & Apple Pie?

I did it by using festivals, and then a small theatrical release. I made a movie, a comedy-drama with no names, and I started submitting to film festivals. I knew I needed to get press and quotes from the media. I did a bunch of festivals, built up a pedigree, and by the time I was done, I'd won six top awards. I had a lot of press and now with this pedigree, I made the decision to open it theatrically in as many cities as I could afford.

Did you four-wall your film and can you say a little about that concept?

When you four-wall, there are really two distinctions that I tell producers you need to make, especially when you're dealing with theatres. Four-walling is when you buy the theatre out for a week. You're paying the owner or the chain an amount of money up front, and you get the theatre and all the box office. However, I didn't want to four-wall as I didn't want to pay out money up front. I wanted to make deals with the theatres. And these deals are percentage deals, where you and the theatre (or chain) are splitting the ticket sales on some percentage basis. Of course, the theatre is sharing the risk with this type of deal, so they have to believe that you'll put butts in seats. So this is what I did. I made deals with the theatres, paid no money up front, and we split the box office. Frankly, if you can make a good percentage deal, this is generally the better way to go; the money you might have budgeted to buy out the theatre can now be spent on marketing.

So I decided to open in Chicago first because that's where I grew up. I planned to use the "local boy" angle to gain press, and it's one of the top three cities in the country, so it's a good market.

Please keep in mind – and this was a mistake I made in Chicago – it's important to choose the right theatre. Number one, be aware of what the theatre is known for showing, whether that be mainstream fare, arthouse fare, or second-run/revival fare. This will have a direct bearing on how your film is perceived in the community and affect attendance. Which type of theatre is right for your film? Number two, choose theatres that have foot traffic. If you pick a theatre everyone has to drive to, you're probably doomed. Obviously, there will be people who will drive to you, especially if your marketing is good. But you also need the spontaneous, impulse-purchases of people walking by. And if you or someone from your team is standing outside the theatre pitching the foot traffic coming to the theatre, you will convert a lot of this traffic to your film. This was how I sold many tickets in my New York City run. Lastly, it's also important that the theatre chosen be in the right area of town for your type of film. For example, if you have a Latino-flavored film, you must take into account the demographics of the area where you plan to open your film, making sure that it makes good business sense.

Did you have the money for this in your initial budget?
No, I learned my lesson the hard way. I recommend that you raise *everything* you need, including festival money, marketing money, P&A money, everything you need! I tell people, budget and raise money for P&A so that you have options if you don't get the deal you want. Since I didn't do this, I had to raise money separately to open theatrically in Chicago and New York.

My marketing was approached in two ways. I hired a PR firm for their traditional approach to PR, and then I personally handled all the grassroots marketing. I knew from my festival work that I needed to do a lot of grassroots marketing, but also knew many PR firms don't understand how to do this. I worked my ass off. I go to stores in the neighborhood, getting posters in store windows, postcards on store counters, I talk to people everywhere, I get on the radio and do radio shows, I work the Internet. I do everything I can. This is just a necessity if one is going to open theatrically and you don't have the money the studios have.

This is great info and I'd like to ask you about mixing traditional distribution with self-distribution. What are your thoughts?
For many independent filmmakers, I feel using the best of both worlds is the way to go. Unless one of the studios' specialty arms or one of the major independent distributors like Lionsgate or Summit or the Weinstein Co. is cutting you a nice check for your film, the best way to maximize revenues is market by market (i.e., home video, VOD, cable, foreign, online platforms, etc.). However, exploiting your movie market by market all by yourself is a huge amount of work. The filmmakers who think, "I'll just put my movie online and make a fortune" – most don't realize how much work it takes to actually make significant sales. It's not just putting it online and then going to the beach.

So if one can partner with some of the traditional distributors for some of the markets, this can make the road to recoupment and profit easier. (Just be sure your butt is covered thoroughly in any contracts signed; too many filmmakers make fatal mistakes by signing bad contracts.) I have a lot I can say about this, but here's an example of what I mean.

Let's say you want to make a deal with a home video distributor, and for the sake of this example, it's not one of the studios' home entertainment divisions. It's a smaller home video distributor. You should negotiate the right to sell your movie *from* your own website, and you allow the distributor the rest of the marketplace (which in North America would be the United States and Canada). This way, you are utilizing their ability to mass-market your film and leveraging that to drive online traffic to your website to buy directly from you at retail price. So you utilize the market penetration and awareness that a home video distributor can do for you – and hopefully they'll make good sales – but if they don't, you still have the power to make your own sales. And each of your own sales is a much bigger piece of the pie, since they're not shared with the distributor.

Now, there are a lot of filmmakers nowadays doing home video on their own without a distributor. Some have had very good success at it. Just know, it's a hell of a lot of work, so don't expect it to be easy.

Also, be aware that many home video distributors are now wanting Internet rights as well. Frankly, I prefer to keep those separate and exploit them myself (or make a deal with a different company). Not only do you want to avoid "cross-collateralization" (where distributor losses in one market are covered by profits in another), but most online platforms are taking anywhere from 30–50 percent of a sale. After a distributor takes their cut of a digital sale, what's left? By the way, when you make a deal with a foreign sales company to handle your film in the overseas territories, I recommend holding back the Internet rights. Why would you want people going to some website in Germany, for example, to download your film? You want them to come to your site, or your Facebook page, or wherever you have your film for sale online that *you* control. However, if you do make such a deal where you are granting Internet rights in a foreign deal, be sure that your film can be viewable/downloadable only within the territory the deal is for. This has to be in the contract.

Any additional suggestions as to how we can take advantage of the Internet?
The Internet right now is not making most filmmakers a tremendous amount of money. But it is making some money and growing every year, so we need to take the potential very seriously. One thing I would recommend is building your fan base and collecting email addresses. You've got to be able to draw eyeballs and traffic to wherever your film is. Second, I feel that a lot of producers charge too much for their films. Pricing is really important. And look for ways to give added value. For example, the movie *Twilight* released a special edition on DVD with some additional perks, one of which was a charm bracelet. My friend's wife spent $50 for the charm bracelet. She already had the DVD but she bought the special edition just because of that item. Even offering the poster signed by the stars of your film gives added value. My third piece of advice here is to pay close attention to your key art (your movie poster artwork). The key art is extremely important. Too many independent filmmakers don't understand that if your key art is kick-ass, people will buy your movie just based on that. Your potential customer, Joe Consumer, who knows nothing about you or your movie, is generally *not* going to spend time researching it or you. You must grab their attention in an instant. Bad key art doesn't do this. Excellent key art does. And once you've got their attention, you're halfway – or more than halfway – to the sale.

Try to get some great quotes from critics as well. Let's say *Fangoria* loves your horror film. *Fangoria* is well known. You get a good quote or review from them, you will likely want to put that on your artwork. It becomes a "stamp of approval" or endorsement – and this is pedigree. It tells people who like or trust *Fangoria* that your movie is good and worth their money. Remember, you're asking people to give you $10 (or whatever your price point is) and two hours, so you have to sell them immediately with your key art, your pedigree, and anything else you can come up with.

Any final piece of advice for today's film producer?
Currently, to make distribution successful, I feel producers need to use everything. (Unless you're getting a big check from a major distributor, as previously mentioned.) DIY, Internet, and traditional distribution – use them all. Map out a distribution strategy – ideally before you actually make your film. But if you're at the finish line of postproduction and you didn't do this, then sit down and map out a

strategy. Even *before* doing film festivals if you're planning to do those. Educate yourself about distribution, and don't buy into a lot of the misinformation circulating out there, such as "Distribution is impossible" or "DVD is dead" or "If I get into Sundance, my job is done." Not understanding distribution and the viable options available is the *real* reason most films never see the light of day.

For more info about producer and distribution expert Jerome Courshon and his three-day DVD program, "The Secrets to Distribution: Get Your Movie Distributed Now!" visit www.Distribution.LA.

JC Calciano

Writer/Director/Producer

JC, I know that you put a lot of thought and work into both self-marketing and packaging your film right from the very beginning. Why did you decide that this was the way to go? Why did you decide to take charge of this area?

The reason that I self-market my films is because I believe that no one is going to care more about my film then I do and that if I want it to be done the way I want it done, then I need to do it myself. It's not to say that having help isn't great, but the simple truth is this: there are a lot of films being made and the competition is fierce, so if you want to find your audience, you need to be proactive in finding them and telling them about your movie. Marketing is expensive, and often distributors are just interested in selling the movie to the markets and not publicizing and marketing it appropriately. That's why if you want it done to your satisfaction, you do it yourself.

When you work with a distributor, they charge fees not only for their distribution services (and expenses) but also for marketing, promotion, and packaging. So say you want to distribute an independent film, they'll take approximately a 20 percent fee for their services, with an extra $50,000 in expenses for marketing, promotion, and materials. There is often no way to audit the $50,000 or get a breakdown of what those expenses were. That means you have no proof or idea if that money was actually spent on your movie or what it was really for. I like to know what I get for my money. I'm not in the business of making other people money unless I'm making some for myself, and for that reason, I want to make sure that their expenses are real and went towards my movie. I'm a capable person who can handle taking care of what needs to be done and I don't need a third party hiring someone else doing marketing and promotional materials. The more people involved means the more people who want to get paid and have input in my movie (which is something I don't want). I want to control my product and how it looks and is represented, so I hire the designer to design the packaging, poster, DVD cover, and so on. By doing it myself, I now not only control it, but I also know what I'm paying for.

And since it's your baby in a sense, you know what is best and you get to create your brand from the get-go. Is that how you see it?

Well, I have a lot of experience in marketing and distribution. I've worked at both in the past and learned what needs to be done. Since I've got the experience already, what I do is start with grass roots and free marketing like Facebook and Twitter. The Internet is the best value for an independent film-maker looking to build an audience for cheap, so I concentrate my efforts there. One thing that I've done which has been extremely successful for me is to create a webisode. I figured I'd make something simple and sexy that would draw in my target audience weekly. I've build a fan-base on the Internet to market my movies through my webisodes. I started the webisode a year before my first movie, and within two years, each of my webisodes average between 20,000 to 50,000 views a day. On every one of the webisodes, I have the name of my company at the beginning of them, so I'm branding my company, and at the end of the webisode, I show two of my movie posters and where they could find them. That means at least 20,000 times a day minimum, people are seeing my branding, seeing my product, and seeing my movie posters. On top of that, I run a revenue share on each episode (advertising banners served by Google), so each month I get a check for hundreds of dollars for showing my webisodes and advertising my movies and company.

Where does the money come from in this case?
YouTube has several ways of generating revenue from videos. You can charge per webisode, where you can set a price per view. My webisodes are free to watch, so in that case what I do is on the very popular ones, they give me an option to run a 15-second commercial of their choosing in front of my webisode. So I can click on the option to let YouTube run a 15-second spot before my webisode and they pay me more money for that view. Or on the less-popular webisodes, I don't run a commercial; all I have to do is allow them to serve ads (Google) to put a banner with a click-through the lower quarter of the screen. By allowing those ads, I make money, and they pay to place the ads on my videos as well as if someone clicks on the ad; when that happens, I get a larger revenue share.

I shoot ten webisodes in one day, and it cost me nothing. I'm a one-man crew, so I cut them myself on my home computer with Final Cut Pro and post them once a week. The cost of feeding my nonunion actors is a $50 lunch once every two months. There are no expenses on top of that. Because of these webisodes, I have millions of people who have seen my posters and advertisements for both my movies, the brand of the company as well as becoming fans of my webisodes. Also, those webisodes all have subscribers who I can email about my projects and keep them informed of what I am doing (and selling). Often bloggers pick up my webisodes and promote them on their websites because they think they are funny or sexy. A blogger could have tens or hundreds of thousands of fans to that blog, and when they post my webisode, those fans see my marketing.

And this serves your film?
Yes. The viral component of the Internet is amazing. Once it's out there, if it's clever and/or funny, people will pick it up and promote it for you. It's a remarkable tool for promotion and marketing.

By just using Facebook, Twitter, blogs, and my webisodes, I have built a huge fan base for both myself, my brand, and my products. My YouTube channel now has thousands and thousands of people who know me and my movies. When a new film comes out, I go over to my YouTube subscribers as well as my fans on Facebook and Twitter and tell them that I just released a movie on DVD or VOD and tell them how they can click on the link (which I have an affiliate program built into) to watch or buy it. They click on my link and not only buy my movie, but also because I have an affiliate link built in to the link to the seller (Amazon or iTunes), I get a percentage of that sale from the seller.

Does Amazon charge quite a bit of money?
Amazon works in a lot of different ways. You can sell a video on demand and/or streaming as well as a rental or DVD purchase. Amazon takes percentages of those transactions. You could also sell DVDs from another manufacturer or use a service they provide called CreateSpace, where you can actually generate a DVD product and sell it – you upload your movie through their site and it not only helps you create a physical DVD to sell but also provides the shopping cart to do the transaction.

Does the fact that we have the Internet access these days make it all a lot easier for the independent producer?
Yes, before the Internet and all the information out there, the distributors really were in control of marketing, production, promotion, and sales, but now, with the Internet, the market is open to everyone and the information is out there for all who seek it.

Online companies like iTunes, Amazon, and CreateSpace have made selling more accessible to filmmakers. There are many services like that available now like DVD Baby – you can go to DVD Baby, create a store and manufacturing system to sell your DVDs, and customers can click on your shop and buy a DVD straight from you. It's all done online now.

Your numbers are amazing. How long did it take you on that site to get to those numbers?
It took me basically two years to reach 4 million unique views on my webisodes. Those webisodes really fueled the marketing and the numbers grow exponentially. I also use other social networking websites like Facebook and Twitter. My new movie *eCUPID* has nine actors who are constantly promoting themselves and the film; each actor brings his social network to the film's marketing and adds to the numbers. The more popular the actor, the higher the numbers. For example one of my actors is a star from last year's MTV's *Real World*. He's a popular character as well as an advocate for the community; he's got a large fan base from the *Real World* as well as the important causes he speaks of; his fan base is tremendous; and he helps promote himself and the movie. I also hired Morgan Fairchild, and she's got her own fan base, which is tremendous. If you consider nine actors, with their own personal fan base promoting the film, you can see how quickly things can grow exponentially.

That is excellent, and it sounds like it's a win/win for everybody.
Yes, and all this marking and promotion is not only free, but it's also making me money. This is a big difference from the old days when a distributor would charge to market and advertise your film. In my model, *I'm making money while promoting my product*. I'm not saying that there aren't times to spend money. I think paid online advertising is great and very effective as well, as long as you do it in a targeted way. YouTube and Facebook have great affordable, targeted marketing engines and by being smart about how you place your ad, your keywords, and

your metadata, you can target your demographic in a very focused and strategic way. I believe if I'm going to be spending money on marketing, it's going to be a wise investment and yield a return. When I place ads online, those ads are going to sell rentals of my film and make me more money than I've spent on the ads.

If $50,000 is going to be spent, I can assure you that that $50,000 is going to be spent very, very wisely. And it's going to be servicing the audience who I know are going to watch my film. And that's going to be what I consider the most cost effective advertising, and from what I have available to me, it's web-based.

There is a distinction between domestic and foreign sales of movies. However, when you are doing something on the Internet, isn't that worldwide? Is that going to prevent you from having a sales agent come on board to do your foreign sales for you? Especially since the Internet is worldwide? Why would Brazil give you money if you are already tapped into people from their territory, for example?

You know that's a very good question, and I think that answer is that although my last film, *Is It Just Me?*, came out in the United States first, the foreign markets want their own version that is subtitled or dubbed as well. For example, *Is It Just Me?* came out domestically in November of last year. Then we had a foreign seller come on board. The foreign seller then went out and sold overseas territories. They converted the film into foreign DVD formats (SECAM and PAL) as well as adding subtitles and packaging in their local language. There is also overseas television that will want the film with subtitles or dubbed in the local language. Local DVD and the TV/theatrical sales are still somewhat viable in the rest of the world. I would imagine, yes, if there was a fan that wanted to see (or order) the English version, nonsubtitled, from Amazon, they might be able to find that online, but if not, they can get the film in their language locally as well.

Have you used your great fan base as leverage?

It's like a band looking for a record company. If a band has lots of fans, the company is far more likely to sign them to a record deal than the band with no fans. I think it helps that I come off of previous successes and have a large fan base of buyers. If you are going to be working with someone (sales agents, investors, distributors, anyone) and they know that you are going to work to promote and sell that film so that it's profitable, then you'll be able to excite an interested partner better. When I talk to investors and show them my fan base and the number of people who subscribe to me as well as the profitable numbers my films make, it puts me in a much better position to negotiate for the money I want to borrow. In that case, yes, it's leverage. Everyone wants to do business with someone who is going to make him or her money.

Any other tips for us regarding marketing?

Another thing I do as far as marketing is to promote my product in the niche markets that it represents. By that I mean my films are GLBT [gay, lesbian, bisexual, transgender] movies. I will Google GLBT movie blogs and I contact them. If my film were about vintage motorcycles, I'd search for groups/blogs about vintage motorcycles. Whatever it is, I look for a group that is interested in that subject matter and then I will write to those bloggers and offer the people that control those blogs content for their blog. I tell them that both my actors and myself will be available for interviews and that I will provide them with exclusive footage and stills. I ask them, "Would you like to do a story on me and/ or my movie?" Bloggers need content; I need promotion and marketing of my film; we basically need each other – the same goes for radio (and Internet radio).

I love it. Have they been taking you up on it?
Absolutely. Here is an example – my actors are good-looking guys. Yesterday, I contacted a website called Hunk DuJour. They have 1.5 million viewers a day! I offered them an interview and photos of my actors in exchange to promote my movie. They said, "This is great; we'd love to help you out!" I told them to send me ten questions, so they sent them and had my actors answer them. I also sent five stills. So within 24 hours on their blog, they wrote a special section for us where their audience could "meet the *eCupid* stars." They talked about my screening, my website, my webisodes – all 1.5 million viewers saw it! I have nine stars, so every other week I'm going to roll out another star. I'm going to do one each week, so you do the math and that's huge numbers that are going to aggregate to my web-site, my movie, and my webisode – all the time seeing my brand. That is just one example of how this works . . . and I do this kind of stuff every day. Last week, I contacted mostbeautifulman.com, and my lead was featured on the blog the entire day. I speak to online magazines like *OhLaLamag* and Bellomag.com, and they did a special campaign with my trailer and pictures of my guys. I contact all these publications and offer them content – and most of them take me up on it.

This self-marketing takes up a lot of time on your part. Is that a problem? Or do you feel that the new game is this and we all need to get with the program?
That's a fantastic question. That question has bred a new animal, and that is what they call a *media producer*. Basically, this kind of situation has created a prob-lem that someone like myself has been forced to deal with. I struggle with the dilemma of not having enough time to do all the social interacting and online marketing every day. I cannot move forward onto my next movie because I'm so busy with the marketing of my movies, so yes, I do have that problem.

There is a certain amount of things that I have to do myself; for example, if I'm going to create a webisode, I have to be the source of that webisode. But by working with a media producer, I could have somebody take the burden of the constant blogging and constant outreach of tweeting, Facebook, blogging, and so on off me. Reducing that workload is a huge benefit and help to me and a person who can do that is what I would consider a worthy investment.

This is really interesting. So a media producer is someone who has mastered those qualities? Not someone who wears both hats?
It's the person who comes in just to handle the media, press, marketing, and social networking associated with the movie. They are there to help the producer market the film, because the problem that the producer already has – wearing a number of hats – is that they often don't have the time to service the social media aspect of promotion and marketing of the movie. The media producer does that for you.

These days, investors are looking to invest in films that have an additional safety net – anything innovative or different that will draw attention and therefore dollars. It sounds like you were really on top of this from the beginning. Is there anything else that you did in the planning stages that you knew would get investors excited?
My movie, which is called *eCupid*, which stands for Electronic Cupid, is a movie about an app that comes to life and helps this couple in jeopardy fall in love.

So what I did is I went out and I actually designed an eCupid app that is part of the movie. So you can actually go to iTunes, download the eCupid app, and in the movie, Morgan Fairchild is the voice of the app. So Morgan Fairchild's voice talks to you and in the integration of the game (or love tester), you can play with the game on the app or can go on "About the Movie" and it takes you to the website, Facebook, Twitter, screening times, and trailer. I've created this app that is not only a fun device, but it is also a tool that integrates the marketing and promotion of the film – all of these things talk to each other.

Wow, your innovation is great because it shows investors a better possible return for investment!
Yes, I'm very pleased and excited to be able to say that. My first movie, *Is It Just Me?*, within six months of being released my investors were paid back 100 percent and I've already started to enjoy the profits from it.

Specifically where did your initial return come from?
For *Is It Just Me?* I made my initial money back within three months from festival fees, DVD sales, and download/rent/VOD alone.

And that was only through the Internet? Is that right?
Mostly online sales, Netflix, Amazon, DVD, and download. That does not include TV or foreign sales.

So, the only time you want to include a sales agent as you mentioned earlier is when it comes to foreign sales.

Not necessarily in all cases, but for the most part I think that domestic can be more "DIY" – overseas is harder in my opinion to "do it yourself." The problem with the foreign territories is the servicing of all the foreign territories. The challenge also comes with collecting money from the foreign territories. I don't have the relationships with the foreign buyers. For me to deal with the legality of contacts and leveraging the payments is not something I want to take on. There's a big difference between them paying a distributor with whom they have a relationship and want more product from in the future and paying out to a filmmaker directly.

I think, for overseas sales, it's worth having the convenience of somebody who has the expertise in that market and has the relationships with the buyers who they know are trustworthy and will pay for a film. If they are charging a reasonable percentage for their knowledge, legal advice, and to handle the deliverables to all the countries, it becomes worth it for me to have the convenience of their services. But I would caution anybody: if you make a domestic deal with a US distributor, be careful that they don't to go out and subcontract it out to a foreign sales agent for an additional percentage of your movie – there will be a lot of fingers in the cookie jar when you do that. So what I would say is that every filmmaker should find a foreign sales agent yourself. Find a foreign sales agent who deals just as a foreign sales agent and deal with him directly and then give them a fair percentage for their time and work to sell to the overseas buyers.

Any final words of wisdom?
Yes; before I make a movie, I find out what the movie is going to sell for. For example, when I made my first movie *Is It Just Me?* I called a sales agent who had sold a film similar to the one I was about make and asked him point blank, what are your fees? Then I asked him, "If I produce a film similar to that film for

X dollars and gave you your fees, could I make my money back in two years?"
He said yes, so then what I did is produced *Is It Just Me?* for half of the amount
of X. I felt that with that information, I was comfortable walking up to an investor
and showing him a movie, explaining to him that I'm going to make a better-
looking, higher-quality movie for half of the amount of money that the distributor
told me he could easily make on it (the other half would then be my profit).

That's what I would encourage independent filmmakers to do: know what
you are going to sell that movie for before you make it. Because a lot of people
think, okay, I'll make a movie that is going to cost me $500,000 to produce. They
make the film and then they take it to the market place and their $500,000 film
doesn't recoup $1 million. (You really need to make at least double what that
production budget is in order to get the money back.)

Every time I make a movie, the first thing I do is I go to a sales agent, find the
numbers the film will sell for (minus theatrical), and make the movie for a quarter of that number.

As far as marketing and distribution: I look at making a movie like being a
parent. The fun part is making it and the tough part is raising it. And when you
make an independent movie, the work starts after it's born. It's a lot of time that
gets invested in an independent movie and it's a tough road to travel, but if you
do it well, there is nothing more gratifying.

For more information about JC and his films, see the following sites:

Is it just me? (isitjustmeTHEMOVIE.com)
eCUPID (eCUPIDthemovie.com)
www.steamroomstories.com
Company website: www.cinema175.com
More info on IMDb.

Chapter 14

You've Delivered . . . Now What?

Just a few years ago, when you had delivered your film and all necessary delivery items to your sales agent, you were pretty much done. It was the sales agent's job to do the trailer, poster, and additional marketing. They did the festival submissions, and if your film was accepted, you would attend the festivals, but the paperwork was left to the sales agent. Well, things have changed.

You may very well decide to self-distribute your film, in which case you are 100 percent responsible for sales and marketing. These days, even if you have a sales agent, the producer is far more proactive than ever before. And that's a good thing. No one knows your film better than you do, so it makes complete sense that you should be more involved with the marketing and promotions.

A WHOLE NEW WORLD

Today, we have our film website up months and months in advance. Even before we start raising the funding for our films, our websites and social media networks are active. In the last chapter, as JC noted, he started a year in advance. And as Marc mentioned, there is now software available to track your followers, so that by the time your film's in the can, you've got a built-in fan base. You can use these numbers to approach sales agents and distributors or for your own self-distribution purposes. It's a whole new world, and technology today offers producers opportunities that weren't available even five or six years ago. In fact, you may well decide to use the number of fans you have to entice a domestic distributor, putting you – the producer – in the driver's seat, giving you the leverage to do a better deal and to take full advantage of a possibly split rights deal where you get to hold on to partial rights of your film. What a great opportunity we now have available to us.

FESTIVALS

As noted in an earlier chapter, in the case of *Candy Stripers*, *Séance*, and *Portal*, there were a number of festival deadlines that happened while we were still in post on our films, so I sent off the pre-postproduction DVD with a note explaining that the final copy would follow as soon as it had been completed. Once each film was ready, I sent them off to the various festivals that we had submitted to with a note telling them to now replace the old version with this final copy.

We also keep our eyes open for other festivals that were a good fit for our genre. Our sales agents on each of those films were on the lookout as well. If you do get accepted and think that you have a good chance of winning, I recommend that you attend. It's great press and an excellent place to meet buyers if you're self-distributing (and sales agents and producer's reps if you need them), and the networking you'll be doing is well worth the time and effort. If you do decide to attend, make the most of it and make a point of going to parties and other screenings. If any of your actors go along with you, make sure there are plenty of photo opportunities. Really prepare for the festival in advance and talk to other producers who are old pros with festivals and get some advice and suggestions from them before you go.

COMMUNICATE WITH YOUR SALES AGENT

Just because you might have done a deal with a great sales agent doesn't mean that you can assume that you are the number-one film on their list and that they are out there selling your film at every market. Like everything else, it's your job to stay in communication. Call them a month or so before each market and discuss their plans and strategy at length.

I happened to be at the American Film Market a few years ago, and I stopped in to see our sales agent on one of our films. They had had our film for less than a year at that point, so when I walked into their suite,

I couldn't believe that there was no poster, no trailer, not even a postcard or one-sheet highlighting our film. They said, "Oh sorry, but a few bigger projects came our way and we are focusing on those." If I had been on the phone with them a couple of months before discussing their plans and strategy for selling our film, I could have found out early that they had moved on and were no longer interested. That way I would have had time to take it to a new sales agent who would have had a fresh approach to selling our film. So be in communication with your sales agent long before each market and find out what they are planning; also ask if there is anything that you can do to help.

ATTENDING MARKETS

Like festivals, film markets are an excellent venue for networking and an invaluable source of up-to-date knowledge of what's happening in the industry. Try to get to at least one market a year – and I would highly recommend that you attend the American Film Market (AFM). Even if you just get a day pass and then spent a few additional days setting up meetings, attending a couple of parties, and even just hanging out in the lobby, it is all extremely valuable. Also what is great about the AFM is the fact that it is exclusively a film market. There is no film festival happening simultaneously, so it is the buyers and sellers – and all the suites are located in two hotels in Santa Monica. It's the first week of November, so the weather is excellent as well. Check out their website at www.americanfilmmarket.com and make plans to attend.

PROMOTING YOUR DOMESTIC SALE

It's always great to get a domestic sale (United States and Canada) of some sort. Whether it's a DVD, VOD, theatrical, home video sale, or whatever, it's all good news. Not only is it nice to get the money from the sale, but as any sales agent will tell you, a domestic sale helps increase the amount of money you can get from the foreign territories and helps sell the foreign territories. When you do get a domestic sale, be sure to get a press release out about it right away. I had a friend of mine who was an actual publicist write it and get it out on our behalf. I strongly recommend that you have money set aside in your operating budget to handle this sort of publicity. Figure 14.1 shows the press release we did about our *Séance* release.

FOR IMMEDIATE RELEASE
WINDCHILL FILMS' HORROR FEATURE SÉANCE SECURES U.S. RELEASE;
SIGNS LIONSGATE'S GRINDSTONE ENTERTAINMENT TO U.S. DISTRIBUTION

Burbank, CA – October 2, 2007 – WindChill Films, an affiliate of Snowfall Films, today announced it has signed Grindstone Entertainment Group for domestic distribution of its award-winning horror/thriller feature film, Séance.

Grindstone was launched earlier this year by Mandate Pictures, the highly regarded film finance, international sales and production company which itself was acquired last month by Lionsgate.

Séance has received numerous awards and industry recognition, including Winner Best Dramatic Feature Eureka Springs Digital Film Festival, Official Selection Best Screenplay and Best Visual Effects Indy Horror Film Festival, and Official Selection Horror Fest U.K. The film's synopsis and trailer are available at:
http://www.windchillfilms.com.

"Given its remarkable heritage, Grindstone is a domestic home entertainment distribution powerhouse and an ideal partner for Séance – a standout low budget indie with exceptional creative and production value that continues to garner industry recognition," said Séance producer and WindChill Films exec Kate Robbins. "We are confident Séance will do exceptionally well in the U.S. home entertainment market."

A favorite with film fest audiences, Séance is billed as "Five kids trapped in a dorm. One deadly killer. You do the math." First time director Mark L. Smith wrote Séance; he also wrote Vacancy, a Screengems feature film that debuted in theaters this past spring.

Smith describes the film's unique award-winning persona, "What if those shapes you glimpse in a dark room... the ones that disappear as soon as you can turn on the light... what if those shapes are still there, but you just can't see them with the light on?"

"That was the driving concept behind Séance," Smith explains. "To take that natural fear of darkness and turn it upside down, so that darkness is necessary to see the things you fear. Then you take that dark empty room... actually twenty floors of dark empty rooms, and you add a young woman with a past that haunts her even in the daylight. Then you surround that young woman with a few friends dealing with their own issues, and just for fun, you drop the ghost of a murdered little girl into the mix... along with the ghost of her killer. And then you give them all one single night to sort things out."

Séance stars Adrian Paul star of the 'Highlander' television series and the upcoming Highlander: The Source. Séance also stars AJ Lamas, son of Lorenzo Lamas; Chauntal Lewis who plays Lindsay in the short 'Lindsay Fully Loaded,' which received an amazing 750,000 hits; Kandis Erickson, 'Her Morbid Desires;' Joel Geist, 'Windfall;' and Tori White, 'Careless.'

About WindChill Films and Snowfall Films
Snowfall Films, Inc. was founded by producers Suzanne Lyons and Kate Robbins. In just six years they have produced or executive produced eight movies. Windchill Films is a Snowfall affiliate that produces low budget horror, thriller, and sci-fi films. For more information, see www.snowfallfilms.com and www.WindChillFilms.com.

Contact:
Margot Black, Black Ink Public Relations
(323) 993-7171
Margot@BlackInkPR.com

FIGURE 14.1

INFORM INVESTORS ALONG THE WAY

Of course, you will be updating your investors in the letters you send to them with their payments from territory sales. However, it's important to keep them up to date on any other news that happens along the way – for instance, if one of your actors gets another film or TV series of note, if you or your sales agent are doing any new types of marketing of the film, if the film has been accepted at festivals, and certainly if the film has received any awards. Be sure to copy them on any press releases that go out and update them on every bit of great news that relates to the film.

SAG RESIDUALS

If you decide to use SAG, or the actors' guild is in your country, then you will have to be responsible for the residuals that come with being a signatory. Something to note here is the fact that you will be paying residuals on the entire amount of the territory sale. I realize that sounds a bit crazy, but it is part of the guild rules. So let's say that your first sale comes in at $75,000; what happens is that your sales agents takes his or her full agreed-upon expenses off the top and their commission as well. So if the amount of their expenses is $30,000 and their commission is 20 percent, you are not getting $75,000 into your account – you are getting $30,000 from that first money in. But you still have to pay residuals on the entire $75,000.

Also, these residuals should be handled through a payroll company. As soon as you choose your payroll company, you'll be required to send them the list of SAG actors from your film with all the pertinent information regarding each actor. As soon as your sales agent sends the check and territory payment report, you will send the report to your payroll company. In a couple of days, they will send you back the amount that is due plus their fee. It is fast and easy and all you have to do is send them the check and they will handle all dealings and paperwork with the guild. Even if you are self-distributing your film and handling all the money that comes in, it's still important and efficient to use a payroll company for any and all guild payments.

ACCOUNTING AND TAXES

Stop crying – it's not that bad. The most important thing here is to be extremely organized. Even if you are able to set money aside from your operating budget, there is absolutely no reason to now spend it all on an accountant. It makes me crazy when I hear that a producer took their box of check stubs, receipts, and all related tax information to an accountant to sort out and organize. That bill will be $5,000! You can do the basic work yourself and save a ton of money.

When I was doing the first set of taxes for *Séance*, I took an entire week and sat down with the checkbook and my detailed check stubs and proceeded to create categories of all the different departments and aspects of the film. I then totaled up the amounts that related to each area. I made a point of listing every possible category and I trusted the accountant to sort out which areas were taxable and which were not. Here are the categories for *Séance*:

Accounting fee
Advertising and promotions (EPK)
Audience testing
Bank credit card finance charges
Bank charge/check charge/processing fees
Camera expenses
Casting consultant
Cast salary (includes payroll services and pension/health)
Crew salary (includes design salary, makeup effects salary, teacher salary, and post sound and music salary)
Craft services on set
Catering
Color correction on film
Copyright film registration cost
Director salary
Editing equipment (includes hard drives)
Executive producer fees
Film tape stock
Film tape transfer
Executive and finder's fees
Gifts
Insurance (film)
Insurance (office)
Legal costs (includes title report)
Lighting for film
Make-up and effects items
Meals and entertainment
Medical costs
Messenger
Pan-and-scan, HDD5, DigiBeta, DVDs
Petty cash
Postage
Printing

Producer salary
Production design
Postproduction supervisor
Power and water (office)
Rent (office and table read hotel)
Rent (film location and permits)
Snowfall Films reimbursement (for LLC formation & office expenses)
Sound equipment (production)
Sound design
Supplies (office and film: includes additional production supplies)
Taxes
Telephone
Transportation/rentals/gas for film
Wardrobe
Writers' salary

Once I totaled everything, I moved on to the investors list. I wrote their names in the first column, and under each name, I included all of the information the accountant would need. For example, the investor's address, phone number, email, and Social Security number. Next to their names, I listed the number of units (shares) that they had purchased and what that totaled. In the next category, I listed how much money they had received in that tax year. Given that it was the first set of taxes, I didn't have to worry about this category, as no money had come in from any territory sales yet. Our sales agent had actually done a few sales, but it takes a while for the payments to arrive.

That was it. Once those few pieces of paper were ready, I emailed and mailed them off to the accountant. And just so you know, instead of the $5,000 bill that I'd heard about, the bill we got from our accountant was for $470.00!

Something else you will need to handle regarding your taxes are the 1099s. I didn't need them for the SAG actors because their pay checks had been handled through a payroll company during the shoot. But everyone else on our film who had made over $600 needed to receive a 1099 by January 31. If we had used a payroll company for everyone on the film, this wouldn't be necessary, but at our budget level, the payroll company was used only for the SAG actors. These 1099s are necessary for only the first tax year following the production of your film, and they are extremely easy to do. The tax forms are readily available at office supply stores and come with computer software that is easy to install. This form is required in the United States; be certain to check government regulations in your country.

CLOSING YOUR LLC

Kate and I choose to leave our LLC open for five years from the date we delivered our film, in other words, from the date it was ready and available to deliver and sell. *Candy Stripers* was delivered in the fall of 2005, and we closed the LLC in December 2010. Any sales that are going to happen usually happen within the first two years from delivery, with maybe a few in the third year – if you're lucky. So I think that five years is fair. You don't want to be paying taxes, bank charges, and accountant fees when there is no money coming in the door. Our investors were well aware of this fact when they came on board, and we reminded them well in advance of closing the LLC.

FINAL NOTES

Be Sure To Get A Mentor (Or Two)

You don't have to do this alone. Human beings have been making movies for over a hundred years, so there are plenty of great producers out there who would make excellent mentors. Let's get very clear about what a mentor is and what his or her job entails. A mentor is someone you respect and someone in a position to advise you on how to accomplish your goal. He or she is someone who can give you advice, suggestions, and guidance. Mentors can share what worked for them on their films and what didn't. A mentor is not a coach. They are not there to push you outside of your comfort zone or make you accountable for your actions.

Here are a couple of tips to consider while choosing, contacting, and meeting with your mentor. First, decide who would make a good mentor. If you are producing a horror film in the $200,000 range, then I suggest that you list four or five producers who have done that at least once and preferably a few times. They don't have to be in your city or country because you can certainly have conversations over the phone. Also, make it easy for them to say yes. Ask for perhaps three 15-minute conversations, on the phone or in person. Or ask for a one-hour lunch or office meeting, or two half-hour coffee meetings. Whomever you choose, I'm sure he or she will be busy, and you want to respect their time.

I suggest you write a letter (by email or mail) focusing on three items: (1) start with the request, telling them why you are approaching them in particular; (2) tell them what it means to be a mentor, such as three 15-minute conversations; (3) introduce yourself; tell them what you are doing, what you're committed to, and the general timeline of your film production. Then tell them that you will be calling them within the next day or two to see if they are available and interested in being your mentor.

I want to stress a few items regarding mentor etiquette. Once you have a mentor, follow through. Call when you said you'd call. Be professional. Keep your word at all times. It is a business relationship. Always acknowledge them and always thank them for their time. Please be prepared; it is important that you have questions ready and that you generate the conversation. Finally, don't put them on the spot. Don't ask them to read the script or go over your budget, and so on. If they offer to do that, no problem, take them up on it, but don't be the one to ask.

I never take on a new learning curve without a mentor or two. They truly are valuable, so make sure to give some serious thought to getting yourself a mentor before you launch into producing your film.

Surround Yourself With Winners

Trust your instincts here. Surround yourself with people who are fun to be with. Look for people who are passionate about what they are doing, hungry for the experience, extremely creative, innovative, and willing to put in the hours and go the extra mile.

Keep Your Eye On The Prize

Congratulations; you've made it through the entire book! You're ready. It's time to produce your own movie and spend some quality time patting yourself on the back as you move through this amazing experience. I truly believe that the process of film producing is a joy and can be easy and fun if you follow my lead and take it a step at a time.

What's important is remembering why you're doing what you're doing. When your parents suggested that you be a doctor or a lawyer and you confidently said, "No, I'm going to be a film producer": why? Why did you say that? What made you want to produce movies? It is important that you get in touch with that dream, that vision, that passion before you begin and then reconnect with it repeatedly throughout the entire filmmaking process.

As the producer, it's your job to constantly stay in touch with possibility. Remember, you set the tone, not just on the film set but at every stage along the way. So if you're feeling frustrated, negative, or discouraged, it shows and it affects your team. Keep your eyes on the prize, as the saying goes. There may be some stumbling blocks along the path, so reminding yourself of the possibility of having your film in the can will keep you turned on, inspired, and excited – even if the going gets tough.

It has been a pleasure, an honor, and a joy for me to write this book for you. To share with you all the information, facts, and stories that have gone into the making of *Candy Stripers*, *Séance*, and *Portal* has really been fun.

I wish you the best in your filmmaking endeavor. Remember always that films touch the hearts, minds, and souls of millions and millions of people around the world. What an incredible, magnificent, magical journey you are about to embark on.

To quote Abraham-Hicks, "Like the dog who sticks his head out the car window and risks getting bugs in his eyes . . . it's well worth it for the joy of the ride." That is what film producing is for me, and I hope that your love of and passion for this medium and industry will be contagious as you produce films that inspire, inform, and delight!

Filmmakers Website Resource Guide

When it comes to resources, the internet is amazing. There are literally hundreds and hundreds of websites these days that are invaluable to the independent film producer. It would take an entire book to give you all of them and there are new ones added constantly. So here are a few to get you started. I've included a real variety, from industry related organizations that you can join, to amazing sites that feature current informational articles and fund raising opportunities to sites that focus on movie reviews and what is happening globally.

About.com – Covers independent film around the world.
www.worldfilm.about.com

AFM – The American Film Market is scheduled in November in Los Angeles; its focus is on independent films.
www.americanfilmmarket.com

Assistantdirectors.com – Resource for assistant directors. Features directories of international production companies, productions services, jobs, workshops, resumes, movie reviews, and forums.
www.assistantdirectors.com

Babelgum.com – Short film competition.
www.babelgum.com

Baselineintel.com – Industry articles, movie reviews, movie costs, television reporting, and media analysis.
www.baselineintel.com

Bluegel Media – Offers website templates for download.
www.bluegelmedia.com

California Lawyers for the Arts – Free legal services and advice.
www.calawyersforthearts.org

Cinefinance – A completion bond company.
www.cinifinance.net

Cinematography.com – Forum for technical aspects of filmmaking. News, resources, job postings.
www.cinematography.com

Crackle.com – Watch movies and TV shows for free online.
www.crackle.com

Crewster.com – Network of film, television, and commercial crews. Posts job listings and information on new shows and films.
www.crewster.com

Digital Video Expo – Training, exposition, and networking events, covering all aspects of the HD content creation industry.
www.dvexpo.com

Doculink – A forum for documentary filmmakers with monthly meetings in Los Angeles and San Francisco.
www.doculink.org

Done Deal Pro – Tracks script, book, treatment, and options. Subscribers are able to search the database by title, writer, representation, company, genre, or date.
www.donedealpro.com

Doddle – Mobile application that allows production guides to be read on your phone.
www.doddleme.com

Entertainment Economy Institute (EEI) – In-depth information and data about the entertainment industry.
www.entertainmentecon.com

Entertainment Weekly – Music, TV, Movie News.
www.ew.com

Film Emporium – Full-service brokerage specializing in entertainment and production insurance; also offers film stock, video tape, digital media, and hard drives.
www.filmemporium.com

Film Independent – Resources, screenings, programs, and LA film festival.
www.filmindependent.org

Film Finances – A completion bond company.
www.ffi-web.com

Film Permits Unlimited – Los Angeles–based permit coordination services.
www.filmpermits.com

Film & Television Action Committee – Focused on issues of runaway film production.
www.ftac.org

Film This Production Services – Los Angeles–based location service that helps provide filming permits.
www.filmthis.net

Film Vision – Resources for the independent film producer.
www.filmvision.com

Filmmaker's Alliance – Trainings, seminars, screenings, and writer's workshops.
www.filmmakersalliance.com

Filmmaking.net – Resources and community for indie filmmakers.
www.filmmaking.net

Filmproposals.com – Film proposals and information on financing.
www.filmproposals.com

Filmtools – Film supplies.
www.filmtools.com

Filmunderground.com – Helps match film producers with private investors.
www.filmunderground.com

Filmventure.com – Film fund-raising source
www.filmventure.com

Foundation Center – Provides information on foundation grants
www.foundationcenter.org

Google Groups – Resource for projects seeking investment, as well as investors seeking projects.
www.groups.google.com/group/filmproposals-forums?hl=en

Hollywood Production Center – Provides office rental space for films in preproduction and postproduction.
www.hollywoodpc.com

IMDB.com – The Internet Movie Database. Resource to search movie titles, actors and watch trailers.
www.imdb.com

IMDBPro – A database of industry professionals, agents info, company directory, industry news, and more.
www.imdbpro.com

Independent Cinema Expo – A Las Vegas based informational seminar for Indie producers.
www.icexpo.com

Independent Film and Television Alliance – Worldwide trade association.
www.ifta-online.org

Independent Filmmaker's Alliance – Resources and information for the independent filmmaker.
www.filmalliance.com

Independent Feature Project – Through workshops, seminars, conferences, mentorships, and *Filmmaker* magazine, IFP schools its members in the art, technology, and business of independent filmmaking.
www.ifp.org

Independent Television Service – Funds, presents, and promotes documentaries on public TV.
www.itvs.org

Indieclub.com – Networking site, message boards and local groups.
www.indieclub.com

Indie Film Page – Networking forum for the independent filmmaker.
www.indiefilmpage.com

IndieGoGo – Funding, promotion and self-distribution opportunities.
www.indiegogo.com

Indie-Pictures – Direct to DVD distribution company.
www.indie-pictures.com

IndieProducer.net – Networking resource.
www.indieproducer.net

Indie Scene – Marketing information and industry updates.
www.indiescene.net

Indieshortfilms.net – Short film competition.
www.indieshortfilms.net

Infolist.com – Industry opportunities, events and information.
www.infolist.com

Inktip.com – Networking source for writers and producers.
www.inktip.com

International Film Guarantors – Completion bond company.
www.ifgbonds.com

iofilm.co.uk – Information on films and filmmaking.
www.iofilm.co.uk

Kickstarter.com – Fundraising platform for all types of creative projects.
www.kickstarter.com

Kodak's Information Server – Products, releases, policies, order prints online.
www.kodak.com

LA411.com – Independent film crew and vendors.
www.LA411.com

Library of Moving Images, Inc. – Has film clips from 1870s to present.
www.libraryofmovingimages.com

Masterguide.com – A great resource that lists film markets, TV market, exhibitions, and trade shows.
www.masterguide.com

Maxfilmpro.com – Production resources, location scout, production activity and daily news.
www.maxfilmpro.com

Millimeter – The professional resource for production and post.
www.millimeter.com

Motion Picture, TV, and Theatre Directory – Independent film crew and vendors.
www.mpe.net

Movie Magic Budgeting – Film Budgeting software.
www.entertainmentpartners.com/Content/Products/Budgeting.aspx

Movie Magic Scheduling – Film Scheduling software.
www.entertainmentpartners.com/Content/Products/Scheduling.aspx

Movie Maven List – Review of foreign and indie films.
www.moviemavenlist.com

Movie Plan – Informational software on business plans and funding.
www.movieplan.net

Planet Shark Productions – A full-service Los Angeles–based film and
video production company specializing in social media. They also provide forums for job listings, casting calls, events, resumes, loglines, and
more.
www.planetsharkproductions.com

Producer's Guild of America – Non-profit organization representing the
interests of motion picture and Television producers.
www.producersguild.org

Production-central.org – A filmmaker's community, vendor discounts and
benefit organizations.
www.mypco.com

Production Hub – "Where production meets the Internet." Production
resource directory, classifieds, equipment, news, jobs, events, and services.
www.productionhub.com

Production-Tube.com – A social network for the industry.
www.production-tube.com

REEL Ladies – A Los Angeles–based organization that offers events,
workshops, and networking opportunities for women.
www.reelladies.ning.com

Reel Women – Provides support and networking opportunities for women
in film and related industries.
www.reelwomen.org

SAG Indie – Resources across the United States to help with your low-
budget production, including contracts, casting, local organizations, workshops, and interviews.
www.sagindie.org

Science & Entertainment Exchange – Resource for experts/consultants in
science, engineering, health, and other areas.
www.scienceandentertainmentexchange.org

Set Wear – Site offers gear for set, gloves, bags, and the like.
www.setwear.com

Shooting People – United Kingdom–based online network for low-budget
filmmakers with New York branch and newsletters.
shootingpeople.org

Shoots.com – The international production crew resource: post messages and find jobs, cast talent, film festival information, and other information.
www.shoots.com

ShortFilmsWanted.com – Opportunities for makers of short films.
www.shortfilmswanted.com

Studio Systems, Inc. – Script log program: logs script submissions and project drafts; in Hollywood, program tracks film developments and breaking news, studio system program offers searches of television and film information.
www.studiosystemsinc.com

Sundance Institute – Provides year-round creative and financial support for the development of original stories for the screen and stage. Includes information on the Sundance Film Festival and Film Forward Programs.
www.sundance.org

Tape List – Platform for filmmakers, distribution, and exhibitors to find distribution.
www.tapelist.com

The Independent – Workshops, resources, and advocacy for the independent filmmaker.
www.aivf.org

Urban Filmmaker's – A nonprofit organization that supports all types of independent media.
www.urbanmediamakers.com

Webmovie.com – Search engine of resources for production services, facilities, stock footage, post-production, music, educational resources, animation, visual FX and more.
www.webmovie.com

Withoutabox.com – An online application submission service for film festivals.
www.withoutabox.com

Women Helping Women – Provides opportunities and connections in the entertainment industry.
www.whwnetwork.com

Women in the Director's Chair – Organization providing support for female directors.
www.widc.org

Women In Film (WIF) – Provides events, mentoring, screenings, and other supports. There are WIF chapters in numerous cities and countries. www.wif.org

Women Make Movies – A multicultural distribution service. www.wmm.com

Women's Image Network – Hosts seminars, screenings, and special events with the aim of empowering women; hosts the WIN La Femme Film Festival. www.thewinawards.com

Books: Some of My Favorites

I have a few suggestions in different categories for you to consider. I think the first thing to look at is developing a screenplay. That is too often overlooked, and I believe it's an area in which we, as producers, need to get more educated. The first thing I did when I moved to Hollywood was enroll in workshops on screenplay development, and my favorite book at the time was *Getting Your Script Through the Hollywood Maze: An Insider's Guide* (Acrobat Books) by Linda Stuart. I took her workshop at AFI (American Film Institute) at the time, and to this day, I think that book is essential for a producer's library. I would add Michael Hauge's *Selling Your Story in 60 Seconds* and *Writing Screenplays that Sell* (Michael Wiese Productions); the brilliant Blake Snyder's *Save the Cat! The Last Book on Screenwriting You'll Ever Need* and *Save the Cat! Strikes Back* (Michael Wiese Productions); and my mentor Pen Densham's *Riding the Alligator* (Michael Wiese Productions). Obviously, keep yourself up to date and educated, but I think this selection will give you a great basis from which to begin.

For more great information on the world of film producing, check out Eve Light Honthaner's *The Complete Film Production Handbook* (Focal Press). I am a big fan (and close friend) of Eve's, and I also highly recommend her book *Hollywood Drive: What It Takes to Break In, Hang In, and Make It in the Entertainment Industry* (Focal Press).

If you've just finished reading my book, you'll know that I talk a lot about the business of show business, and I think buying books that focus on that – like Eve's first book – will be a great source of information, as are *The Independent Film Producer's Survival Guide: A Business and Legal Sourcebook* (Schirmer Trade Books), by Gunnar Erickson, Harris Tulchin, and Mark Halloran, and *The Movie Business: The Definitive Guide to the Legal and Financial Secrets of Getting Your Movie Made* (Simon & Schuster), by Kelly Charles Crabb. I also feel that watching Dov S-S Simens's *2-Day Film School* DVD collection (www.dovsimensfilm-school.com) is a must for the new film producer. Dov was one of my first mentors when I moved here, and I am one of his biggest fans.

Let's not forget the money. Show me the money! Unless you're using your own credit cards, if you can't raise the money, you're not making a movie. So you really want to take a serious look at your own relationship with money. I am not kidding here. It you've got issues in this area, clean them up . . . now! A couple of books I recommend are Lynne Twist's *The Soul of Money* (W.W. Norton & Company) and Ester and Jerry Hicks's *Money and the Law of Attraction* (Hay House, Inc.). I have had people who want to take my workshop on Indie Film Producing and tell me that they can't because they don't have the money for the seminar. That always blows my mind. If you can't raise the money for a seminar, how the heck can you raise $200,000!? We all need to master the art (yes, it's an art) of enrollment. If you want people to play with you, then handle your own relationship to money and start to have fun with it. Lighten up about it, be generous, and people will want to play. That much I know for certain!

When it comes to raising money for your film, there are two other books that I suggest. One I read a few years ago, *43 Ways to Finance your Feature Film* (Southern Illinois University Press), by John W. Cones, and more recently *Bankroll: A New Approach to Financing Feature Films* (Michael Wiese Productions), by Tom Malloy. I have to say that I really loved Tom's book. It is inspiring as well as informative.

I also want to make a point here of mentioning a few of Mark Litwak's books. One of the first things I did after launching Snowfall Films, Inc., is take his workshop on how to read contracts at UCLA. Some his books that you might want to add to your collection are: *Risky Business: Financing and Distributing Independent Films, Dealmaking for the Film and Television Industry*, and *Contracts for the Film and Television Industry* (Silman-James Press).

As you know by now, I feel very strongly about getting educated on film distribution, so I think picking up Stacey Parks's book *The Insider's Guide to Independent Film Distribution* (Focal Press) is a must. In addition, take a look at Jerome Courshon's DVD collection *The Secrets to Movie Distribution: Get Your Movie Distributed Now!* (www.distribution.la)

ADR Additional dialog recording is often required and is done during post. The actors come back and lip sync and loop (re-record) dialog that wasn't sharp or clear during filming.

Breakdown services A company that receives audition material (called "sides") from the production company and distributes it to talent agents and managers.

Callback A second audition. Generally, a callback means the actor is seriously being considered for the role. A "chemistry callback" allows the director, producers, and casting director to see ensembles of actors and determine whether they would make believable relatives, love interests, etc.

Chain of title Written proof (in the form of legal contracts, copyright certificate(s), assignments, and other documents) that you (the producer) control the rights to all the elements in your film.

Character breakdowns Descriptions of the characters in your film, including age, gender, race, and any other key characteristics critical to the film (i.e., the character must be able to ride a horse, play the piano, speak French, etc.).

Color correction specialist A postproduction professional who digitally improves and unifies footage that might have been taken at different times of the day, on different cameras, or even in entirely different locations and "corrects" them to match seamlessly.

Credits The title you get for the work you did on the film. Films often have a few key credits that roll at the beginning of the film and the full credits at the end. A "single-card" credit means that your name appears by itself on screen.

Deal memo A short-form contract that lays out the essential elements and terms of the agreements.

Deferments Postponed payment(s) promised to cast and crew until a particular time or event (defined profit or box office is achieved, distribution contract is consummated, etc.).

Development The time during which the screenplay undergoes any necessary rewrites.

Delivery The list of items "deliverable" to a distributor to enable them to promote and distribute your film, such as proper chain of title, script clearance report, E&O insurance, various digital or film masters of your movie (with and without music and dialog for subtitles, etc.), production stills, key art, and other items.

DGA The Directors Guild of America.

Dialog list A transcript of every word spoken in the film used to translate it into other languages. A combined dialog and spotting list (CDSL) is an efficient cross-reference; the spotting list is a list that contains the actual subtitles, in and out times, and calculated duration.

Distribution The screening of your film for the general public. Domestic distribution refers to releasing the film in your home country; International distribution covers selling the film to other countries or territories.

Errors & Omissions insurance (E&O) An insurance policy that indemnifies (protects and holds harmless) producers (and distributors and other partners) from lawsuits alleging libel or slander, invasion of privacy, plagiarism, unauthorized use of trademark, etc. Usually a prerequisite to distribution, this policy will pay any and all liability (and cover legal fees) in the case of mistakes.

Editor's assembly This, the first rough edit of the film, is usually done by the editor, alone, with a fresh set of eyes, often oblivious to any of the drama or challenges of the shoot or the politics or intentions of the parties involved thus far. He or she simply selects the best of the material actually available "in the can" and puts them together in the most satisfying order to him or her and prepares for the director to join him or her to work side-by-side from this as a starting place to create the director's cut. The producers often add their input, sometimes based on feedback from test audiences. Final cut is when the picture is "locked" and (ostensibly) no further changes are made.

Film festival An organized competition, series of screenings and often a celebration of films (with parties, panel discussions, workshops, etc.). Typically of films completed that year (or the year prior), sometimes focused on a particular genre (ScreamFest for horror films) or type (Frameline for LGBT).

Film markets Trade shows for the film industry where filmmakers, distributors, and sales agents meet with the main purpose to sell or license films.

Four-wall Renting out a cinema by paying for all (or a minimum number of) the seats to show your film to the public. This is sometimes done to qualify undistributed movies for Oscar candidacy or to pique distributor's interests.

Headshots A professional, close-up photo of an actor's face. Some actors have several variations that show their different "looks" and submit according to the role they hope to secure an audition for.

Keys Heads of the various production departments (hair, make-up, wardrobe, etc.).

Line producer The professional who breaks the script down into a reasonable schedule and manageable budget and coordinates and oversees all the details of the physical production to ensure both are adhered to.

LLC (limited liability company) Arguably the most common business entity chosen to make independent films, as it isolates the project as a separate entity distinct from all your other business and personal assets, and if anything goes wrong, all liability is contained by the LLC.

Lock picture The final edited version of the film. You need to lock picture before you can add the soundtrack and other elements, such as sound effects. It becomes extremely difficult and expensive to make any changes after the picture is locked because of the "domino effect" that occurs when new edits affect all the other elements such as sound, music, special effects and so forth.

Locations Structures and settings "on location" that your cast and crew will have to physically travel to in order to shoot (as opposed to movie studio sets).

Making-of photographer The making-of is a featurette, usually a bonus for the DVD or website, of behind-the-scenes interviews and footage chronicling the making of the film.

One-sheet The color poster or 8½ × 11″ sell sheet for your film.

Operating agreement The legal document that everyone signs that spells out the bylaws of your LLC.

Option An agreement between you and the rights holder (usually the screenwriter, but could be the novelist, playwright, journalist – or the individual whose true story you're adapting, etc.) that gives you exclusive rights to buy (and ostensibly shop and raise money and secure attachments for) their intellectual property or life rights for a certain amount of time, usually for a token amount of money against a larger purchase price (which may be spelled out or left to further negotiation). Exercising the option means paying the full price to legally fully acquire the material. If the option is not exercised in the allotted time period, control of the material reverts back to the writer (or subject matter).

Pan-and-scan TV screens are smaller than movie screens, so when a movie is reformatted for home video/DVD, the editor must decide what part of the frame will be seen by the viewer and what will be cut off.

Pick-up shots Critical missing shots that an editor determines he or she needs in order to satisfactorily edit the story. These may be close-up inserts of objects or reaction shots of characters that allow the editor something to cut away from the master shot or underline something of importance in the storytelling that the audience might otherwise miss.

Postproduction Everything that happens after the "martini shot" (the last scene shot) to make a movie out of the raw footage. This includes editing, sound design, music, color correction, and special effects.

Preproduction The time period when you have your team on board – and on salary – preparing everything (from casting, securing locations, and building sets to fitting costumes) leading up to the physical shooting of the film.

Principal photography The time during which the film is actually being shot.

Private placement memorandum (PPM) If you decide to raise funds from a small number of private investors (without an initial public offering), your fund raising efforts will be subject to the Securities Act of 1933, typically Regulation D. This specific legal document will spell out what the terms of the film investment opportunity are, what exactly it is you're selling (shares of common or preferred stock, membership interests, promissory notes, etc.), how and when they'll get their money back, and the associated risks and how you plan to mitigate them.

SAG The Screen Actors Guild is the union for actors, stunt people, and extras.

SAG delivery book A binder delivered to SAG after production that details all their required accounting of your actors' deal memos and schedules. To ensure you honor this request, they require a deposit before they allow you to start shooting with any SAG actor.

SAG signatory A production company that has signed the Screen Actors Guild contract and has agreed to abide by the rules set by the union for employing their actors. If you want to use SAG actors, you – or more likely your project's LLC – must become a SAG signatory.

Sales agent A salesperson, middleman, or broker who may be able to help you market and sell your movie, especially to international distributors.

Script clearance report A certificate that confirms (usually to a distributor) that an independent third party has done sufficient due diligence to ensure that all the legal concerns of your script have been vetted and your project is eligible for errors and omissions insurance (to protect the distributor from being sued – or to pay the damages in the case of an oversight). This could range from the right to show a particular brand to defamation of character (if a real person has the same name as one of your characters) or if copyright infringement has occurred (i.e., perhaps you used a song that you thought was in the public domain but the recording you used isn't). Your film (or ideally the script) must to "clear" this legal hurdle before it can be distributed (sometimes before it will even be shot).

Sound designer The postproduction professional in charge of all the sound in your film. He or she will make sure we can hear and understand the dialog, but will also make sure that you are as audially-emotionally engaged as you are visually and that the sound effects and music don't compete with the dialog.

Spotting list The spotting list is used for creating subtitles and closed-captioning. A full transcript of the dialog as well as a blueprint of when and where the subtitles should appear. (See *dialog list*.)

Subscription agreement The actual legal document that allows your investor to become a part of your LLC (based on the terms spelled out in your PPM) and invest in your movie. This and all binding legal agreements should be drafted or at least vetted by your attorney.

Table read Unlike a staged read, where there might be some blocking or pantomimed action, a table read collects as many of the actors as possible for them to run through the script together, just sitting around a table, reading from the script, sometimes to rehearse but often for the writer to trim and punch up the dialog and for all the department heads to familiarize themselves with the project.

Trades The nickname for the trade newspapers (or magazines) in the entertainment industry. Traditionally referencing *The Hollywood Reporter and Daily Variety*, there are several websites, daily e-newsletters, and social media platforms that cater to movie professionals (The Wrap, Deadline Hollywood, Twitter feeds, etc.) that are changing how Hollywood gets its news.

Units Also called *shares*, these are the percentages of your film that you sell to investors. The amount of money you need to raise will determine how much each unit costs.

WGA The Writers Guild of America is the union for writers.

Wrap book A binder created by the line producer at the end of principal photography that contains the final script, schedule, crew, case and vendor list, call sheets, and production reports.

Printed and bound by PG in the USA